DEDICATION

This book is dedicated to my wife, Cecilia; my daughter, Ysabel; my mom, Modesta Rosario Sabeniano; my sisters, Myriam, Judith and Carol; my brother, Joy Dennis; my niece, Ciarra; and nephews, Ennio, Hamilton, Nathan and Seth.

I also dedicate this book as a remembrance of my son, Miguel Antonio; my dad, Ernesto Vinoya Martinez; and a special friend, Etta May, who taught me the value of life... there are bigger and better things in life than just life itself.

ACKNOWLEDGEMENTS:

I would like to express my deepest appreciation and gratitude to my family and friends who gave me the inspiration to write this book; to my staff, publisher, and to all who contributed in making this book possible. Most of all, I would like to thank our Almighty God for giving me life and the energy to finally publish this book after four years struggling to put it together.

I hope that the ideas that I am about to share with you, will make a difference in your life as well as in the lives of others that you will meet and help in this business.

Romwell Martinez Sabeniano, MBA.HCM
Author-Publisher

CAREGIVING

How to Start a Small Business of Providing Personalized In-Home Care Service

Romwell Martinez Sabeniano, MBA.HCM

authorHOUSE®

AuthorHouse™
1663 Liberty Drive
Bloomington, IN 47403
www.authorhouse.com
Phone: 1-800-839-8640

First published by AuthorHouse   11/18/2009

ISBN: 978-1-4490-4496-1 (e)
ISBN: 978-1-4490-4509-8 (sc)

Library of Congress Control Number: 2009911834

Printed in the United States of America
Bloomington, Indiana

This book is printed on acid-free paper.

The information presented in this book is readily accessible from public agencies and deemed reliable at the time of printing. The reader must seek advice and consultation from other health care professionals, experienced entrepreneurs in the caregiving business, legal counsel and other entities relative to his/her particular business and financial situation prior to getting deeply involved in this type of undertaking. The author is not rendering professional advice but merely presenting useful resources and materials that are possibly helpful to individuals who despite of their lack of knowledge and experience in establishing a start-up caregiving business are determined to explore the income potentials of the business. As individual results may vary, the author does not guarantee the success of each and everyone's undertaking, nor does the author guarantee the accuracy of the information presented in this book. The reader must consider varying factors such as state, federal and local regulations that could affect the course and nature of the business. Personal budget allocated for the initial phase of the undertaking and other related factors can affect the future results of the business. The information presented in this book are acquired from existing local regulations, general principles, guidelines, and practices observed in a typical caregiving business setting and are deemed in effect at the time this book was printed. Each state requirements on licensing and permit provisions relative to the caregiving business is different. The reader of this book is personally responsible in keeping abreast of the latest information, local laws, regulations, and guidelines in his/her respective states, counties and cities that could affect his/her views, understanding and operation of the business. The reader purchased this book with the understanding that the author and its publisher are not engaged in rendering legal or business advice on the business. Notwithstanding anything to the contrary stated or implied in any of the materials available herein, the author, its agents, affiliates, employees, and contractors cannot, and do not make any representation, warranty, endorsement or guarantee, express or implied, regarding (i) the accuracy, completeness or timeliness of any such information, facts or opinions or (ii) the merchantability or fitness for any particular purpose thereof, nor shall any of such materials be deemed the giving of legal advice by the author, its agents, affiliates, employees or contractors.

TABLE OF CONTENTS

WHY DO YOU NEED THIS BOOK?

Are you looking for a "part-time" business or an alternative to what you already have besides your current jobs? Stop looking and start working! To those who are very motivated to embark in a new business or career but is discouraged by limited available funds for start-up capital, or perhaps lack the experience in operating a small business, this book is for you. The DOT.COM era is almost DOT.GONE. Enter the new business of the 21st century by providing personalized care to the aging and the ailing population. Actually, this business is anything but new. It has been around for so many decades now. Caregiving has hundreds of success stories and gross billions of dollars in revenues for the nation. It once was an unpopular business in the early 1960's and late 1970's but made a great come back in the mid 1990's to early 2000's to meet the needs of more than 87 million Americans that belong to the baby boomer population in desperate need of this service. With these recent developments, things gradually changed and it appears to be for the better. With these growing trends in aging, health care, and technology, people are taking advantage of these changes by gradually trading-in their lucrative careers and professions to enter into a more personalized care type of business, such as health care and other caregiving related careers.

In challenging economic times or even during boom times, service-oriented businesses will always be in demand when it is compared to product-oriented businesses. Everyone that has the talent, determination and the drive to do something that other people are unable to do for themselves, will always be in demand despite economic downturn. Caregiving is a unique type of business that will thrive in any economic situation. As we will all live through our lifetime, we are always prone to getting sick and age accordingly. Most of the time when we are challenged by an illness that keeps us bed bound, we try to get by on our own for a limited time, but at some point, we will need to humble ourselves to the aid of a caregiver. The aging population will continue to outgrow itself and with the advancement in technology, we shall continue to live longer and healthier lives. With this in mind, the potentials of caregiving business are endless, thus it is up to our creative imagination, patience, and determination to make it work in our favor.

This book contains information about the business of providing personalized care in a private "in-home" type of setting. It aims to help the reader in realizing the common variables and the challenges of the business as it parallels with his/her understanding of the earning potentials and benefits of owning a caregiving business.

The goal of the book is to literally hold the reader's hand and guide him/her through the whole process of setting-up the business from start to finish by simple illustration and in a manner that is easy to understand and realistic to accomplish.

The reader will benefit from this book by learning the simplest way to establish a small business, realize that even without experience and with very limited money as start-up capital, one can establish a caregiving business. In times of economic downturn when millions of people loose their jobs and there is lack of available business or employment opportunities to turn to, establishing your own "low cost", personalized caregiving business is one of the best ways to go. Tough times call for tough decisions. Getting involved in this type of business will not only generate revenue for the community but also addresses the chronic problem prevalent in the health care delivery system pertaining to the sub-standard quality care. Setting up the business will be a win-win solution to a tough financial situation in a sense that the business will not only generate revenues to the sagging global economics but will also meet the service demands of the growing "baby boomers" population of the country and of the globe. Whatever global economic challenge we face, there will always be a high demand for the caregiving service.

This book will also address the alarming global problem that the aging population is facing... lack of availability of quality in home care service. As millions of "baby boomers" will surge into the first wave of this aging generation, we must be able to address their needs and services now. Otherwise, we will face the serious consequences later as this enormous task continues to escalate at an alarming level.

Upon completion of this book, the reader will be able to accomplish three important things: to realize the unlimited potential of the caregiving business, to explore various types of caregiving business alternatives that are available and to learn easy steps in establishing a small low-cost enterprise. The reader will understand the different types of businesses related directly and indirectly to caregiving. In the event of a sudden change of plans to expand the business alternatives or should one become indecisive, the reader will have a variety of options to choose from to make an intelligent choice... to either move forward with the initial intended plan or shift to another type of business without incurring heavy financial loss.

The book will present common errors and scenarios that most start-up entrepreneurs experience when setting up their first caregiving business. In this manner, the reader may be able to avoid or even spot possible flaws by learning from the mistakes of others who have gone before him/her.

The book contains sample forms and actual documents that I prepared when I established my first caregiving business. The reader may be able to utilize these sample forms to jump-start the business and save thousands of dollars in consultation fees and costs.

Do you currently have a job but the income is not even enough to pay for all of your bills? Did you recently loose a job? Do you feel like you are working at a "dead-end" job or worried sick about your financial future? Do you feel like your retirement fund is insufficient and you need other means of income as a supplement in order to support a humble lifestyle for yourself and for your family? Are you looking for an opportunity to establish your first caregiving business or do you simply want to make considerable changes in life or in your career? Do not worry. You are not alone. For whatever reason or challenge that is keeping you from reaching out to accomplish your dreams while you are hoping that the right opportunity will come along to help you jumpstart those plans into action, it is all up to you. There are literally hundreds and thousands of people out there that are in similar or worse situations like yours who may keep complaining about their life and yet, do nothing about it. If you do not make the initiative of taking the first step beyond reading this book, you will never know.

The book might hold important solutions to most of your unanswered questions about the business of providing care. Remember that in life, there is no single answer to all our questions. Man has yet to discover that perfect solution to achieve what it is that he wants in life be it success in a career, having tons of money or simply having a real life. There are literally millions of ways and means to achieve your goals and surprisingly enough, you may not realize that the solutions are just right in front of you. All you need is an open mind to embrace those solutions. Make those solutions work for you by focusing on those changes that needs to be done within you and let the special force of nature take you to where you need to be and where you want to be. Those changes had to start within you and from you alone. Nothing will happen until you make that commitment in your mind when you will actually take that crucial first step to implement those changes. You can read all the books and listen to hundreds of "how to" motivational CD's all your life, but everything still depends on that day when you will decide to put those plans into action and use the acquired knowledge and experiences to work in your favor. You will need to find a way to focus and channel the energy and enthusiasm to convert ideas into productive results that may lead you to whatever it is that you aspire to do or want to be in your lifetime.

To those of you who want to set up a caregiving business but do not know how to start or simply afraid of that unknown factor, maybe this book can help. It contains important information, especially made for those who are ambitious, those that have the passion to help others and have the commitment to achieve the goal of owning a piece of the great "American Dream." If you feel confused and frustrated because of your previous experience in setting up a business or the lack of experience in dealing with the unknown factor of the business, you are not alone. It is normal to be afraid, particularly when you are about to embark on a new business where it involves financial risks; when just about everything you have saved, including your retirement funds, or perhaps equity from your home, or even your lifetime savings are at stake.

In life, there are no guarantees. Whatever you do in your lifetime, you will always have to take risks. Every waking moment of our day and every second of our lifetime, we will always take risks. At this point and time, you have to consider and weight the risk against the odds. It is up to you to answer: "To risk or not to risk", that is your question.

Caregiving business is not for everyone. It takes a lot of patience, courage, determination, persistence and financial creativity not only to be able to start up the business, but most importantly, to make it survive. As results may vary, you have the responsibility to find ways to make your business fit within your busy schedule and of course within your tight budget.

There are no words to describe how you will feel after conquering your most difficult challenge in setting up this business. This book does not guarantee your success, as it only offers basic information about the business based on practical and cost effective approach that I have experienced when I started a small caregiving business quite similar to what you are about to start up. The rest is up to you.

As the author of this book, I do not guarantee your success in this business nor am I aware of any proven formula that you can use to succeed in this business. If only there is such a magic formula for success and if the whole world finds out about it, perhaps no one will be out there cleaning our dishes or cars, no one to serve our meals or even worse, we will all be crowded in the same beach drinking our favorite cocktail drink. Then, life would be miserable, would you agree? That is why this is not for everyone. It takes a special type of person to do this business.

Let me ask you this ...."Where will you be in a few years from now, and how is it different from where you are today"? If you keep doing whatever it is that you are doing now, how do you see your life different a few years down the road?

In 2006, I wrote my first book, "*An Easy Guide on How to Establish Your First Residential Care Facility*" (ISBN: X-4208-3357-X, now available at your local bookstores, the Internet and thru my publisher Authorhouse.com). During my past book signings, I had the opportunity to accommodate numerous requests from my audience seeking advice and information on other types of caregiving businesses that are less taxing and simple. The overwhelming requests inspired me to write this book.

After reading this book, you may literally start the business at your own phase. It is the only "service oriented" business I know that requires the most modest amount of start-up capital and that it can even be initiated and managed while working at your current business or job. For now, there are few state and federal requirements, but as future demand for the business grows, so is the potential for errors, and perhaps, lawsuits which eventually will lead to more cautious scrutiny by regulatory boards or agencies that oversee this type of business. Although there may be other businesses that are more simple and cost effective than this, nothing can come close in comparison to a caregiving business when it comes to the start-up capital requirement and ease in operation as this "service based" enterprise and versus other enterprises out there that are both "product and service based".

As clients' needs and the aging population continue to grow exponentially, expect to make necessary adjustments in order to be able to meet the overwhelming demand for personalized care services. In the years to come and as the aging population trend expands vertically, the health care service delivery system will outgrow itself becoming less complex and specialized type of business.

❖ This book will guide most beginners in the business by illustrating easy "to do" steps in setting up the business. You will learn the simple process of starting and managing the business as a home-based enterprise, initially operating from the comfort of your home giving you the option of maintaining the start-up business without sacrificing your current business or job.

❖ Learn the different techniques on how to improve the income potentials of the business within weeks from initial operation.

ARE YOU READY YET?

Well, if you have not made up your mind, another option for you to consider is save more money towards your business and try to earn the experience that you might need, and perhaps later on, you might have a clearer mind to decide what you need to do for yourself. To me, any business is as good as all other businesses as long as it is legitimate, legal, moral, and ethical. The business of caregiving definitely meets all of the above expectations, which explains why it is one of the best. There are only a few available businesses, I am aware of, that can give you the personal satisfaction of both earning a generous income, and at the same time feel good about yourself while making an enormous impact in other people's lives.

To some, it could be an excellent opportunity to petition a family member or a friend from a foreign country to work within the business.

And, most importantly … DREAM. This is what makes this country so great and powerful. It is the land of opportunity where people from all "walks of life," regardless of age, gender, religious belief, orientation, and status, have an equal opportunity to survive, compete and be successful in whatever they do and can dream to be in their lifetime.

When you are ready to decide and commit yourself to do this business, remember the reason why you are in it, "service first and money will come in volume more than you can expect". Keep your goals and dreams together. Maintain your passion to help other people.

THE DREAM:

It starts with a DREAM, then, believing in it to give you the courage to make it work. There are so many business opportunities that could fit just about anyone's lifestyle and dreams. To those who are looking for a "quick fix" type of business that will make them wealthy overnight, honestly, they will be terribly disappointed in this business. Caregiving business requires a lot of hard work and dedication that could take at least a couple of years before one can see the fruits of their labor. First, one needs to focus on the best quality of service to provide. Then, nurture it and watch it grow, slowly. Most of us have that goal of achieving the great "American Dream" to own a business, to be free from the bondage of being just a plain employee for the rest of our lives and earning the respect that we deserve in the family as well as within the community. Some of us might just be contented with what we do for now, going home from work everyday then going back to work the next day for the next 30 to 45 years. Perhaps, quite a number of us will decide to work for someone else and help make that person become wealthy instead of us. Some will prefer to do the daily grind and maybe an option to get a second or even a third job to supplement their income in order to support a family. If we do nothing about our current financial situation, we might end up with nothing, but working for the rest of our lives even beyond our retirement age. Perhaps, the question remains… how long can our body physically tolerate what we are doing now? All of us will eventually get older and cannot go back in time to correct the past. We are not getting younger, so we need to ask ourselves… how long can we keep doing what we are doing right now for perhaps, the rest of our lives? This, my friend is my Million Dollar question for you. Unless we embrace the winds of change, we will be where we are. We all make choices in life and I hope you have made yours.

It is sad to know that thousands of people prefer to just sit around and wait for history to unfold right before their very eyes. Are you willing to make history or are you going to wait for history to make you? I do not know about your plans, but for me I will not sit down and wait or rely on someone else to decide on what my destiny will bring. Honestly speaking, I know that deep inside you, you have that burning passion to create a positive result out of your current financial situation. You have the power to decide for yourself what your destiny will bring. Otherwise, you will not buy this book.

Together, you and I will hope that some day the business you aim to establish will grow to become your biggest break in getting out of your current financial situation; whatever it is whether it be unemployment or possibly just to get rid of your unwanted job. Perhaps you might want to retire and do something while in retirement. Others may simply want to help and share their blessings with the community.

No matter what reason that drives you to set up this business, it is important that you understand your goal and the mission that you are trying to accomplish. It does not matter how grandiose or small your dream business may be, whether it be a "small mom and pop type of business" or a store that sell widgets. What you need to understand is that in any type of business, it will take a lot of hard work, patience and sacrifice in order for that dream business to even possibly come true. Even if you try your best in getting the business together, even if you have all the resources and the talent that qualify you to become successful in the business, there is still no guarantee that the business you have in mind will succeed or even make it through the first year. Studies show that 95% of start-up businesses fail during the first three years of initial operation. A huge portion of those who succeed in the first year might not make it by the fifth year in business. It is quite depressing, but if you do not try to find out for yourself, you will never know. Not having any idea at all on what to do and how to go about it may even be more depressing to some especially to those who have limited cash and very little experience at the beginning.

Realistically, at this stage, the hardest part is making the decision when to start. Later on in the process, you will realize how much you have accomplished after going through the challenges of the business.

Let me make it clear, this book does not contain all the answers to your questions neither does it have all the secret tricks of the trade nor the magic potion to make a successful caregiving business. However, a lot of people became independently wealthy and has a good life out of the business. Some expanded their services and made millions in establishing a franchise business as a spin off to caregiving. But, there are also hundreds who lost their business for reasons that you will find out for yourself as you will read from this book when I present the pros and cons as well as the common mistakes that most people make in the business.

By purchasing this book, you have practically made that BIG DECISION to start and set the wheels in motion, which is a good sign. You will need to evaluate your finances, make a plan on how you can accomplish it, and most of all commit yourself to making your dream a reality.

As you embark for the first time in accepting the different challenges in your new business, you will realize how important your role is as a provider of care. In due time, you will experience a unique and indescribable feeling that no one else can express unless they themselves have been through it. You are taking care of the future need of the aging population today, here and now.

WHAT IS THE FUTURE OF THE BUSINESS?

DEFINITELY, the future of caregiving business is very bright. I do not need to put icing nor cherries on the description. Look around you, you can tell what I mean. There will always be a need for the service no matter what. Everyone will, from time to time, get sick and eventually get old. We will all get old no matter what, and when we do, we will need some help in getting by through the days when we are unable to do things, from a simple task to a more complex undertaking. Imagine life without caregiving, it will be the most horrifying stage in our lifetime unless we prepare for it now. The bottom line is that no matter what the global economy brings, there will always be a need for the business. There is an estimated 87 million Americans and migrants most of them belonging to the "Baby Boomers" generation including those born before them in other countries migrating into the US that will turn 65 years old between 1990 and 2020. These are the people in this generation that will determine the fate of the global economy. If you look around you and meticulously observe the messages on the news, advertisements, products being marketed to the public, I guarantee you that most (if not all of it) is geared to benefit the aging population. These are the same group of people who have been through most of it all (world wars, the great depression, real estate boom and bust, etc…) and hopefully, have saved enough money to take care of themselves when they age gracefully. All you need is to serve a small fraction of this aging population by providing a safe, convenient and accessible environment and in return make a decent income for the business.

Picture their situation in your mind. The fact of the matter is that, gradually, we will all get old. But, when we do, we will have to make that decision to prepare ourselves for the inevitable stage in our aging life either to welcome our age at our private homes and have someone take care of us or live with a group of people in a retirement home, or in an institution. Every day in our lifetime, we all face that uncertain factor about the condition of our health. At any moment or time, and for any unknown cause or reason, we could get sick or face the challenge of developing some form of disability through other means beyond our control, such as diseases, accident or by some genetic fluke. All of a sudden, we confront a medical challenge that confines us to our bedroom for an indefinite time, and without caregivers, imagine how miserable our life would be! It may sound like a scary line from a horror movie but it is the truth. Without caregivers, who among us can survive a day without someone assisting us with our special needs such as feeding, medication reminders, transportation to and from appointments, bathing, meal preparation, cleaning, etc… that requires physical, emotional and even psychological support in order to get through the days when we are unable to perform such urgently needed tasks. Try to imagine it and figure out how you could survive the minutes, hours, days and even months of agony without someone assisting you with your basic needs or simply just being there for you when you need help.

Although it may sound like the business is prying on helpless individuals, it is not. It is simply providing a service that is almost identical to what is offered in hospitals or skilled nursing facilities except it is provided in the privacy of the individual's home, which could improve the quality of life and to respect the person's dignity. There is an urgent need for the service, which explains the infinite potential of the business. It is all up to you to explore the potential. How many millions of Americans, beside those who are in their retirement age will be in need of your services? All you need is to serve a small fraction of that population to earn a modest profit. Undoubtedly, there is a need for your services no matter what your respective states, and national budget dictates on a yearly basis. I honestly believe that this is the business of the future today, here and now.

This business is different from providing care in a residential care setting such as a Group Home for Children, Adult Residential Care , Residential Care for the Elderly and the Chronically Ill; A Day Program, Adult Day Care, Adult Day Health Care, Senior Day Care and Senior Day Health Care Center. The information on these types of business is available through my other book: *"An Easy Guide on How to Establish your First Residential Care Facility"*. (ISBN: X-4208-3357-X, now available at your local bookstores and through my publisher Authorhouse.com)

How did I learn about the caregiving business?

Getting started in any type of business is not as easy as it seem particularly for those who are in it for the first time. It is normal to be concerned and confused every time you do something new particularly when you get into a first time business. I felt anxious when I established my first caregiving business. Each of us may have different experiences in setting up a business for the first time and hopefully, most of these experiences end with a positive result.

When I first started in the business, I did not know exactly what to do. What I knew then is that caregiving is second nature to me particularly where I grew taking care of our elders. In 1988, when I was living with my parents in Los Angeles, California, I established a strong friendship with my neighbors particularly with a charming elderly couple in their 80's. We knew each other well and shared fun times together. One day, the elderly gentleman who had a history of diabetes, vision problems, high blood pressure and other medical issues fell ill and I was asked to drive both of them to their medical and dental appointments. Then, I was given the broad task of preparing meals, gardening, medication reminding, errands, household maintenance and repairs, and sometimes sleeping over to make sure they were both fine. Their ages caught up with them and simple tasks, such as going to the bathroom and getting something from the kitchen, became a major challenge. Then, both of them eventually were unable to perform most of their daily tasks. I treated them well with a lot of dignity and respect just like I treated my own grandparents. I asked myself what if I could turn my passion of helping others and my skills in human relations into a business? So, I did my research and looked into the potential of the business, but due to my lack of information, experience and resource, I was too afraid to try it. As years went by, I volunteered in various group homes that provided care for children, adults and seniors with mental health issues and developmental disabilities. With all those years, my experience once again asked me the same question, Am I ready to start-up a small caregiving busines? As I was studying for my Masters Degree in Business Administration, I wrote a business plan on establishing a caregiving business and received an excellent grade for the thesis. Once again, the nagging question kept coming up… what if?

When I became a social worker/case manager for a state agency, I realized that it was time to start on my own business. After a couple of years teaching on the different subjects related to caregiving, I compiled all of my resources and information in anticipation that one day I would be able to share the knowledge and experience I gained, so others will benefit from it. On May 1, 2000, I established my first caregiving business and named it **Angel Care Respite and Home Support Service,** and the rest is history.

Come along with me as I walk you through the detailed process on how I established my first caregiving business and learn how you too could benefit from the process.

DO YOU NEED TO HAVE EXPERIENCE AS A CAREGIVER OR AS A STAFF TO GET STARTED IN THE BUSINESS?

NO, but in a service-oriented type of business like this, having actual experience in a health care setting would definitely be beneficial to the start-up individual. To some, caregiving is second nature but to others, it will be quite a challenge.

Do Not Quit Your Day Job Yet. Volunteer to acquire the experience. The initial process could take from at least a month to six (6) months of massive advertising and marketing prior to acquiring your first client. For the mean time, in order to be able to supplement the initial operating cost of the business, it is best not to quit your regular jobs until the business is able literally stand on its own.

Check Out Your Management Mentality

What type of management mentality do you need to start up? Since you are starting with very limited capital, consider yourself at the bottom of the payroll list as the only staff to do all the hard work. You will be wearing a couple of hats for a while but once the business picks up and have more than two customers in your roster, then perhaps you might need someone to help you on a daily and consistent basis. As your client base continues to grow, so is your staff. I will be discussing more on this subject in the succeeding chapters of the book.

Comparing yourself to someone who may have deeper pockets and can afford to hire a staff immediately on board; your challenge may be a little bit different but the outcome shall remain the same. Do not worry, you will do well just like they did.

"What do you need to know in running the business?"

To start with, you have this book as a reference to build the business. The rest shall depend on your own initiatives and what your daily experiences will bring. Managing a business is a learning process that never ends. You will need to make the necessary adjustments on a daily basis depending on what challenges the business brings. It is amazing to observe how many people that have never worked in this field at all and yet do well in the business. With enthusiasm, sheer optimism, patience and self-motivation they impulsively invested their hard-earned savings into the business. Call it luck or whatever, but I think most of it is hard work and proper planning.

The message is clear. If you do not have the experience in this type of business, try not to start the business right away. Defer it until you can obtain valuable "hands-on" experience as an employee or at least you can hire an experienced manager to help you run the business.

Consider these options:

1. Get the experience that you need.
2. Hire an experienced staff and a qualified manager who can temporarily help you start the business.
3. Join a group of successful individuals who have the expertise, experience and the funds for the business.
4. Become a mentor or be mentored by someone who knows the business.

If you do not have the experience but you are eager to get this business started, fear not. You can do it with the following approach:

a. If you are a "go-getter" and motivated to meet the challenges, it takes patience and humility to learn from your mistakes.
b. Try to survive and learn one day at a time.
c. Be resourceful and network with a lot of people, senior centers, attend seminars, consult with an SBA representative, chamber of commerce, etc... and let the whole world know that your business is out there. Your business relies on marketing and advertising.
d. Be responsive, compassionate and always listen to your clients.

e. Keep a strong list of staff that are reliable, background checked and well-trained staff. This element is the lifeblood of the business as it could either make or break your business.

f. Keep your records straight.

g. Maintain a high ethical standard and expectation.

Another way to approach this challenge is to tighten your belt and do not expect so much at first. Nobody can actually predict how successful your business will be 2 to 5 years from now. It is purely up to you. In every enterprise, the start-up years are often times difficult.

WHAT ARE YOUR OPTIONS IN THE CAREGIVING BUSINESS?

You have quite a number of possible combinations of options to consider:

1. The business may consider branching out to supply caregiver-staff to support under-staffed group homes, residential care facilities, day programs, senior centers etc…

2. Provide short or long-term support, or job specific assignments such as transporting seniors to their medical-dental appointments, 3-hour service.

3. Establish a Residential Care Facility.

4. Establish a caregiving business franchise where you can collect a pre-determined percentage of income on a monthly basis.

This business is all about providing readily available staffing service to support the needs of individuals living in private homes and facilities. With this business, you have the flexibility of sending a caregiver/staff even on a short notice. The unfathomable demand for caregivers is attributed to factors such as the younger generations' lack of interest in providing the care, people prefer to concentrate on other job opportunities, caregivers are paid at a low cost possibly at a minimum wage, caregivers are always at risk of contracting forms of illness related to their job of providing care. In short, caregiving is not a very attractive job that family members themselves would refuse to provide the care. These issues shall be discussed later on in the succeeding chapters.

With your list of available staff, you are not limiting your service to meeting the needs of those living in private care, but also having the flexibility to meet the needs of those in residential care facilities, hospitals, skilled nursing facilities and hospitals.

As your network of available caregivers grow exponentially and with the growth in your income, you may consider the possibility of establishing a residential care facility that will cater to the needs of seniors, children and adults in need of the care service.

After establishing the caregiving business, you may also have the option of selling your network of services in a form of a franchise wherein you will be able to collect a pre-set percentage of the business income on a monthly basis. When you feel that you need to retire, you may sell the business at a lucrative price.

These are just a few of the simple ideas that you can come up with to branch out with the potentials of your business.

The best thing is that, while you are setting-up or running your new caregiving business, you may have the option of keeping the job that you love so much without compromising your income potentials.

"I wish you the best in this new found business interest and looking forward to hearing about you and your successes in the near future…."

Rmwell M. Sabeniano, Mba.Hcm

CHAPTER ONE:
CAREGIVING

A. WHAT IS CAREGIVING?

Caregiving is commonly known as the provision of care to a recipient known as the *care receiver* by the provider of care known as the *caregiver.* Care-providing is personalized in such a way that it may come in varied ways and forms depending on the particular need and service that the recipient or client requires. The type of care including expectations and standard of personal service requirement is mostly dependent on what is established or recommended by a licensed professional such as a physician, nurse, therapist, social worker/case manager, psychologist etc...which the caregiver will maintain to provide accordingly for the benefit of the **Care receiver.** For intents and purposes, **Caregiving** will be defined specifically and referred in this book as the business of providing care in a private "in-home" setting. In California, there are numerous forms of caregiving business that are available and some of them will be enumerated in this chapter. Although in other states, they may be called differently, but their service models are similar in nature. For discussion purposes, we shall limit our topic to cover the particular type of caregiving that we will provide which is an "in-home" care setting also known as private care. Our caregiving business is all about providing compassionate, trained and experienced staff to care and support the needs of seniors, adults and children with medical issues that are living in the privacy of their homes. Depending on the client's needs, the service may vary from home companionship, respite care, hourly chores including meal preparation, simple errand, driving to medical, dental appointments, grocery, assisting in prescription medication, hygiene, etc.... The exciting part about this business model is that you can initially operate it from home, at work or where ever you are with the use of a cell phone and even without the need of an office which translates to low initial capital and operating cost. This also means that you do not necessarily have to invest so much money to start up the business nor do you have to sacrifice your current job(s) or business. Even when your business starts to expand to at least 20 clients, you can still keep up with the management of your business affairs with the use of a cell phone.

By the time you finish reading this chapter, you will realize the huge potential of the caregiving business (All these subjects to be discussed later on in this book).

B. WHAT IS THE DEMAND OF THE SERVICE?

Between now and the year 2030, America will be in need of more than four million caregivers to meet the increasing demand of the aging population. In the US alone, there will be more than 87 million Americans including those migrants coming into this country that belong to the "baby boomers" generation not to mention those born before them that are turning 65 and will be in serious need of personalized care. If we do not address this urgent demand now, we will all be facing a critical shortage of competent and compassionate caregivers by the time we will actually need them. About 40 percent of people over 60 and 1.9 million privately paid caregivers share the burden of providing home care for older or disabled Americans. This does not take into consideration the significant number of people who live independently without support and care from relatives and friends. That is just the beginning of the problem. With the advancement in research and technology, today's aging population are living longer healthier lives. Back in 1907, the average life expectancy was 47 years, but now it is beyond 87 years old. With this in mind, the aging baby boomers generation will more likely provide care for their parents and eventually for themselves. The question remains: Are we one of those that will provide the care or are we the ones that will receive the care?

Our current health care system is at a very critical stage that we need to address this problem now. The quality of care goes down as the price and cost of providing it go up. As this disturbing issue of price vs. comfort in the health care delivery system spirals out of control, the people that gets squeezed in between are the seniors and the patients that needs help the most and are left with very limited choices. The aging and the medically fragile prefer to live the rest of their lives in the comfort of their homes instead of being in an institution or a group care setting. Ironically, this social disadvantage contributes to the increasing demand for our caregiving services.

For most families, the major problem in providing care for their loved ones is the cause and effect of caregiving itself. It is difficult to provide care to the aging and the ailing family members particularly if the caregivers themselves have their own personal, financial, medical issues to deal with besides the strain and the impact that the responsibility contributes in meeting the needs of their own families and loved ones. The households of today will make a difficult choice between earning a living to survive or to care for a bed-bound family member.

Statistics show that the U.S. economy losses more than $ 35 Billion each year in lost revenues, absenteeism and production cost due to the fact that most employees that are family caregivers frequently miss their work schedules to attend to their responsibilities at home and that these employees will eventually be replaced and new set of people to retrain. This is a chronic problem not only affecting America but also globally as it is happening around the world.

There is no such thing as job security. Every nation, no matter how economically stable and geo-politically powerful, is prone to every possibility of an economic meltdown. Just like what happened in the US, Europe and Asia in 2008-2009, when millions of jobs were lost due to contributing factors that led to the collapse in the real estate market, high fuel cost, deep recession, high inflation, thousands of private and multi-billion dollar businesses closed, bank failures, stock market plummeting to their lowest depths, jobs shipped overseas where cost is cheaper, millions of families displaced by lack of resources and services etc... These are grim reminders of our time that we all need to diversify not only with our income potential but also with our ability to harness our creative skills in producing external revenues that can supplement our current income. By establishing a small business, we may be able to help pull ourselves up and in return, contribute in stimulating the economy no matter how menial but daunting task might be.

Everyone that has jobs today could loose them tomorrow. Having a back up plan is always a great idea no matter how wealthy or stable you are today. Each of us may have different alternative ideas depending on other factors besides cash and skills. Some of us might prefer investing in stocks, futures, CD's, money market funds, real estate etc... But, to those among us that have very little cash reserves left, establishing a small business might not be a bad idea after all. There are hundreds of business ideas out there, but nothing can compare caregiving business. Between now and within the next decade to come, there will be millions of people approaching their retirement age. Thousands of people will get sick on a daily basis and those with serious illness may end up in hospitals or specialty care. Healthy seniors, adults and children are no exception. Some are lucky to have family members or friends that will provide the much needed care and support, but what about those that do not have that type of support system? They will need help from other contracted sources such as home-health agencies or private caregivers like you. With the ridiculous high cost of healthcare and the lack of quality personal care in an institutional setting, people would undoubtedly prefer to live and die in the comforts of their home where they can benefit from personalized caregiving. The only drawback to this is that, only a few can afford the cost of the service. Between the choice of cost, service and the convenience of living "life", it is obviously a personal preference based on convenience, affordability and urgency. By setting up the caregiving business, you are doing your share in stepping up to the plate by providing a solution to this alarming problem and to help improve the quality of care in the healthcare delivery system and reduce the spike in the cost of care on a long term basis. This is your unique response to the stimulus package, to contribute in improving the global dilemma.

C. HOW DO WE SOLVE THE PROBLEM?

Comparing other industrialized nations, America does not have an effective healthcare system. As the global population and economy expands, the burden on caregivers will continue to grow, and so will the shortage of paid services worsen. The critical shortage of available caregivers are partly attributed to factors such as low wages, few fringe benefits, lack of training and experience, lawsuits, lack of affordable insurance to cover personal health and well being, unpleasant work conditions and lack of career development.

In most cases especially in families, the adult children find it financially impossible to give up their current jobs to secure a lower paying salary in exchange for down time just to provide care for an aging or ailing loved one. They also have bills and other responsibilities too, just like what we all do.

The answer to this problem may be too obvious. One feasible solution is to set up the business of providing personalized care at a cost that is affordable and easily accessible to everyone in need of the service. To keep the cost down, the service may either be privately paid and or subsidized by insurance companies and the government sector. The cost of the service is always relative to the cost of providing it.

We must face these challenges soon otherwise by the time we reach the year 2030, you and I will confront the dilemma as to "who will take care of us?"

D. THE DIFFERENT TYPES OF CAREGIVING BUSINESS

This section will enumerate the different types of caregiving businesses currently available in the market. These various types of services are available in California and may also be available in other states, presumably under a different service category, so you need to check with your local phone directory. The purpose of this section is to give you several options to consider as alternatives to your current plan. You might also be able to utilize this information as possible leads in providing and securing staffing services and caregivers, solicit new clients that you will be able care for and other creative ways you can use for your purpose or business. Get a copy or place an ad to announce your business in the local hospital directory of services and phone book for a minimal monthly fee. A business card or a company flyer needs to be out there in every publication, night stand, reception desk, parking lot, groceries, senior centers etc… to get other people's attention that might spark some interest in your service.

THE DIFFERENT TYPES OF CAREGIVING BUSINESS:

1. **Home Serviced Based**
   a. Personalized In-Home Care Service (Non-Licensed)
   b. Home Health Agencies (Licensed)
   c. Hospice Care (Licensed)

2. **Facility Based Services (All Licensed)**
   2.1 LONG TERM CARE
   a. Medical
   a.1. Hospital
   a.2. Skilled Nursing
   a.3. Sub-Acute
   b. NON-Medical
   b.1. Assisted Living/Continuing Care
   Retirement Communities
   b.2. Institute for Mental Health
   b.3. Intermediate Care ICF
   ICF-DD
   ICF-DDH
   ICF-DDN
   b.4. Residential Care for Adults,
   Elderly and the Chronically Ill
   b.5. Group Home for Children
   b.6. Congregate Housing

In the distant past, when we talk about long-term care, most people think of custodial care only for the elderly in nursing homes or skilled nursing facilities. As we learn through the years, long-term care as we know today includes a wide variety of settings and services available to meet special needs not only for the elderly but also the needs of children and adults with medical, behavioral, psycho-social issues and developmental disabilities or self help needs.

1. Home Serviced Based:

a. Personalized In-Home Care Service (Non- Licensed):

The provision of personalized care in private homes for people with non-medical issues vary from providing companionship, minor household chores, medication reminders, transportation, and other basic personalized care. Most of the clients in need of the service are seniors living independently, but are unsafe if left alone without supervision; seniors, adults and children with minimal medical health issues.

- Regulation: *No State or Professional Regulatory License requirement. Only Local Business Operating License from the City Hall.*
- Payment: Private Pay, Insurance, HMO, SCAN, County In-Home Support Services Funds for those eligible, Some Medi-Cal, for those eligible, Dept. of Aging.

Respite Care: Respite care provides short-term inpatient or home care to an individual adult, child or elderly person as a temporary substitute for their regular caregiver.

- Regulation: No separate license required of existing licensed providers.
- Payment: **Private Pay,** Funding through home and community based waiver and the Department of Aging.

b. Home Health Care: (Licensed) Home health care provides medically-oriented care for acute or chronic illness in the patient's home, usually as a follow-up to acute or other discharge.

- Regulation: Licensed and Medicare and Medi-Cal certified by DHS.
- Payment: Funded primarily through Medicare, with limited coverage through Medi-Cal, private insurance and private payments.

c. Hospice: (Licensed): Hospice provides care and support for the terminally ill and their families. It can be provided in a facility setting or at home.

- Regulation: Hospice license required for in-home care. Dual license required in a facility setting. Medicare certification required for Medicare or Medi-Cal payments.
- Payment: Funded through Medicare, Medi-Cal, private insurance and private payments.

2. Facility Based Care: (All Licensed)

2.a MEDICAL:

a. **Hospitals:** Provide comprehensive medical attention which services include medical and nursing care during an emergency, rehabilitation and therapy for the ill or short-term clients of all ages.

- Regulation: Licensed and Medi-Cal and/or Medicare certified by the California Department of Health Services (DHS).
- Payment: Funded primarily by Medi-Cal. Some funding provided through Medicare, managed care and private payment.

b. **Skilled Nursing Facilities** (SNF's). SNF's, or nursing homes/convalescent hospitals, provide comprehensive nursing care for chronically ill or short-term clients of all ages, along with rehabilitation and specialized medical programs.

- Regulation: Licensed and Medi-Cal and/or Medicare certified by the California Department of Health Services (DHS).
- Payment: Funded primarily by Medi-Cal. Some funding provided through Medicare, managed care and private payment.

c. **Sub-acute Care Facilities**. Specialized units often in a distinct part of a nursing, sub-acute-care facilities focus on intensive rehabilitation, complex wound care and post-surgical recovery for clients of all ages who no longer need the level of care found in a hospital.

- Regulation: Licensed and Medi-Cal and/or Medicare certified by DHS.
- Payment: Funded primarily by Medi-Cal. Some funding through Medicare, managed care and private payment.

2.b NON-MEDICAL

a. **Assisted Living/Residential-Care Facilities for the Elderly** (RCFEs). Assisted living facilities provide personal care and safe housing for people who may need supervision for medication and assistance with daily living but who do not require 24-hour nursing care.

- Regulation: Licensed by Dept. of Social Services, Community Care Licensing Division.
- Payment: Funded primarily though private payments. Nearly 30% of RCFE clients rely on SSI/SSP non-medical out-of-home grants.

b. **Continuing Care Retirement Communities** (CCRCs). It includes three levels of care: independent, assisted living and nursing care. CCRCs require an entrance fee paid by the applicant upon admission and includes services for more than one year and up to the lifetime of the client.

- Regulation: Licensed by Dept. of Social Services, Continuing Care Contracts Branch. Skilled nursing level licensed by the Dept. of Health Services.
- Payment: Private Payment

    c. **Intermediate-Care Facilities** (ICF's). These facilities provide room and board, along with regular medical, nursing, social and rehabilitative services for people not capable of full independent living.

- Regulation: Licensed by Health Care Licensing and paid thru Medi-Cal and/or Medicare certified by DHS.
- Payment: Funded primarily by Medi-Cal. Some funding through Medicare and private payment.

    d. **Intermediate-Care Facilities for the Developmentally Disabled (ICF/DDs).** This is known at the federal level as ICF's/MR (mental retardation), these facilities provide services for people of all ages with mental retardation and/or developmental disabilities. ICF/DD's have 6 to more than 16 beds; ICF/DD-H (habilitative) and N's (nursing) have 15 or fewer beds and average six beds in a home setting.

- Regulation: Licensed thru Health Care Licensing and Medi-Cal certified by DHS. The Department of Developmental Services and Regional Centers are responsible for placement and quality assurance.
- Payment: Nearly 100% Medi-Cal.

    e. **Institutes for Mental Health (SNF/STPs).** Designated in California as "special treatment programs," these facilities provide extended treatment periods for people of all ages with chronic mental health issues; many of the clients are younger than 65. Specialized staff serves clients in a secured environment.

- Regulation: Licensed and Medi-Cal certified by Department of Health Services DHS. Local mental health departments are responsible for placement and program content.
- Payment: A combination of state and county funding.

Community Care-Based

    f. **Community Care Facilities:** Community care facilities provide 24-hour non-medical residential care to children, adults and seniors with developmental disabilities including seniors and adults without disabilities unable to care for themselves and those with behavioral/mental illness. This category may include the care for high risk-assaultive children in a group home setting.

- Regulation: Licensed by Dept of Social Services, Community Care Licensing Division.

- Payment: Funding through home and community-based Medi-Cal waiver program. Regional Center funding for the developmentally disabled.

Residential Care Facilities:

1. Small Family Homes (SFH)
2. Foster Family Homes (FFH)
3. Foster Family (FFA)
4. Transitional Housing (TH)
5. Group Homes (GH)
6. Adult Residential Care (ARF)
7. Residential Care for the Elderly (RCFE)
8. Residential Care for the Chronically Ill (RCFCI)
9. Adult Day Care (ADCF) / Social Day Care (SDC)

g. **Congregate Housing:** Housing with a common living area and non-medical support services to meet basic needs of older people.

- Regulation: Dept of Social Services, Community Care Licensing Division.
- Payment: Grants provided through the Federal Government (Housing & Urban Development). Some funding through SSI/SSP for those eligible.

If we discuss each subject I mentioned, it could take us more time than necessary and it could become too confusing to read. For our intent and purpose, we shall focus our discussion on PERSONAL CARE SERVICES which is the business that we are about to engage. For those of you who have heard of group homes and are interested in these types of business, allow me to introduce them to you briefly.

Different types of Facilities Available Through Community Care Licensing?

1. **Small Family Homes (SFH)**
2. **Foster Family Homes (FFH)**
3. **Foster Family (FFA)**
4. **Transitional Housing (TH)**
5. **Group Homes (GH)**
6. **Adult Residential Care (ARF)**
7. **Residential Care for the Elderly (RCFE)**
8. **Residential Care for the Chronically Ill (RCFCI)**
9. **Adult Day Care (ADCF) / Social Day Care (SDC)**

As a matter of common practice, the manner of establishing any of the mentioned facilities are very similar to each other. If there is a slight difference, it may be easily detected depending on the specific type of facility. The higher the standard of care and service expectations there is on the particular type of facility, the stringent the requirement. But generally, procedures, steps and guidelines in establishing any residential care business, are very similar if not oddly identical. So, do not feel confused while researching the type of facility you are considering.

The first five categories of facilities are namely: small family home, foster family home, foster family, transitional housing, and group home involves placement for children who are victims of family abuse, neglect and/or the family's inability to care for their children. This temporary living arrangement where children will live in a family like setting, often times with another group of children from different families, in a 6 bed home supervised on a 24-hour non-medical basis is operated by either a mom and dad type of setting or by a staff member representing a private or non-profit organization directly responsible for their care and supervision.

Most, if not all, of the placements in these homes are undertaken as a result of a mandate from the family court advocating for the rights and interest of families particularly the children.

SMALL FAMILY HOME (SFH)

Provides 24 hour-a-day care in the licensee's family residence for six or fewer children who are abused and neglected; mentally disordered, developmentally disabled, physically handicapped, and who require special care and supervision as a result of such disabilities. Majority of these homes are situated in single-family residences or apartment units that are typically run by a mom-dad and their adult children who themselves comprises the staff that takes care of the clients. The placement is either for a short term or long term basis depending on the reason why the client is placed. It is similar to the set up of a foster family home but the difference is that it is managed on its own, for its own, and by its own. In order to become a small family home business operator, one must secure licensing from the local Community Care Licensing office of the Department of Social Services or Health Care Licensing and secure vendorization from the placement agencies such as the Child Protective Services, Regional Center, Dept. of Health, and Dept. of Mental Health

FOSTER FAMILY HOME (FFH)

Provides 24-hour care and supervision in a family type setting in the licensee's family residence for no more than 6 children. Care is provided to children who have been removed from their home due to neglect or abuse, children who require special health or who are mentally disordered, developmentally disabled, physically handicapped, and who require care and supervision as a result of such disabilities.

FOSTER FAMILY (FFA)

A non-profit organization engaged in the recruiting, certifying, training, and providing professional support to certified parents, or finding homes for placement of children for temporary or permanent care for children who require the level of care as an alternative to a group home setting. This is the agency directly responsible to the placement of children typically done by the Dept. of Children and Family Services, Child Protective Services

TRANSITIONAL HOUSING (TH)

An extension program intended for children coming from group homes who by age (exceeding 17 years old) and, by maturity, are almost ready for emancipation but are still in need of a short term support from government agencies. These adolescent children are provided with housing and support until they achieve self-reliance and independence. Typical transitional housing is in apartment complexes and single-family homes where the child-client lives responsibly with other children in a home-like setting where they learn to transition into responsible adulthood.

GROUP HOME (GH)

A group home provides 24-hour non-medical care and supervision to children in a structured environment. Services are provided, at least in part, by staff employed by the licensee. Group home licensees are responsible for the care and supervision of the children placed in the group home. Group homes are licensed by the California Department of Social Services (**CDSS**), Community Care Licensing Division (CCLD). CCLD monitors group homes by making unannounced visits at least once per year, and as often as necessary to make sure that the facilities meet the regulations.

The children are placed in the group homes by the county social services and probation departments (they make the greatest number of placements of children in these residential facilities), county mental health agencies and regional centers.

ADULT RESIDENTIAL (ARF)

It is a residential care facility of any capacity (typically 4-6 bed) that provides 24-hour non-medical care for adults, ages 18-59 years, who are unable to provide for their own daily needs, physically handicapped, developmentally disabled, and/or mentally disordered. Adult Residential Care Facilities are either operated by a family member or by staff representing a placement organization.

RESIDENTIAL CARE FOR THE ELDERLY (RCFE)

Residential care of any capacity that provide non-medical care to persons 60 years of age and over or persons under 60 with compatible needs; elderly clients requiring varying levels and intensities of care and supervision; and protective supervision or personal care; elderly who may be frail and/or disabled, and cannot, or do not desire to take care of their own daily needs.

RESIDENTIAL CARE FOR THE CHRONICALLY ILL (RCFCI)

This is a facility with a licensed capacity of 25 or less, that provides care and supervision to adults who have Acquired Immune Deficiency Syndrome (AIDS) or the Human-Immunodeficiency Virus (HIV).

ADULT DAY CARE (ADCF) / SOCIAL DAY CARE (SDCF)

A facility of any capacity that provide programs for frail adults, elderly, developmentally disabled individuals, and / or mentally disordered in a day care setting.

In order to simplify our discussion on the business, the book will be limiting its scope on understanding the In-Home Care Services. If you need to know more about these types of business, my other book: "An Easy Guide on How to Establish Your First Residential Care" is available at your local bookstores and the internet through my publisher Authorhouse.com.

CHAPTER TWO: STARTING THE BUSINESS PLAN

A. Steps in Setting up the Caregiving Business

In order to start the business right, the single most important step is to create a business plan. The business plan serves as a road map to where you are and how you will get to where you need to be. You must have a general idea or a guideline to follow as to how you will go through the whole process of establishing your first caregiving business. Cited in this book are practical steps in a form of a check-list that you may follow at your own pace. As regulations in other states may vary, you have to make the necessary adjustments to fit your own objectives. All the steps mentioned here are general guidelines only for purposes of establishing expectations. The guidelines may be interchangeable as other steps may not be necessary depending on particular situations that you will encounter that also depends on the county or state regulations or requirements. However, it is important for you, the reader, to be flexible and to observe the guidelines set forth by the local regulation in your respective state or county. For those who are new in the business, the guidelines provided will definitely serve as a useful tool.

HOW TO STEPS IN SETTING UP THE CAREGIVING BUSINESS

Step 1:   Create a Business Plan.

(Time line: 30-90 days)

Step 2:   Set-Up a Business Entity and Register with the Secretary of State

(Time line: 30-90 days)

- Establish your Entity: Corporation, Sole Proprietorship, Partnership, Limited Liability Company
- Secure a business address and a dedicated business telephone number
- File for a Fictitious Business Name Statement
- Register the business entity with the Secretary of State

- Secure a Tax Identification Number (TIN)
- Contact your local IRS, Franchise Tax Board, City Hall, etc... Secure For Profit or Not for Profit Status through IRS-Franchise Tax Board
- Open a business bank account
- Advertise in the local newspaper for clients, job applicants, staff, consultants who will work for you
- Provide a Minimum 8-Hour Introductory Staff Training before sending your staff to their respective assignments

Step 3: Finance the Business

(Time line: 30-60 days)

Step 4: Secure a Business License from you local City Hall

(Time line: 30-60 days)

Step 5: Create Policies and Procedures

(Time line: 10 days)

Step 6: Create the Forms in the Operation of the Business

(Time line: 15 days)

Step 7: Get Fingerprinted by Live-Scan and secure a background check clearance from FBI-DOJ or your local police department for yourself and your staff.

(Time line: 3-15 days)

Step 8: Secure CPR-First Aid Certification.

(Time line: 3-15 days)

a. All staff must secure eight (8) hour HIV-Hepatitis certification course. (To be explained later)

b Direct Support Professionals: Direct support professionals in Service Levels 2, 3, and 4 facilities employed before January 1, 2001 must satisfactorily complete the first 35-hour training segment (Year 1) by January 1, 2002; and satisfactorily complete the second 35-hour training segment (Year 2) by January 1, 2003. Direct support professionals in Service Levels 2, 3, and 4 facilities employed on or after January 1, 2001, have one year from the date of hire to satisfactorily complete the first 35-hour training segment; and, two years from the date of hire to complete the second 35-hour training segment.

Step 9: Protect Your Business by securing Insurance Coverage.

(Time line: 30 days)

- General and Professional Liability Insurance should include abuse and allegation and other blanket insurance to protect yourself and your staff
- Property and Transportation Coverage
- Other related Insurance coverage (ask you local insurance broker)

Step 10:   Provide 40 hours of staff training on an annual Basis

(Time line: 5 days)

Step 11.   Advertise the business.

(Time line: 5 days)

- Produce flyers, business cards, and other handouts
- Promote the business by attending community events that promotes the interests of seniors
- Senior Centers
- Distribute flyers in hot spots such as groceries, strip malls, gas stations, parking lots, etc...
- Advertise in local magazines and newspapers
- Create an activity to sponsor local events and community gatherings
- Knock on doors and distribute flyers and mailers in your local community or neighborhood
- Yellow Pages, Phone Books and Local Newspaper clip ads

Remember that in advertising, it is purely a numbers game. The more frequent your business name is out in the community, the higher your chance is in securing local interest.

Step 12:   CREATE A STAFF DATABASE:

Always maintain a list of engaged/active employees and have an applicant database. Replenish the database with fresh new names and prospects. Keep in touch, and if possible, retain the part-timers and the on-calls for emergency purposes.

- Advertise regularly for job placements and employment opportunities to have a continuous database of available employees and interested applicants
- Categorize the job applicants by addresses to cover certain areas and communities, special assignments, etc...

You need to sacrifice a lot of your time and resources in order to market the business to the public. This is one of the essential elements in keeping your business active and profitable.

CHAPTER THREE: THE BUSINESS

STEP 1: CREATE A BUSINESS PLAN

(Time line: 30-90 days)

A. BUSINESS PLAN

A business plan is a formal statement illustrating a set of ideas and goals written and drawn in a form of a plan to indicate the cause and reasons why and how to achieve them in order to determine the possible results or directions of the business. Preparing a business plan is the most important first step that a beginner needs to take regardless of the size, or the amount to be invested in the business. Even if it is just a small mom and pop type of business, you still need a business plan. To those who do not have any experience in setting up any type of enterprise, there is no other way to emphasize the importance of preparing a business plan. Obtaining research on the business that you are planning to get into may take a lot of work, but it is all well worth it. There are self-help books out there that you can use or you may ask help from a friend who can do it for you. You may also seek assistance from the Small Business Administration (SBA) in your local area. Any local chamber of commerce can be a useful resource in preparing a business plan. Also available to the public are computer software that is "user friendly" even the most computer challenged individual may be able to use in creating a decent plan. It does not have to be elaborate nor intensive. What is important is to determine the basic information in current demand, its profitability and of course the possible challenges in the operation and success of the business.

To give you an idea as to how a business plan may look like, a sample plan is found on EXHIBIT ONE: BUSINESS PLAN page 138 of this book.

Below is a general outline of a typical business plan. It indicates the topics or items that the preparer will need to discuss in order to present an informal plan.

A Business Plan Guide
1. Cover Sheet

    2. Statement of purpose

    3. Table of Contents

I. The Business

   A. Description of the Business

   B. Marketing

   C. Competition

   D. Operating Procedures

   E. Personnel

   F. Financial Data

II. Financial Data

   A. Capital equipment and supply list

   B. Balance Sheet

   C. Break even analysis

   D. Pro-forma income projections (profit and loss statement)

   E. Three year summary

      Detail by month, first year

      Detail by quarter, second and third years

      Assumption upon which projections were based from

   F. Pro-forma cash flow

III. Supporting Documents

   A. Tax returns for last three years

   B. Personal financial statement

   C. Resume of all professionals and their respective services

   D. Others

The Business Plan also serves as an entrepreneur's introduction to the business. The best part about having a plan is that one will have a clearer understanding of the whole undertaking before making the commitment to the business. The financial information presented on the plan will help the prospective entrepreneur in making an intelligent and meticulous evaluation to determine if the project is viable or not. When seeking financing for the business, the plan can be a useful tool for bankers, venture capitalists, investors in their evaluation of the benefits and the risk potential of their investment. In some cases, the business loan applicant may be required to provide financial statements as well as the proof of financial ability to sustain the business on a long-term basis. Some investors or stakeholders may require equity participation on the part of the entrepreneur for at least 50% before interested parties may even consider in reviewing the proposal. Investors and bankers will even verify all pertinent financial information that the applicant submits including tax returns, bank statements, and verification of deposit. However, do not be alarmed because the business concept that you are about to learn from this book requires very minimal capital, that you might not even need financial help from any one except from your own pocket or from that of your relatives who may show interest in your business idea. The answer to the question, how much money do you need to start this business is purely dependent on what you want to spend initially for your own business. There is no simple answer, nor is there a right or wrong response to this complex question.

Depending on factors such as business location, equipment etc..., the **lowest start-up cost may range between $ 1,000.00 to about $ 3,500.00 only,** depending on your budget for your start-up equipment cost and other unexpected start-up expenses of the business (depending on the state, city and other regulatory fee requirements). However, after combining all your cost and expenses, your total start up cost can be **$ 8,764.00.** It is important for every start-up entrepreneurs to have cash reserves to cover other unforeseen cost of maintaining the business for at least three to six months or until the first solicited client make their initial payment/deposit.

There are several ways to finance your start-up business. Some of them may come from securing a loan from local banks using equity on real estate property, IRA, 401K, 457, Savings Bonds, Mutual Funds, stocks, bonds etc... Try to consider creative financing by pulling in a business partner (s) or a group of professionals who are willing to invest their experience, time, and money into the project.

B. THE START UP COST

Part of the requirements in the initial research process is for the entrepreneur to come up with a budget proposal which is reflected on the business plan. The stated amount may be verified (or maybe not) by the investors/bank financiers.

Included in this section is a sample budget statement for the reader to review in order to have an idea as to the type of format and the basic contents of a budget proposal.

SAMPLE START UP COST	Amount
Reservation of Corporate Name	$ 10.00
Live-Scan Fingerprinting	$ 184.00
Market Research and Consultation (Optional)	$ (3,000.00)
Articles of Incorporation	$ 100.00
Gas /Mileage	$ 80.00
Law and Business Software	$ 100.00
Hep/HIV Certification	$ (80.00)
Accounting Software	$ (80.00)
Fictitious Business Name/	$ 100.00
Business License/City Registration	$ 100.00
Business Insurance/Site Deposit	$ (300.00)
Automobile Insurance Deposit	$ 100.00
Professional/General	
Liability Insurance	$ (600.00)
Workers Comp. Deposit	$ (800.00)
Non-Hire Transport Insurance	$ (800.00)
Others	$ 200.00
Computer and Quickbook software	$ (1,500.00)
P.O. Box /Address	$ (200.00)

Telephone-Fax	$ 150.00
10-Key calculator	$ (25.00)
Answering machine	$ 40.00
Software/Database	$ 65.00
Pens/pencils/Supplies	$ 50.00

Equipment and supplies cost

Others	$ 100.00

Total Start-Up Cost:

Excluding Fixed and Variable Cost	**($ 8,764.00)**

If you are to start on a bare bones budget, you can cut down on a few start-up expenses that you may need to substitute later on:

a.   Business Plan Research
b.   Computer software
c.   Insurance
d.   Computer
e.   Office address (use your residence as business address)

All these are equally important to the business. However, since you are barely trying to survive during the initial stage of your business, you need to focus on your essential start-up expenses such as:

1.   Register your Corporation with the Secretary of State
2.   Secure a Business License
3.   Background check and fingerprinting
4.   Business Telephone Contact Number
5.   Secure a Business Address
6.   Business card and flyers
7.   Policies and Procedures
8.   Service Agreement
9.   Business forms

As your business expands, later on you can stretch your budget to cover the remaining essentials such as insurance, computer and others things that you may deem important to the operation of your business. In short, your initial "bare to the bones budget" as a start-up capital can be only less than **$ 3,500.00.**

The **$ 8,764.00 is your total projected start-up cost**. However, you do not need to have all that cash to start the business. All you need is approximately **$ 3,500 or less to start** with just the basics to market the business and gradually increase your expenses on "as needed basis only" to keep your expenses under control. Later on, as the business starts to generate revenue, you will need to cover important expenses such as professional and general liability insurance to protect your personal assets, and the business in the event of an accident, allegation, and other unexpected situations that could bind you, your staff, and your agency in a lawsuit that could seriously hurt your business. The projected cost may seem intimidating because of the cost of the research in the business plan. To offset this cost, you can do the research yourself using the library, Yellow Pages, Internet or by interviewing the competition. This is when you can be creative to find out about your competitors, type of services available, and prevailing price. Demographics, population, pricing, marketing strategies, demand, and general practice in the area that you intend to serve, average income, percentages of people by age, and other resources that you may need to utilize within the community.

While at your current job, start saving money for the cost of registering your company, securing a P.O. Box (post office box) or an apartment address to use as your business address, a designated business telephone number represented by your personal cell phone, and an answering machine to start. In order to solicit for prospects, you may need to distribute flyers and business cards in common and heavily populated areas, attend mixers, and other networking groups, sponsor activities at the senior centers, community plazas, etc... These are just a few of the creative ideas you can come up with to reduce your cost to the barest minimum and yet be able to practically start-up the business.

It is always a good business practice to keep sufficient amount of cash reserves to cover miscellaneous but necessary expenses in order for your agency to stay afloat while waiting for your first clients. You must be able to extend your cash reserves to cover expenses for up to at least six months in operating cost in case the process takes longer than expected. Come up with creative financing, aggressive marketing ideas, promotions, gimmicks to attract interest within the community. In order to be able to offset your expenditures and the limited cash, you sometimes must resort to creative spending. Try to extend your patience and finances in order to be able to survive the crucial first year of the business. There is no proven formula as to how soon you will be able generate positive cash flow but most of it is dependent on how determined and motivated you are in marketing the business to the public. It could take your business at least two to six months or even a year before accommodating your first client. That is why it is a good idea to keep your day job(s) until the revenue become stable and predictable. With the use of a business plan, you can draw up hypothesis and projection as to how you will be able to cope up with all the challenges that would confront your business during the initial phase of the business operation.

C. NO CASH RESERVES AVAILABLE YET?

Initial capitalization may come from the following sources:

a. Personal Savings Account
b. Home equity line of credit
c. Credit cards
d. Retirement funds and other investments
e. SBA Loan from a local bank
f. Business loans or equity sharing
g. Loans from friends and family
h. Unwanted Jewelries, personal belongings that can be sold for cash reserves

i.   Angels/Investors

Remember, take your time, save money, and earn the experience that you need before you make the tough commitment to do this business. Gradually purchase your operating equipment such as bond papers, computer, clips, folders, etc from garage sales, auctions, flea markets and just about every where you can to reduce your start-up expenses. An office space may be convenient and prestigious but not a necessity as the business may be operational and fully functioning simply with the use of a cell phone or by maintaining a dedicated telephone line to respond to inquiries on the business. A personal home address such as a room in an apartment unit or a post office box (P.O. Box) can serve as the business address where all correspondence and inquiries may be channeled accordingly. There are tons of benefits in having a home business. In other states, some of the dedicated expenses that are purely for the business such as paper clips, bond papers, telephone bill, coffee maker, rent, meals, etc…may be considered as business expenses write-offs. (Consult your local tax preparer or accountant on this subject). With the advancement in technology and communication particularly the Internet and broadband system, there are tons of advantages in maintaining a home-office, and one of them is cost efficiency, practicality, savings, and most of all tax benefits. However, advantages may come with a price such as the sacrifice for lack of privacy, business persona, etc… What matters is how you can save money, and at the same time start the business in a financially restrictive manner.

CHAPTER FOUR:
THE BUSINESS ENTITY

STEP 2: SET-UP A BUSINESS ENTITY AND REGISTER IT WITH THE SECRETARY OF STATE

(Time line: 30-90 days)

A. Sole Proprietorship
B. Partnership
C. Limited Liability Company
D. Corporation (For profit or Non- Profit)

In order for an entity to acquire official business status, it must register with the Secretary of State where it intends to operate its official business activities. The task of registering an enterprise is probably one of the biggest challenges for most start-up individuals, and since we are not here to learn business law, the discussion on this subject will be simple and brief. In this chapter, you will learn the different types of business entities currently available in most states in the US and it is up to you to make the choice as to what is best for your purpose. With the help of legal counsel (which I urge you to consult with), you will have a better understanding of the choice that you are about to make. Such important decisions will draw serious long-term impact on the business in terms of tax ramifications, legal and business complexities that are involved in the establishment and future operation of the business. If you have a ton of patience and do not mind reading a couple of books from the library on establishing a business entity, you could save yourself a lot of money. There are also useful reference materials available on the Internet and at your local bookstore. Registering your business with the Secretary of State is not as difficult as you think. First, it is very important to know what type of entity that you are interested in and then to have that business name and entity registered in the state or county where the business will be established or located. For residents of other states, you may need to search the world wide web by typing the words "SECRETARY OF STATE" and for California residents check out the California Secretary of State website at: http://www.ss.ca.gov/ under Business Filings.

Generally, in establishing a service-oriented business like this, you have the following choices:

a). Sole Proprietorship

b). Partnership

c). Limited Liability Company, LLC

d). Corporation

If you are to ask what would be the best choice, the answer will depend on your personal preference, and tolerance for risk and benefits. The most popular business entity for small businesses like a caregiving business is the **corporation** and recently discovering the benefits of a Limited Liability Corporation or LLC for obvious reasons, which you will read later on in this chapter.

Can your caregiving business be registered as a non-profit corporation? Yes, for practical reasons, you can. The discussion on this subject will be limited to corporations only. For purpose of illustration, this book presents in *EXHIBIT TWO: Articles of Incorporation and By-Laws found on page 170* a sample format for a non-profit corporation which is almost similar to a for-profit corporation except for a few articles that may seem too obvious due to the non-profit nature of a corporation. To give you a simple explanation on business entities, this book shall discuss in brief narrative each entity for you to make a determination as to what you think is best applicable.

A. SOLE PROPRIETORSHIP:

A sole proprietorship is a type of business entity that does not make a legal distinction between its being as a business as well as its private affairs. The business owner and the business itself are just one single entity or proprietorship. There is no distinction or separation. Therefore, all activities, profits and even **debts** are the sole responsibility of the owner. The person who sets up the company has sole responsibility for the company's debts. *The limitations of liability enjoyed by a corporation and limited liability corporations/partnerships does not apply to sole proprietors.* It is a "sole" proprietorship in the sense that the owner has no partners. A sole proprietorship essentially refers to a natural person (individual) doing business in his or her own name and in which there is only one owner. A sole proprietorship is not a corporation; it does not pay corporate taxes, but rather the person who organized the business pays personal income taxes on the profits made, making accounting much simpler. A sole proprietorship does not have to be concerned with double taxation, as a corporate entity would have to. A sole proprietor may do business with a trade name other than his or her legal name. In some jurisdictions, the sole proprietor is required to register the trade name or "Doing Business As" with the local government or city. This also allows the proprietor to open a business account with any banking institutions. In caregiving, most of the people I knew who started in the business were sole proprietors themselves who eventually shifted their entity into S-Corporation or Limited Liability Company (LLC) as the business grew.

Disadvantages:

A business organized as a sole proprietorship will likely have a hard time raising capital since shares of the business cannot be sold, and there is a lesser sense of legitimacy compared to a business organized as a corporation or limited liability company.

Transactions: It can also be more difficult to raise bank finance, as sole proprietorships cannot grant a floating charge which in many jurisdictions is required for bank financing. Hiring employees may also be difficult. ***This form of business will have unlimited liability, so if the business is sued, the proprietor is personally liable at the same time.***

Life span: The life span of the business is also uncertain. As soon as the owner decides not to have the business anymore, or the owner dies, the business ceases to exist. The business owner is responsible for everything and handles everything. He works for himself and by himself. As the business grows, the risks accompanying the business tend to come with it. To minimize risks, when the business improves the owner may transition it into a corporation or a limited liability company LLC, which would give the protection of limited liability but would still be treated as a sole proprietorship for income tax purposes.

B. PARTNERSHIP:

A partnership is a type of business entity in which partners (owners) will equally or proportionately share with each other the profits or losses of the business. Partnerships are often favored over corporations for taxation purposes, as the partnership structure does not generally incur a tax on profits before it is distributed to the partners (i.e. there is no dividend tax levied). However, depending on the partnership structure and the jurisdiction in which it operates, owners of a partnership may be exposed to greater personal liability than they would as shareholders of a corporation. The cost to register your Partnership is $ 70.00 (Form LP-1), $ 15.00 handling fee and annually, your company needs to pay a minimum of $ 800.00 to the Franchise Tax Board.

A limited partnership is a form of partnership similar to a general partnership, except that in addition to one or more general partners (GPs), there are one or more limited partners (LPs). The GPs are, in all major respects, in the same legal position as partners in a conventional firm, i.e. they have management control, share the right to use partnership property, share the profits of the firm in predefined proportions, and have joint and shared liability for the debts of the partnership. In a general partnership, the GPs have actual authority as agents of the firm to bind all the other partners in contracts with third parties that are in the ordinary course of the partnership's business. As with a general partnership, "An act of a general partner which is not apparently for carrying on in the ordinary course the limited partnership's activities or activities of the kind carried on by the limited partnership binds the limited partnership only if the act was actually authorized by all the other partners." (United States Uniform Limited Partnership Act § 402(b)).

Like shareholders in a corporation, LPs have limited liability, meaning it is only liable on debts incurred by the firm to the extent of its registered investment and have no management authority. The GPs pay the LPs a return on its investment (similar to a dividend), the nature and extent of which is usually defined in the partnership agreement.

C. LIMITED LIABILITY COMPANY:

A limited liability company (abbreviated L.L.C. or LLC) is a legal form of business company offering limited liability to its owners. Often incorrectly called a "limited liability corporation" (instead of company), it is a hybrid business entity having characteristics of both a corporation and a partnership. It is often more flexible, the owners have limited liability for the actions and debts of the company, and it is suitable for smaller companies with a single owner. The primary corporate characteristic is limited liability while the primary partnership characteristic is the availability of pass-through income taxation. The cost to register your LLC is $ 70.00 (Form LLC-1), $ 15.00 handling fee and annually, your company needs to pay a minimum of $ 800.00 to the Franchise Tax Board.

LLCs may either be member-managed or manager-managed. A member-managed LLC may be governed by a single class of members it approximates a partnership) or multiple classes of members it approximates a limited partnership). Choosing a manager, management creates a two-tiered management structure that approximates corporate governance with the managers typically holding powers similar to corporate officers and directors. The LLC's operating agreement (the LLC version of a partnership agreement or a corporation's by-laws) determines how the LLC is managed. Corporations, S-corporations, Limited Liability Partnerships, Limited Partnerships, Limited Liability Limited Partnerships, and LLCs lie along a spectrum of flexibility with LLCs being the most flexible, and thus preferable, for many businesses.

For Income Tax purposes, LLCs that are treated as partnerships use IRS Form 1065. LLCs are organized with a document called the "articles of organization," or "the rules of organization" specified publicly by the state; additionally, it is common to have an "operating agreement" privately specified by the members. The operating agreement is a contract among the members of a LLC and the LLC governing the membership, management, operation and distribution of income of the company.

Under some circumstances, the members (the LLC version of shareholders or partners) may elect for the LLC to be taxed like a corporation (taxation of the entity's income prior to any dividends or distributions to the members and then taxation of the dividends or distributions once received as income by the members). Operating as an LLC form of partnership does not mean that appropriate US federal partnership tax forms are not necessary, or not complex. As a partnership, the entity's income and deductions attributed to each member are reported on that owner's tax return.

With federal income tax treatment as a partnership, LLCs can lose the tax advantage. The possible label, "disregarded entity" for income tax purposes, singles out the one-member owner of a LLC as actually earning income and deductions directly. It is the owner, who reports as a business proprietor, rather than as a LLC operating an active trade or business. A LLC passively investing in real estate and owned by a single member would have its income and deductions reported directly on the owner's individual tax return on a Schedule E tax form. A LLC owned by a corporation/individual. In other words, a LLC with a single corporate member would be treated as an incorporated branch and have its income and deductions reported on the corporate tax return, creating double taxation.

Advantages:

- A LLC can elect to be taxed as a sole proprietor, partnership, S corporation or C corporation, providing much flexibility
- Limited liability, meaning that the owners of the LLC, called "members," are protected from some liability for acts and debts of the LLC, but are still responsible for any debts beyond the fiscal capacity of the entity
- Much less administrative paperwork and record keeping than a corporation

- Pass-through taxation (i.e., no double taxation), unless the LLC elects to be taxed as a C corporation
- Using default tax classification, profits are taxed personally at the member level, not at the LLC level
- LLCs in most states are treated as entities separate from their members, whereas in other jurisdictions case law has developed deciding LLCs are not considered to have separate juridical standing from their members
- LLCs in some states can be set up with just one natural person involved
- Membership interests of LLCs can be assigned, and the economic benefits of those interests can be separated and assigned, providing the assignee with the economic benefits of distribution of profits/losses (like a partnership), without transferring the title to the membership interest
- Unless the LLC has chosen to be taxed as a corporation, income of the LLC generally retains its character, for instance as capital gains or as foreign sourced income, in the hands of the members

Disadvantages:

- Although there is no statutory requirement for an operating agreement in most states, members who operate without one may run into problems.
- It may be more difficult to raise financial capital for an LLC as investors may be more comfortable investing funds in the better-understood corporate form with a view toward an eventual IPO. One possible solution may be to form a new corporation and merge into it, dissolving the LLC and converting into a corporation.
- Many states, including Alabama, California, Kentucky, New York, Pennsylvania, Tennessee, and Texas, levy a franchise tax or capital values tax on LLCs. Texas has replaced its franchise tax with a "margin tax".) In essence, this franchise or business privilege tax is the "fee" the LLC pays the state for the benefit of limited liability. The franchise tax can be an amount based on revenue, an amount based on profits, or an amount based on the number of owners or the amount of capital employed in the state, or some combination of those factors, or simply a flat fee, as in Delaware.
- Some creditors will require members of up-and-starting LLCs to personally guarantee the LLC's loans, thus making the members personally liable for the debt of the LLC.
- The management structure of an LLC may be unfamiliar to many. Unlike corporations, they are not required to have a board of directors or officers.
- Taxing jurisdictions outside the US are likely to treat a US LLC as a corporation, regardless of its treatment for US tax purposes, for example if a US LLC does business outside the US or a client of a foreign jurisdiction is a member of a US LLC.
- The LLC form of organization is relatively new, and as such, some states do not fully treat LLCs in the same manner as corporations for liability purposes, instead treating them more as a disregarded entity, meaning an individual operating a business as an LLC may in such a case be treated as operating it as a sole proprietorship, or a group operating as an LLC may be treated as a general partnership, which defeats the purpose of establishing an LLC in the first place, to have limited liability (a sole proprietor

has unlimited liability for the business; in the case of a partnership, the partners have joint and several liability, meaning any and all of the partners can be held liable for the business' debts no matter how small their investment or percentage of ownership).

- The principals of LLCs use many different titles-- e.g., member, manager, managing member, managing director, chief executive officer, president, and partner. As such, it can be difficult to determine who actually has the authority to enter into a contract on the LLC's behalf.

- A Series LLC is a special form of a Limited liability company that allows a single LLC to segregate its assets into separate series. For example, a series LLC that purchases separate pieces of real estate may put each in a separate series so if the lender forecloses on one piece of property, the others are not affected. (Wikipedia)

D. CORPORATION:
(FOR PROFIT OR NON-PROFIT)

A corporation is a legal entity that you form by filing articles of incorporation (in some states, the term used in the statute is certificate of incorporation) with the Secretary of State in the state in which you have chosen to organize the corporation, along with the required filing and license fees. The cost is: $ 100.00 to file for Articles of Incorporation and $ 15.00 special handling fee. Each year, the company is subject to a minimum Franchise Tax of $ 800.00/year. The fees are subject to change or varies from state to state.

One or more persons can form a corporation. Thus, a sole proprietor can incorporate if he or she chooses to do so. With some exceptions (doctors and lawyers are prohibited by ethical and regulatory constraints from operating in certain types of corporations), corporations can generally operate any type of business. Deciding whether or not to incorporate is an important choice to make when starting your new caregiving business.

Advantages:

Owner Protection from Legal Liability: Once a new business's owner(s) successfully completes the incorporation process, the owner(s) have a limited amount of legal liability for the corporation's business activities and debts, because in the eyes of the law the corporation is a separate entity. In order to maintain this limited liability, the corporation's owners must follow a number of legally required corporate formalities.

Power Structure: The corporate business form has an established power and management structure: directors, officers, and shareholders. Each group has its own set of clearly defined roles and responsibilities within the corporate framework of the business.

Disadvantages:

Time and Cost of Incorporation: The incorporation process can be expensive and time-consuming. A number of documents must be prepared (including the new corporation's articles of incorporation and bylaws), and filing fees must be paid to your state's Secretary of State Office (or similar business filing).

Following Corporate Formalities: Corporations are required by law to observe a number of corporate formalities, to ensure that the corporation is operating as a separate entity and independent of the business's owners. These steps include holding regular meetings of directors, keeping records of corporate activity, and maintaining the corporation's ongoing financial independence.

Potential Tax Liability: The profit from traditional corporations may be "double taxed." That is, the corporation itself is taxed for profits earned, and any individual stockholder who earned profits from the corporation (in the form of paid "dividends") are also taxed. However, in small businesses, owners of the corporations, who often work for the business itself are paid salaries (which are tax-deductible for the corporation) rather than dividends. One solution to the double-taxation problem is electing "S" corporation tax status.

Corporations Compared to Sole Proprietorships and Partnerships, Corporations enjoy many advantages over partnerships and sole proprietorships. But, there are also disadvantages. We cover the most important upsides and downsides below.

Advantages:

Stockholders are not liable for corporate debts: This is the most important aspect of a corporation. In a sole proprietorship and partnership, the owners are personally responsible for the debts of the business. In situations when the assets that belong to the sole proprietorship or partnership cannot satisfy the debt, creditors can go after each owner's personal assets such as a house, car, bank account, salaries, etc. to make up for the difference. On the other hand, if a corporation runs out of funds, its owners are usually off the hook.

Please note that under certain circumstances, an individual stockholder may be liable for corporate debts. This is sometimes referred to as "piercing the corporate veil." Some of these circumstances include:

- If a stockholder personally guarantees a debt
- If personal funds are intermingled with corporate funds
- If a corporation fails to have director and shareholder meetings
- If the corporation has minimal capitalization or minimal insurance
- If the corporation fails to pay state taxes or otherwise violates state law

Self-Employment Tax Savings: Earnings from a sole proprietorship are subject to self-employment taxes, which are currently a combined 15.3%. With a corporation, only salaries (and not profits) are subject to such taxes. This advantage is most significant for stockholder-employees who take a salary of less than $ 72,600.

For example, if a sole proprietorship earns $ 60,000, a 15.3% tax would have to be paid on the entire $ 60,000. Assume that a corporation also earns $ 60,000, but $ 40,000 of that amount is paid in salary, and $ 20,000 is deemed as profit. In this case, the self-employment tax would not be paid on the $ 20,000 profit. This saves the stockholder-employee over $ 3,000 per year. Please note, however, that you should pay yourself a reasonable salary. The IRS frowns upon stockholder-employees who pay themselves too little.

Continuous life: The life of a corporation, unlike that of a partnership or sole proprietorship, does not expire upon the death of its stockholders, directors or officers.

Easier to raise money: A corporation has many avenues to raise capital. It can sell shares of stock, and it can create new types of stock, such as preferred stock, with different voting or profit characteristics. Plus, investors are assured that they will not be personally liable for corporate debts.

Ease of transfer: Ownership interests in a corporation may be sold to third parties without disturbing the continued operation of the business. The business of a sole proprietorship or partnership, on the other hand, cannot be sold as a whole; instead, each of its assets, licenses and permits must be individually transferred, and new bank accounts and tax identification numbers are required.

Disadvantages

Higher cost: Corporations cost more to set up and run than a sole proprietorship or partnership. For example, there are the initial formation fees, filing fees and annual state fees. These costs are partially offset by lower insurance costs.

Formal organization and corporate formalities: A corporation can only be created by filing legal documents with the state. In addition, a corporation must adhere to technical formalities. These include holding director and shareholder meetings, recording minutes, having the board of directors approve major business transactions and corporate record-keeping. If these formalities are not kept, the stockholders risk losing their personal liability protection. While keeping corporate formalities is not difficult, it can be time-consuming. On the other hand, a sole proprietorship or partnership can commence and operate without any formal organizing or operating procedures not even a handwritten agreement.

Unemployment tax: A stockholder-employee of a corporation is required to pay unemployment insurance taxes on his or her salary, whereas a sole proprietor or partner is not. Currently, the federal unemployment tax is 6.2% of the first $ 7,000 of wages paid, with a maximum of $ 434.00 per employee.

What is a non-profit corporation and how is it formed?

A corporation is a distinct legal entity under California law. A new corporation is born when its Articles of Incorporation and By Laws are filed with the Secretary of State. A non-profit (public benefit) corporation is different from a for-profit corporation. A for-profit corporation has owners whose goal is to create a profitable return. A non-profit corporation is created for charitable purpose, (i.e., to benefit the public at large and not for personal gain of certain individuals). But, non-profit does not necessarily mean the company cannot make a profit. You can make a profit.

In incorporating a non-profit organization, here are some important tips to consider:

1. Prepare articles of incorporation and file them with the Secretary of State.
2. Prepare organization by-laws.
3. Conduct an initial meeting of the board of directors. Items on the Agenda usually include adopting bylaws, electing officers, and planning a budget.
4. Apply for federal tax exemption from the Internal Revenue Service.
5. Apply for state tax exemption from the Franchise Tax Board.

WHAT IS AN ARTICLE OF INCORPORATION?

Information contained in the articles of incorporation will provide the Department information concerning who is ultimately responsible for which functions in the business.

The creation of this document signifies the start of a corporation as soon as it is registered with the Secretary of State. The articles of incorporation must at a minimum include:

1) The official name of the corporation
2) A statement that the corporation is a nonprofit or for profit and,
3) The name and address of a person in California who will accept legal notices (California Corporations Code Section 5130). There is more required information, which, if not included in your articles of incorporation, must be included in the bylaws **Officers of the Corporation:**

California corporations must have at least three officers: a President (Chairman of the Board), a Secretary, and a Chief Financial Officer (Treasurer) (California Corporations Code Section 5213). Officers (President, vice President, secretary, and treasurer) are in charge of carrying out the day-to-day business of the corporation. Their powers, duties and responsibilities are set by the articles of incorporation, bylaws, or by resolution of the board of directors. Officers owe a fiduciary duty to the corporation and must act honestly and in the best interest of the corporation. One person may fill one or more of the officer positions. However, the person or persons who hold (s) the offices of Secretary and Treasurer cannot also be President.

What is a Board of Directors?

The board of directors ("board") is the governing body of the corporation. The board consists of persons named in the articles of incorporation or bylaws or elected by the creators of the corporation and later board members to act as members of the board.

Composition of the Board

While it is convenient to have employees or relatives on the board, it is not always in the corporation's best interest because these individuals are likely "interested persons." There is a built-in conflict of interest if too many directors receive money from the corporation or if too many directors are related to employees of the corporation. In the case of a non-profit organization, no more than 49% of the board of directors may be "interested persons." "Interested persons" include any director who has received payment for services rendered within the past 12 months whether as an employee (full or part time), independent contractor, or otherwise. If a director is blood related to anyone who has received payment from the corporation, that director may be an "interested person" (California Corporations Code Section 5227). There is a good reason for this rule. Directors may have to decide whether to use corporate money for their own payment (or other interests) or for the corporation's charitable purposes. By limiting the number of "interested persons" serving as directors, the corporation limits the potential for self-dealing transactions and other conflicts of interest.

Board of Directors Duties:

a. Select, employ, assess and, if necessary, dismiss the Chief Executive Officer.

b. Provide support, comments and criticism, when needed; hold the staff accountable for carrying out plans and policy decisions; provide a formal performance review and appraisal.

c. Adopt and monitor the corporation's operating budget, financial development plan and insurance program.

d. Review and understand the financial statements on a regular basis to ensure the financial health of the corporation and that the corporate funds are being spent appropriately and in accordance with the board's financial plan and budget.

e. Perform its legal responsibilities.

f. To act for the corporation as outlined in the articles of incorporation, constitution and/or bylaws.

g. Protect the assets of the corporation. Ensure that no board member, management, or staffs are overpaid or unfairly or unreasonably profiting from business dealings with the corporation.

h. Ensure the corporation's equipment is not being misused.

i. Ensure all purchases and leases have fair and reasonable terms, and represent the best deal possible to the corporation.

j. Board development (recruiting, orienting and assessing the board).

Standard of Care: Directors must perform their duties in the following manner:

The duties must be performed in a manner that the director believes to be in the best interest of the corporation; and the duties must be performed with such care, including reasonable inquiry, required under the circumstances (California Corporations Code Section 5231).

The directors have the authority and responsibility for managing the corporation. The directors meet and make decisions together as the board of directors ("board"). The board is ultimately responsible for making sure a corporation is ran properly. If it fails to do so, individual directors may be responsible. All corporate powers are exercised under the board's direction (California Corporations Code Section 5210). While certain powers may be assigned to committees, officers, or employees, their use of that power and their actions are subject to the board's review, direction and control. The board must take an active role in overseeing the corporation. The following are some specific duties of the board of directors:

- Make and approve long-range goals and objectives
- Actively participate in the management, authorization of the corporation's long-term protection
- Approve or delegate approval of annual objectives and priorities established to achieve long-range goals
- Develop a financial plan to ensure that there are adequate funds to pay expenses and long-range goals and objectives. This could include fund raising to supplement the program

- Make and adopt policies
- Establish the limits of the Executive Director's authority to budget, administer finances and compensation, and otherwise manage the corporation

Minutes of the Board Meeting:

A corporation must keep a written record of the meetings of its board and committees of the board (California Corporations Code Section 6320). In addition, the minutes of the board meetings must be made available to California Department of Social Services staff, upon request (Health and Safety Code Section 1520l(f)). The law requires the minutes to contain enough information to make a clear written record for future use. The primary purpose for keeping minutes is to have documentation that explains the actions of the board, which may be used later on to defend its actions. Although minutes need not be a word-for-word record of everything said at a board meeting, they must present an accurate record of what was done, such as time, place, who was present, what was discussed, results of all votes taken, and what decisions were made and why. Any documents the board or committee uses to make decisions (including financial statements) should be attached to the minutes if they are non-confidential. If these documents are confidential, they must be clearly identified in the minutes. However, if the documents are usually apart of the corporation's permanent records, they must either be attached to the minutes or clearly identified in the minutes.

Usually the Secretary of the corporation is responsible for preparing the minutes and distributing the minutes either in advance of the next board meeting or at the meeting. A vote to approve the minutes is required only when board members want to make changes to the minutes as presented by the Secretary. Lastly, the minutes should be certified by the Secretary (California Corporations Code Section 5215).

Board Meeting:

Board of directors meetings must be held at least every three (3) months (Health and Safety Code Section 1520.1 (e)). At these meetings, the board of directors shall review and discuss business operations and other issues affecting the business. Board of directors meetings can be held anywhere stated in the notice, bylaws or board resolution. If the meeting place is not stated in any of these ways, then it must be held at the principal office of the corporation.

Voting Requirements:

In order for any act or decision of the board of directors to be official, it must be voted on by a quorum. A quorum is the number of members necessary to take action at a meeting (California Corporations Code Section 5211). The quorum may be stated in the articles of incorporation or bylaws and must meet the legal rules. A quorum can never be less than the majority of directors present.

DUE DILIGENCE:

In exercising due diligence, the directors must conduct a reasonable investigation into the facts. For example, assume the corporation is considering hiring one of its directors to perform bookkeeping services. An independent person or committee should be appointed to conduct an investigation into the facts. At a minimum, the facts considered should include what bookkeeping services are required and what other bookkeepers charge for similar services. The fair market rates should then be compared to that of the "interested director." The directors must review in good faith all of the information gathered by the independent investigation, and all other relevant information, and ask all necessary questions in order to make an honest and informed decision. This review and comparison will indicate to the board whether the transaction is "fair and reasonable" to the corporation.

What are By-Laws?

The bylaws provide the rules for governing and operating the corporation (California Corporations Code Section 5151). If you have this information in your articles of incorporation, you do not need bylaws. However, if you make any changes to your articles of incorporation, you must file the changes with the Secretary of State. Bylaws must state the number of directors of the corporation, unless stated in the articles. Unless restricted by law or the articles of incorporation, the board of directors can set, adopt and amend bylaw provisions.

The following are typical provisions included in bylaws:

1. The time, place, and method used to call meetings of members, directors, and committees
2. The duties, powers, method of election and qualification of directors
3. The length of directors' terms
4. The manner of appointment, duties, compensation, and the length of officers' terms
5. The requirements of reports to members
6. The rules for admitting and removing members
7. The appointment and authority of committees
8. The special requirements for the percentage of member and director votes needed to take certain actions
9. The number of directors needed to make a quorum

WHERE TO KEEP THE ARTICLES OF INCORPORATIONS AND BYLAWS?

Current copies of the articles of incorporation and bylaws must be kept at your principal California office (California Corporations Code Section 5160). A copy of the bylaws and articles of incorporation should be kept up to date by filing copies of amendments as they are adopted by resolutions of the board of directors (California Corporations Code Sections 5215 and 5810-5820).

The directors have the authority and responsibility of managing the corporation. The directors meet and make decisions together as the board of directors ("board"). The board is ultimately responsible for making sure a corporation is ran properly. If it fails to do this, individual directors may be responsible. All corporate powers are exercised under the board's direction (California Corporations Code Section 5210). While certain powers may be assigned to committees, officers, or employees, its use of that power and its actions are subject to the board's review, direction and control.

The final action is to register the business entity with the Secretary of State of the county where the business is located. To register the organization, forms are available through the local county agencies and the Office of the Secretary of State.

Registration cost may vary from State to State so the reader is advised to contact his/her local State office that handles the registration of business organizations.

The life of a corporation begins upon the filing of articles of incorporation with the Secretary of State's office. Prior to filing the articles of incorporation, the following issues should be considered:

WHERE SHOULD I FORM THE CORPORATION?

Wherever you prefer, you can incorporate in any of the 50 states. Delaware is a popular choice because of its history, experience, recognition and pro-business climate. In fact, over half of the companies listed on the New York Stock Exchange are incorporated in Delaware. Recently, Nevada has also gained popularity due to its pro-business environment and lack of a formal information-sharing agreement with the IRS. Neither Delaware nor Nevada has corporate income taxes, and business filings in these states can usually be performed more quickly than in other states. Many people also choose to incorporate in their home state. Doing so may save them money because corporations are required to register as a "foreign corporation" in each state where it does business, and there is often no need to pay another person to serve as the registered agent. For example, a Delaware corporation that has its main business office in Texas must register as a "foreign corporation" with the Texas Secretary of State.

However, if your home state has a high corporate income tax or high state fee, and your corporation will not "do business" in that state, it may be wise to incorporate elsewhere. "Doing business" means more than just selling products or making passive investments in that state. It usually requires occupying an office or otherwise having an active business presence.

Choosing a name

In general, the name of a corporation must end with "incorporated," "corporation," "corp." or "Inc." A name will not be accepted if it is likely to mislead the public or if it too closely resembles the name of another corporation formed in that state.

If the name of your corporation will be used in connection with goods or services, you may wish to consider obtaining federal trademark protection for the name. This ensures that no one else in the U.S. may use that name in connection with the same general type of goods or services (except in areas where someone else is already using that name).

The Board of Directors

A corporation is managed by the board of directors, which must approve major business decisions. A director can be, but is not required to be, either a shareholder or an officer. Like representatives in congress, directors are elected by the shareholders and typically serve for a limited term. Each corporation must have at least one director.

Examples of procedures which must be approved by the board of directors include:

- Declaring a dividend
- Electing officers and setting the terms of their employment
- Amending bylaws or the articles of incorporation
- Any corporate merger, reorganization or other significant corporate transaction

Directors of a corporation owe duties of loyalty and care to the corporation. Generally, it means that directors must act in good faith, with reasonable care, and in the best interest of the corporation.

Registered Agent

Each corporation must have a registered agent, the person designated to receive official state correspondence and notice if the corporation is "served" with a lawsuit. The registered agent must be either (1) an adult living in the state of formation with a street address (P.O. boxes are not acceptable) or (2) a corporation with a business office in the state of formation which provide registered agent services.

As previously mentioned, one of the advantages of forming a corporation in your home state is that any officer or director can act as the registered agent. However, there are some advantages to having another person or company act as your registered agent. First, this adds an extra layer of privacy, since the name and address of the registered agent is publicly available. Second, this ensures that if your corporation is named in a lawsuit, no one will surprise you at home on a Sunday night with court papers.

Corporations compared to LLCs

Limited liability companies are a relatively new type of business entity that combine the personal liability protection of a corporation with the tax benefits and simplicity of a partnership. However, there are still other important differences. The following discusses the main advantages and disadvantages of corporations versus LLCs.

Advantages of Corporations:

Profits are not subject to social security and medicare taxes: Salaries and profits of a LLC are subject to self-employment taxes, currently equal to a combined 15.3%. With a corporation, only salaries, and not profits, are subject to such taxes. This advantage is most significant for stockholder-owners who take a salary of less than $ 72,600.

For example, if an owner-employee of an LLC earns $ 40,000 in salary and is distributed $ 20,000 of the LLC's profits, a 15.3% tax would have to be paid on $ 60,000. For an S-corporation, social security and medicare taxes would only have to be paid on the $ 40,000 salary. This saves the stockholder-employee over $ 3,000 per year. Please note, that the IRS frowns upon employee-owners of an S-corporation not paying themselves salary and simply distributing the profits. In situations where the IRS feels that shareholders are taking too little in salary, the IRS will characterize all or part of the profits as salary.

Since limited liability companies are still relatively new, not everyone is familiar with them. In some cases, banks or vendors may be reluctant to extend credit to limited liability companies. Moreover, some states have restrictions as to the type of business that a LLC may conduct.

Greater variety of, and fewer taxes on, fringe benefits.

Corporations offer a greater variety of fringe benefit plans than any other type of business entity. Various retirements, stock option and employee stock purchase plans are available only for corporations. Plus, while sole proprietors, partners and employees owning more than 2% of an S-corporation must pay taxes on fringe benefits (such as group-term life insurance, medical re-imbursement plans, medical insurance premiums and parking), stockholder employees of a C-corporation do not have to pay taxes on these benefits.

Tax Flexibility: Although C-corporations are subject to double taxation, they also offer greater tax flexibility. A C-corporation does not have to immediately distribute its profits to shareholders as dividend.

Disadvantages of Corporations:

More corporate formalities: Corporations must hold regular meetings of the board of directors and shareholders and keep written corporate minutes. Members and managers of a LLC need not hold regular meetings, which reduce complications and paperwork.

Ownership restrictions for S-corporations: S-corporations cannot have more than 75 stock-holders, and each stockholder must be an individual who is a client or citizen of the United States. Also, it is difficult to place shares of an S-corporation into a living trust. None of these restrictions or difficulties applies to a LLC.

Shareholders of C-corporations cannot deduct operating losses: Members who are active clients in the business of a LLC are able to deduct operating losses of the LLC against their regular income to the extent permitted by law. Shareholders of an S-corporation are also able to deduct operating losses, but not shareholders of a C-corporation.

The most common entities in this business are corporations for obvious reasons discussed earlier in this chapter. For discussion purposes only, I am assuming that you will be registering your business as a corporation. So, I am presenting for your review a free sample of Articles and By-Laws of a company I set up years ago. Feel free to review it and modify it according to what you feel is important to you. Then, you may have to register your company with the Secretary of State in your area. Because state rules on establishing your business may vary, you need to consult with an attorney or the Secretary of State in your area. Preparing By-Laws and Articles of Incorpora-tion is not difficult as there are books out there to aid you for this purpose. You may even check the website of the Office of the Secretary of State and be able to download samples of corporate documents for your personal use.

SECURE A BUSINESS ADDRESS AND A BUSINESS TELEPHONE NUMBER

After drawing a business plan, you will need to establish a physical location for your business because almost all your formal documents, state and local district applications, bank accounts, business license, credit cards, contracts etc... requires a business address. Initially, you may use your home address or the services of a Mail Box Etc... wherein with a minimum monthly fee of about $ 50.00 to $ 80.00, you will be provided with a post office box (P.O. Box) representing a designated physical business address for your enterprise. If you want to have a fancy looking address/location such as an executive office, some big buildings offer the same services as the Mail Box Etc.. whereby for a set monthly fee, you are permitted to use its office building address and a designated mail box inside the building. You may come on a daily basis just to pick up your mail and to check on your messages, but no regular or physical office location for you to sit in. With this in mind, big office addresses provide you with a physical legitimate location for your business and to appear like you have a huge office in one of the high rise buildings downtown when in fact it is just an office address where you come on a daily basis to pick up your mail or messages.

In actuality, you do not need a physical office to operate this business. You can start-up by using your home address until the business is starting to make some serious income. It is imperative however, to have at least a P.O. Box where you can direct the communication, as well as, to make your business more professional and appealing to the public as compared to operating out of an extra room in your house. In line with this thought, you must at least have a dedicated phone line purely for your caregiving business. You could get a business cell phone and answer all your calls like…"ABC Caregivers", Thank you for Your Business… this is John speaking…. You can meet this objective within the comforts of your break while at your other job. If your job requires so much of your time, you can forward your calls to your answering machine or through a local answering service for a minimal fee. Separate your personal calls from your business. This also great because your business expenses may include your telephone bill which you will need to declare in your tax return for the business. You will need a professional sounding message, answering machine/ answering service or a communication system that will appropriately represent who you are and what your business is all about. Relative to formally introducing your business, you will need a professional looking business card and pre-printed flyers that you can pass-out in public places, parking lots, homes, senior centers, etc… to let people know you are in business.

1. FICTITIOUS BUSINESS NAME STATEMENT

A. File for Fictitious Business Name Statement

After a company is registered with the Secretary of State, the next step is to apply for a fictitious business name statement to properly identify the applicant's business name under the statement…"Doing Business As", DBA. An example would be… "ABC" Corporation, duly registered with the state of California, Doing Business As "Angel Personalized Care Services". Do you need an attorney to do this? Consulting with an Attorney would be a great idea. However, you can do it yourself by going to your local County Recorder's Office and pay the required fee. The application itself will illustrate what you need to do. Once again, as state regulations may vary, you will need to ask questions from professionals. A Corporation name maybe the same or different from a Business Name depending on what is available or the choice of the business owner. Technically, one may need to research whether the business name you have in mind exist and if does, the name cannot be used by another entity. In applying for a fictitious business name statement, the applicant must submit an application with the County Register's Office in the county and city where the business will operate. The County Registrar's Office is most of the time located in the City Hall. One may have a company based in Nevada and may operate in California, but the company needs to be registered in California under a "DBA". Upon approval, the application shall be published in a local newspaper to announce to the community that there is a stake claim of ownership right over the applied business name applied for. If no one comes forward to contest it within at least a couple of weeks or so, (typically 30 to 60 days) then the business name applied for will officially be registered under the requested name. After registering your business name, you will be instructed to contact your local newspaper publication of your choice and pay for a fee for the cost to publish your fictitious business name statement.

2. SECURE YOUR TAX IDENTIFICATION NUMBER (TIN) AND EMPLOYER'S IDENTIFICATION NUMBER (EIN) WITH THE IRS AND THE FRANCHISE TAX BOARD

After registering the business entity and filing for a fictitious business name statement, the next step shall be to contact your local Internal Revenue Service (IRS) office to notify them about your new business. There is an automated number that you can contact or check your local phone directory listing for Government Agencies and look specifically for IRS. For convenience, one can register either by phone or online and you can secure your Tax Identification Number and Employers' Identification Number within minutes. Within 15 to 30 days, you will receive a confirmation letter indicating your official business numbers. These numbers are essential especially when you apply for tax exemption or tax benefits and also when you open a corporate account at a local banking institution and when you apply for a business license in the area where you want to establish the business.

3. OPEN A BUSINESS BANKING ACCOUNT

In order to fully function as a business, you have to have a business that have banking capability to handle your revenue, the deposits, the advances made by your clients and your venture capitalist and investors. You also might need an account to show your credit worthy enterprise. This is optional at this time. In order to open an account with your local bank, you will need original copies of the following:

1. Articles of Incorporation and By-Laws registered with the Secretary of State
2. Tax Identification Number/ Employer's Identification Number
3. Business License
4. A Board Resolution authorizing the opening of a business banking account
5. Fictitious Business Name Statement Business address
6. Other forms required by the bank or institution

4. ADVERTISE IN THE LOCAL NEWSPAPER FOR CLIENTS, JOB APPLICANTS, STAFF, CONSULTANTS WHO WILL WORK FOR YOUR AGENCY.

At this stage in time, your business already has the legal personality as a business entity. Every caregiving business relies significantly on its staffing professionals to send to private homes or facilities on a regular basis. It is important to advertise on a regular basis, the need for available staff on a consistent basis. The more available staff that you have on your pipeline, the more convenient your operation will be. Advertising may come in various ways depending on the available funds in the budget. Since, you are barely starting-up the business, you need to keep your cost down to the minimum and as income grows, so is the cost for advertising. The advertising ad may look like this:

> "Caregiver wanted: Live-in / out to care for seniors and adults at home.
> Call: LISA (800) 123-4567"

Having a pipeline of available and reliable staff to cover a variety of shifts and clients needs is extremely important to the business. This is one of the most popular mistakes that entrepreneurs make, and I could say is the major cause for the downfall for most caregiving business start-ups. Your ability to produce a long list of staff to meet the demands of the service will determine whether you may be able to keep or loose the business. Depending on the type of services provided and company that provides the services, rates of pay varies. Most caregivers are paid at a minimum wage and on a per hour basis without benefits and are some times considered as "independent contractors". The word independent contractors are intended for IRS purposes and you need to read more on IRS regulation as far as the subject on employment is concerned. Staff categories may be determined as employees or independent contractors. As an employer, you will need to determine how your operation will be and how you will need to treat your employees for tax, insurance and benefits purposes. Depending on the available service to cover, the basic services varies from a companion rate which is per hour/minimum wage to cover a full 8-hour AM-PM shifts. If the service requires overnight stay, for obvious reasons that not a lot of caregivers will take the shift, the cost of the service may be a little higher to serve as an incentive. Some services requires that the staff be on live-in basis which means that the staff may be required to stay for a determined number of days (Monday-Friday) then a break for (Saturday-Sunday) to be covered by another staff who is willing to take the shift, the cost of the service is pro-rated sometimes ranging between $ 150-180 per day. This numbers are not set in stone as the price of the service may be determined by the owner of the business based on actual cost and margin for profit. This information is mostly apparent on the figures illustrated in the business plan.

The business of providing caregiving staff includes not only staff sent to private homes but also staff in residential care facilities, skilled nursing facilities, hospitals etc... To give you an idea, there are private individuals who prefer to receive nursing and individualized care from the comforts of their home instead of the hospitals and skilled nursing facilities. Some people just want to have that sense of immediate care in the event that the nurses are unavailable. In the case of 6-bed residential care facilities, where staffing can become a major problem (most of the times) when a line staff suddenly calls in sick and no one can cover the shift. The business must also cover advertising for professional positions such as physical therapist, occupational therapists, dieticians, recreational therapists, physicians etc needed in special situations.

WARNING:

"It is extremely important for every caregiving business to have sufficient staffing to cover the services required by the clients regardless of time frame, day of the week, holidays, night shift, emergencies, short notices, absentee staff."

Needless to stress this enough but "your ability to supply readily available staffing even on short notices will determine the success of your business and reduce your chances of getting involved in lawsuits resulting from injury or negligence relative to the care of a client". When your agency signs up for a service contract with a client or a family member, your responsibility is to make sure, that there will be an available caregiving staff (even on a short notice) at the client's home on the designated time and day as the contract promised to provide. A staff absence or tardiness is never an acceptable excuse particularly when the client decides to take care of himself and gets hurt in the process while under your agency's contract schedule, then you will have a very serious situation that could cost you big bucks in incidental cost, lawsuit or even a closure of the business. You must always be vigilant in your quest to have a long list of back-up staff willing to take shifts on emergency basis, but of course it will cost you so much that you would be willing to sacrifice the loss in income instead of a lawsuit. This is one of the most important challenges of the service business.

Another type of mistake commonly encountered on the subject of staffing is consistency in the quality of the service, and the timeliness of the staff.

Cost of the service is always relative to the price. If you find that the price of your competitor's service is sometimes cheaper than what you offer, they are somehow cutting their cost to maintain their staff. To the extreme, sometimes caregiving agencies hire undocumented aliens that they pay at a "below minimum wage", no insurance, no taxes deducted and unreported expenses which in turn lowers down their cost and in general reduces the over-all price of the service. What is frustrating is that people do not realize the long-term effects of their scheme. The price for the service is mostly dependent on the cost of maintaining the staff including training, identification, documentation etc. If the competition offers a price lower than what is realistic, they are in a way lowering the standards of expectation in the business, and undermine the quality of the service business in general. It is normal and expected in this type of business for people to make their choices based on price, but what they do not know is that, "the price dictates the quality of the service". The clients' pay for what they get which equates to cheap and low quality service.

There are factors that caregiving agencies have to consider in determining their prices:

- The cost of advertising and promotions
- Fingerprinting, background reference check
- Documentation
- Cost of training to deliver high quality service
- Insurance cost (General and Professional Liability)
- Transportation Insurance and Blanket Insurance
- Medical and Other Employee Benefits
- Uniform and identification

CHAPTER FIVE:
FINANCING THE BUSINESS

Where to secure financing, SBA loans, venture capitalists, grants, gifts donations, etc... to finance the business

STEP 3: SECURE FINANCING FOR THE BUSINESS

(Time line: 30-60 days)

After making financial a decision based on the feasibility plan of the business, the next move would be to figure out whether it is worthy to continue on to the next level. Should you decide that this is not the right business for you, this is the right time to quit. At least your overall cost is still at a minimum which is limited to the cost of this book and the loss of your leisure time reading. However, if you decide to move forward to the next level, the dilemma would be to figure out where to get the necessary funding for the business. This section will help you understand most of the questions that start up individuals encountered when setting up their business. The suggestions presented in this chapter are not guaranteed effective as they may not be applicable to all cases at all times since solutions to every situation may vary. Nevertheless, figure out what may or may no apply to your particular situation.

Finding start up capital is never easy. Even if you have an excellent business idea to present but do not have sufficient collateral funding to support it, tough luck. It is not impossible but it is quite a challenge. Believe in the business, perseverance, and commitment to your business idea are important elements to unlocking these challenges. The unique thing about the business is that you do not really need a lot of money as a capital to start the business. All you need is funding to support the business until you get your first client. That is why, I will keep telling you "DO NOT QUIT YOUR JOBS". A big bulk of your start-up money goes to establishing your business entity and marketing/advertising cost. The rest is up to you. Another common mistake that people do is quit their jobs to start a business which is not really a good idea in this type of business. You have to have that steady stream of income coming in to supplement for the house bills and other business expenses.

Here is a list of resources that you might want to explore:

1. PERSONAL FUNDS, MONEY FROM FRIENDS AND RELATIVES, GET A BUSINESS PARTNER, LOOK FOR AN INVESTOR:

Then it comes to financing your own business, the first thing that you as a start-up entrepreneur need to look into is your personal finance, how much money you saved or is expecting to receive while you are getting this business started. Perhaps you need to check your savings, income from your jobs, retirement funds, IRA, stock and bonds or even monies from a long lost uncle etc… Sell your unwanted personal collections such as jewelries, clothes and/or furniture.

2. US SMALL BUSINESS ADMINISTRATION (SBA).

SBA is the largest source of long-term small business financing in the nation. Check with your local banks that support SBA Loans. Many start-up individuals have used SBA loans to start or expand businesses. In order to be eligible for a loan, a business has to be for profit and qualify as a small business under the SBA standard criteria:

a. Use of proceeds: The loan proceeds are intended for a variety of business purposes including working capital, inventory, machinery and equipment, leasehold improvements and the acquisition of business property.

b. Loan term: The maturity of the loan is dependent on the use of the loan proceed and varies from five to seven years for working capital, ten years for fixed assets or 25 years for real estate acquisitions depending on the bank or institution that will finance the deal.

c. Interest rates: The interest rates are variable and negotiated between the lender (the bank) and the borrower; however, the lenders generally may not charge more than prime rate. Approach a local bank that provides SBA loans and the SBA shall guarantee the payment of the loan when due.

d. Collateral: SBA requires that sufficient assets be pledged or use as collateral for the loan to ensure that the business owner has a substantial interest in the success of the business. Although, most SBA will not decline a loan application due to lack of collateral, lenders will require a reasonable amount to provide as a secondary source of repayment.

SBA will help you obtain conventional financing through loan guarantees or loans made by private lenders or banks. To cite a few sample available programs:

- Small loan guarantees
- Seasonal line of credit guarantees
- Handicapped assistance loans
- Venture capital
- Loans for disabled and Vietnam Veterans
- Long term loans

In addition to these programs, SBA offers training, technical help and counseling with their partner organizations namely:

- Service Corps of retired Executives (SCORE) that provides free training and one-on-one counseling from volunteers.
- Small Business Development Centers (SBDC's) providing training, research, counseling and other kinds of assistance.
- Small Business Institutes providing free management studies provided by business students under faculty directions at more than 500 universities.

3. VENTURE CAPITALISTS, INVESTORS AND PRIVATE MONEY.

Funding for the business can also be acquired through interested private parties who share your vision and the potential of the business. These entities commonly known as "ANGELS" are found in newspapers, trade magazines, business fairs. Angels are groups of people with tons of discretionary funds who are always on the look out for businesses and ideas that they think will provide a good return on their investment typically at 20% or more instead of a bank at 1%. Their paradigm is "more risk equates to higher returns". It is up to you if you want to give up a chunk of interest on your business. It is always a good practice to participate in networking clubs where you can associate yourself with a group of people that have money, and are willing to takes the risk with you. You can also find these types of people at your local chamber of commerce, library, the Internet, business magazines, banks, etc... Investors will of course read and discuss with you the business plan that you created, look at your background and experience, etc... to assess if they can trust you with their money.

WRITING A GRANT PROPOSAL

In requesting for financial support or a grant, you must research on how to prepare a grant request. The format presented in this book is a "sample only" and you may come up with your own format depending on the project, company or entity with whom the grant is proposed to, the purpose, and of course the mission/objective. For foundations, or corporations, when applying for a grant the writer should always prepare a cover letter describing who you are, what the plan is trying to accomplish and specific amount of funds you are requesting. Try to limit the proposal letter to about three pages of narrative and it must be signed by the Executive Officer. It is also a wise idea to attach a copy of your company's annual budget for the past year and an audited financial statement, an IRS letter of Determination (for non-profit), a cover letter and a business plan/grant proposal will be sufficient.

Preparing a grant is somewhat similar to a business plan as it indicates the amount of money needed and for what purpose. It must also present a schedule or a window as to how the funds will be spent, what it aims to accomplish and a timeline when the funds will be re-paid back with the compromised interest on the return on investment. Included in this section is a Summary Draft of a Grant and what a grant proposal should contain.

Components of a Proposal/ GRANT

I.   Summary
II.   Introduction
III. Problem Statement
IV.   Objectives
V.   Methods
VI.   Evaluation
VII. Future or other necessary funding
VIII Proposal Budget Estimates
IX.   Time Chart

Tips in writing a Grant Proposal:

1. Include a cover letter
2. Be brief and positive
3. Avoid unsupported assumptions
4. It must be written in clean, neat paper and must be in English
5. Write to an organization that supports your objectives and mission statement
6. Budget estimates
7. Business Plan
8. Good luck and be positive

INTERNET: Another excellent place to check is the world wide web and you just type in the words: Money, loans, investors, business, etc and you will be surprised what you will end up with. There are a few Internet sites that I would like you to check:

1. missingmoney.com
2. Grants.gov
3. Free Government Money
4. Unclaimed Properties
5. California State Controller's Office

There are tons of websites that are available for you to surf to find out if there is any money out there that you actually own in behalf of a missing or a long lost relative who might have left something for you, a former employer that gave you entitlement under their profit sharing program, it could also be a bank deposit that you use to have, etc.

You might want to search your local chamber of commerce, hall of records, County/State Controller's Office, ask your local city for available grants/programs that could fund your business.

All you need to do is ask around and search for other ideas from other people who might have done it too.

CHAPTER SIX:
THE BUSINESS LICENSE

STEP 4: SECURE A BUSINESS LICENSE

(Time line: 30-60 days)

The next thing to do is to apply for a Business License in the city where you will conduct your business. In certain cities, counties and states, fees for securing a business license may vary. Some cities have a preset amount for a business license, but to some, a set fee based on projected or actual income, a set fee schedule is available as a basis for the cost of your business license fee. Contact your local City Hall of Records for more information as fee rates may vary. In California, the average cost of initially registering a business ranges from $ 190.00 to $ 250.00 with a renewal fee every year depending on the city where the business is located. Some cities may require copies of your business records and documentations to confirm address of the business while other may not require anything except for the fee.

BUSINESS MAY OFFICIALLY BEGIN UPON RECEIPT OF A BUSINESS LICENSE.

Other forms of caregiving businesses such as a residential care facilities, home health agencies etc… will require securing a license from public licensing agencies and you have to go through hoop and bumps in bureaucracy to secure a license. In this type of caregiving business providing staffing in private residential homes, or private care for individuals confined in hospitals or skilled nursing facilities, hospice etc… all you need is a business license/permit from your local city hall where the business is located. THAT'S IT! There is no other professional license requirement in order to operate this type of caregiving business. The business license is a permit for you to operate your business in the county/city where your business is located. In other states, operating a caregiving business may require a license from a local state licensing agency besides the business permit/license so, please consult with your local agencies before you get in trouble.

CHAPTER SEVEN: FORMS, POLICIES PROCEDURES

STEP 5: CREATE A POLICIES AND PROCEDURES

(Time line: 10 days)

Every caregiving business must have its own policies and procedures. The sole intention is to serve as a guideline for all employees and staff to follow according to the mission statement and objectives of the agency. It also serves as a basis for employee performance evaluation as well as to define the services and its limitations. Without it, everyone including the staff will be acting on their own standards causing so much confusion and chaos within the operation of the business organization leading to costly lawsuits, employee dissatisfaction and eventually resulting to lack of effective management and possibly closure of the business. In preparing policies and procedures, you must be familiar with current regulation and procedures commonly observed in residential care facilities, hospitals, skilled nursing facilities, etc… as they can be the best guideline to observe since the quality and standard of care is similar if not identical with their operations. You may opt to do your own research by asking for a copy of a hospital/facility's operations manual (which is confidential) or search the Internet. You can also utilize the resources available at your local library or Community Care Licensing, State Licensing Agencies, State Regulatory Websites posting current regulations on proper patient care and services. There are private consulting agencies specializing in these types of services that can design policies and procedures that will specifically meet your agency's standards however, it could cost you at least $ 5,000.00 in consulting fees or manpower hours.

To save you time and money, I included in this book a sample policies and procedures that I wrote for my caregiving business found on EXHIBIT THREE, PAGE 103. Review it and if you find it practical, you may use it for your own purpose and revise it to meet your own personal objectives. I am giving you full permission.

What does your policies and procedures contain?

Every policies and procedures must contain detailed information on what must be observed in the operation of the business. It must contain the following:

a. What your company/agency represents, goals and mission statement
b. General Principles
c. Clients Admissions Policies
d. Proper treatment policies, Dignity and Respect
e. Client safety
f. HIPAA Regulation and Confidentiality
g. Types of Client Activities
h. Emergency Procedures
i. Employee Hiring/Firing Procedures
j. Transportation Safety
k. Staff scheduling
l. Staff Training and Continuing Education

These are just a few of the most basic and yet, very important subjects to be covered under the policies and procedures. Without these policies, the agency will be operating in "whatever" mode, which will keep the business open to lawsuits and other problems. In preparing your own policies and procedures, keep in mind the basic rule in the business..."How do I Prevent a Lawsuit from the Clients, their Families, Staff and from the Local Government?" You can be creative and include anything and everything that you as business owner desire to observe in the operations of your business based on current regulations as long as they are ethical, legal and practical in all senses for the observance of safety and order in the business.

The policies and procedures is the law of the business and must be strictly observed and modified accordingly to meet current issues and events that affects the daily operation of the agency.

Every time an issue evolves, an accident happens, or just about any problem and is not and cannot be resolved by the policies and procedures, it is time to make some changes in the rules of your operating procedure.

STEP 6: CREATE THE FORMS THAT YOU WILL NEED TO USE IN THE OPERATION OF THE BUSINESS

(Time line: 15 days)

In order for the business to operate initially, it must have the basic forms and documents that it can use in its transactions and communications. Depending on the scope and limitations of the service to be provided by the agency, it must have much needed forms and documentations vital to its daily operation including the following:

- Service Contract
- Contract of Employment
- Incident Report
- Client Assessment
- Client Personal and Emergency Information
- Daily Progress Report
- Medication Records Keeping Form

These are just a few of the sample forms your business may need and the rest, you must develop on your own according to what your agency may require in its daily operations.

CHAPTER EIGHT: STAFFING

Caregiving business will never be complete without a caregiver/staff. In this type of business where it relies heavily on personalized interaction among people from all types and cultures, there will always be a probability for conflict, miscommunications, and other issues relating to its management and operations. As a business owner/operator, you must take precautionary steps when choosing the right employees for your business all the way from hiring, training, promoting, and termination of employment contract services. All your staff must undergo background check and fingerprint clearance prior to being given a work assignment or engaging in any form of interaction or communication with your clients.

STEP 7: GET FINGERPRINTED BY LIVE-SCAN AND SECURE BACKGROUND CHECK CLEARANCE FROM FBI-DOJ OR YOUR LOCAL POLICE DEPARTMENT.

(Time line: 3-15 days)

Everyone in the staff roster including the owners of the business must have proof of background check clearance through the local police department and LIVESCAN prior to checking in to work on the first day. Part of the hiring process is to require applicants to complete an application form that includes personal questions such as criminal history, background check and test questions to indicate the applicant's mental health and well-being. You may also conduct your own immediate background check on your employees by logging on to **backgroundchecks.com or integrascan.com** to get results in less than 5 minutes for a cost ranging from $ 8.00 up to $ 50.00 for your peace of mind. These are excellent tools for your business as well as for your clients.

To assure the clients and their families safety, it is very important to conduct the following on your staff prior to hiring:

- Personal Interview of the staff
- Personality check and testing

- Character review
- Stress test
- Background check
- Credit check
- Criminal Records Check
- Verify references.
- Provision of 3 letters of recommendations.

In order to complete the task of verifying background and history, all prospective staff/applicants must fill up pertinent information on the employment application and a pre-formatted authorization letter must be signed by the applicant/staff allowing the agency to conduct background and credit history check as a requirement for the application process. The fastest and most convenient way to verify information about an applicant is thru the use of a computer and the Internet where in less than a minute, you will receive a spread sheet of information that you can not believe you can find about the individual. There are readily available computer software and hundreds of websites that can provide background checks and or credit report for as low as $ 8.00 per item/inquiry or up to $ 50.00. If you want to take your search to another level, there are websites that even verifies addresses, previous employments and people searches. With a pre-paid membership fee and a software cost of $ 100.00, one can have unlimited searches and inquiries on all prospective applicants regarding their past, present and pending criminal history, (misdemeanor, criminal and civil action filed with the local courts) sex offender check, lien and civil judgments, previous addresses, relatives etc... Here are some useful website to explore:

a. Sentrylink.com
b. Intelius.com
c. USA People Search.com
d. **backgroundchecks.com**
e. **integrascan.com**

Searches may include the following categories:

a. Statewide Criminal Background Check
b. Current and Previous Addresses
c. Phone Numbers
d. Property Records
e. Bankruptcies
f. Pending Civil/Criminal/misdemeanor Cases
g. Driving Records

If you do not have any access to a computer or the Internet, you may request an applicant to secure a background clearance from the local police department for just about the same cost using the traditional fingerprinting methodology and a network information database. There is also a private company called LIVESCAN that is contracted through the Dept. of Social Services and

Community Care Licensing that provides fingerprinting services using the FBI-DOJ-Homeland Security Records database. The results may be procured almost instantaneously or at least within three-clearing days from the Department of Justice and the Federal Bureau of Investigation.

This business has the highest incidences in allegations, abusive practices, neglect, loss, injuries, malpractice, theft and worst, even possibly death. These factors including inefficient staff management and training could lead to numerous lawsuits which in turn results in business closures due to lack of oversight, ineffective training practices and records keeping, lack of insurance and liability coverage including insufficient risk management which factors are directly related to poor business practices. Staff hiring is a very crucial element in the business. Despite of all the preventive maintenance in assuring high quality staffing, there is no guarantee as to the character and personality of the staff. One could portray a perfect character during the interview then, after the interview process, the individual can turn into a very different personality. As much as possible, you will need to do your best in weeding out the ones that are good from those that your gut feeling will dictate otherwise.

In every caregiving business, the availability of staff to work on certain short notices is also very crucial to the survival of the business. It also helps when you or your manager conduct random and unannounced client visits and regular communication with the families as to the quality of the care provided by the staff. This approach may keep staff on their toes in delivering the highest quality services that clients duly deserve. Old fashion detecting and proper training is an important key in maintaining the right staff for the business. Always check them out, surprise them with unannounced visits, talk to other staff members, consult the clients and their families, be open and observe their attitudes and general demeanor. Look around for signs that could show concerns for your client's safety and well-being. It is always better to be safe than sorry later on. After all, this is your business. You need to be the first to know what is going on.

STEP 8: SECURE CPR-FIRST AID CERTIFICATION.

(Time line: 3-15 days)

It is a common practice in licensed residential care facilities and institution type of facilities to require all their staff to be CPR and First Aid Certified prior to their initial contact with the clients. The most important responsibility of a caregiver is to provide an environment where the clients feel safe and secure. In order to achieve it, part of their role is to be able to assist the clients in any way they can in the event of an emergency. Staff may be required to attend the certification classes every three years or less to reinstate their certification cards. CPR Classes are available in schools, universities, adult schools etc… and there are some service providers that can come to your home to provide the certification classes at a cost of $ 50.00 per person or sometimes free when you attend seminars at your local Red Cross Chapter.

a) All staff must also secure eight (8) hour HIV-Hepatitis certification course.
b). Direct Support Professionals: Direct support professionals in Service Levels 2, 3, and 4 facilities employed before January 1, 2001 must satisfactorily complete the first 35-hour training segment (Year1) by January 1, 2002; and satisfactorily complete the second 35-hour training segment (Year 2) by January 1, 2003. Direct support profes-

sionals in Service Levels 2, 3, and 4 facilities employed on or after January 1, 2001, have one year from date of hire to satisfactorily complete the first 35-hour training segment; and, two years from the date of hire to complete the second 35-hour training segment.

Prior to Initial Client Contact, All Caregivers/Staff Must be Provided with an 8-Hour Introductory Staff Training:

The provision of a compulsory 8-Hour Introductory Staff Training to the staff before sending them on an official work schedule to service your clients is extremely important. Here are some of the suggested basic subjects for the initial training:

a. Agency Policies and Procedures.   (1 Hour)
b. Health and Safety at the Workplace.   (1 Hour)
c. Client Information and Care.   (1 Hour)
d. Emergency in the event of Natural Calamity, terrorism and Earthquake. (1 Hour)
e. Ethics: (1 Hour)
f. Law and Crime.   (1 Hour)
g. Transportation Safety   (1 Hour)
h. Activities, Care Planning and Basic Chores   (1 Hour)

These topics are available in tapes, CD's and DVD's from public libraries and other service providers. It is very important that you as the business owner/manager to provide these introductory training prior to your staff securing their respective assignments. Each staff will sign-in for the attendance sheet and given a certificate of completion on the suggested subjects as part of the conditions for continuing employment with your agency. This practice will at least give you the peace of mind knowing that your staff is competent, professional and responsible in their role to keep your clients safe at all times. This will also reduce the chance of a possible lawsuit from all the parties involved in the service. Besides the 8-Hour Introductory Training, your agency shall maintain a continuing education requirement for all your staff consisting of minimum 40-Hours of Credentials Training or Continuing Education Units. All these important training topics reflects the quality of the service and the paradigm that your agency believes in …"Safety and the Best Quality Care at All Times". The 40-hour training may provided by an independent instructor who may come to your agency or arrange meetings for your staff. These required training hours are also important in reducing the cost of injury and loss in manpower hours including lawsuits as a result of providing the care that can range from injury, abuse and lack of knowledge on the part of the caregiver and in behalf of the client-recipient of the care. Despite of all the steps you take, you and your agency will always be open to possible lawsuits no matter what preventative measures you take. However, with this practice of regularly training your staff, you are observing the role of a "good father in the family" which you can use as an argument when the right time comes that you need to defend your business. People will always find creative ways to make a fast buck out of you. Therefore, it makes a good sense to train your staff and empower them with the knowledge needed in the business.

CHAPTER NINE: INSURANCE

STEP 9: PROTECT YOUR BUSINESS BY SECURING INSURANCE COVERAGE.

(Time line: 30 days)

There is no better way to secure your business financially other than providing insurance coverage for your operations. We live in the real world of lawsuit happy people. The most common thing you hear out there is…"I will sue you". It is sad, but true to the bones. There are different types of lawsuits: a). Legitimate claims to address a wrong deed, b). Malicious and contrive claims c). Claims to just annoy and clog the justice system, d). Claims to collect serious amount of money for personal gain, or fame, and; e). Claims for whatever reason one can imagine. Jokingly aside, as a business owner, caregiving is very vulnerable and open target for lawsuits. In order to be able to mitigate rising costs resulting from a lawsuit is to blanket the business with insurance coverage to secure:

- General and Professional Liability Insurance to include abuse and allegation and other blanket insurance to protect yourself and your staff for up to $ 1Million Dollars
- Property and Transportation Coverage
- Other related Insurance coverage (ask you local insurance broker)

Insurance company representatives and brokers can provide these types of insurance at a package cost of $ 200/month depending on the ratings they observe in the business based on risk assessments, credit report, etc… Farmers Insurance, Lincoln and other east coast based companies do underwrite these types of coverage. During the initial phase of the business, it may be a costly undertaking, but it is well worth every penny considering the responsibilities that your business may carry on a daily basis. You can arrange for limited coverage at a low cost, but try to negotiate for a price that would give you a dependable coverage. A common mistake that businesses do is to take this warning lightly. You must have a very strong insurance coverage for your business to include your daily operation, staff, transportation, accidents, allegations, loss of revenue, which must cover at least $ 1Milion Dollars. In order to achieve this, your insurance broker will quote you a minimal percentage that you need to pay on a monthly basis. The average cost to you per month is approximately $ 300.00 to cover the necessities in your operation. You must also secure a blanket insurance just in case. Most insurance carriers such as All State, State Farm, etc do provide the coverage. With the enormous cost in operations alone, I agree with you that this requirement may be outrageous. But, without insurance, this business will have a difficult time surviving. Most caregiving businesses that fail to observe this requirement are prone to closing its doors. In order to meet this requirement at a low cost, you may negotiate with your insurance carrier to provide you with the most affordable plan with a reasonable coverage which you may be allowed to upgrade when the business improves.

BONDS:

Bonds also play an important role to secure the business from lawsuit in the event of financial theft or loss. There are instances when the client allows the agency to handle their financial responsibilities such as payment of their house bills, rents, gas and electric bills, and if your agency allows staff to assist in the handling of clients' money management needs. In the event that your agency will be authorized to handle clients' monies more than $ 500.00, bond is a must have. Bonds are available through your local insurance brokers and insurance providers by paying a pre-set percentage on the amount that your agency is willing to cover.

Transportation Insurance:

If your staff or the agency will provide transportation for the clients to go to and from their medical, dental and other personal errands, you must require all your staff to have their own automobile insurance that are renewed on an annual basis and the agency shall receive current and active copies on file.

Blanket Insurance

In this business, the larger your insurance coverage, the better you are. That is why, if budget permits, you need to have a blanket insurance to cover incidences that general and professional liability insurance does not cover. It is not a must, but you are paying for your peace of mind.

CHAPTER TEN:
STAFF TRAINING

STEP 10: PROVIDE 40 HOURS OF STAFF TRAINING ON AN ANNUAL BASIS.

(Time line: 5 days)

In a small start-up caregiving business, it is important that you provide an initial 8-Hour Initial Employee Training and supplemented by an annual 40-hours Certified Training (CEU) requirement to all staff. All caregiver staff must be required to attend a compulsory 8-Hour initial training on the basic topics of caregiving prior to initial contact with the clients. The first five days of employment must be dedicated towards training of first time applicants to familiarize themselves with the policies and procedures, ethics, medication, client review and the discussion on the topics of standard of care and abuse. The initial training shall consist of four grueling days. In order to help improve and maintain the high quality of the service, the training topics shall include:

1. Client Knowledge
2. Safety at the Workplace
3. Medication dispensation
4. Transporting clients and road safety
5. Incidence reporting
6. Emergency Response and Drill
7. Fire and Chemicals Safety
8. Social and Recreation Activities
9. Ethics
10. Proper Client Care
11. Lifting
12. Personal hygiene
13. Relationship Building
14. Respect of Clients Rights

15. Health and Welfare
16. Disease and Prevention
17. Falls and Keeping Safe
18. Life and Death
19. Injury Prevention

The more information you can learn and share with the staff, the better your business will be. As a business owner, you may provide these training by yourself or by requiring your staff to secure at least a minimum of 40 training hours on an annual basis. With this practice in mind, you are psychologically and physically preparing the staff about the agencies expectation on the proper care and treatment of the clients.

INITIAL STAFF ORIENTATION TRAINING PLAN:

First Day:
a). Orientation and familiarization with the agency rules and client expectations, b). knowledge and familiarity of the fire exit, emergency shut off of the water, gas and electric, c). review emergency and disaster plans, d). policies and procedures, e). food service, storage and food handling, f). employee manual, g). health sanitation, h). housekeeping procedures, i). hygiene and j) environment safety.

Second Day:
k). First Aid info, l). medications; m). demonstrate how to safely assist the client with the medications that are self-administered; n). client behavior and dynamics, medical/emergency procedures, o). public relations, p). orientation to client's, q). working on the floor or kitchen under supervision.

Third Day:
r). Review "Early Signs and Symptoms of Illness," how to assist in giving a proper shower or bath, s). activities, volunteers, t). supervising client, u). safety and hazards, household duties, w). performing duties with supervision.

Fourth Day:
x). Familiarization of the neighborhood and the other professionals (Hospital, Doctors or Medical Group, Ombudsman, ASP, Senior Services, Dental offices and many more). y). Show how to conduct a fire drill, perform duties with, and without, supervision. The employee must be supervised until he/she can show competency and upon completion of a successful performance evaluation and thorough understanding of the job requirements.

CHAPTER ELEVEN: EARNING THE BUSINESS

Advertising and Promotions

The lifeblood of the business in receiving client referrals is dependent on the amount of effort that is exerted into the marketing and advertising. There are several cost effective ways. You can utilize a medium that can reach hundreds of people from your own personal network of friends and families of friends. And you can do this with a small stroke of a mouse through the Internet or email. When I started with the business, I was literally walking for blocks and miles of houses to meet people and to shake their hands as I introduced the business. I met hundreds of people on the road, malls, parking lots; distributed flyers, attended a number of networking groups and clubs. It is up to your creative ideas as to how you could catch your client's attention. One of the creative ideas I came up with to promote the business was to make 100 pieces of 6 X 10 signboards that I placed on busy streets and corner lots that are high in pedestrian and automobile traffic. I asked permission from property owners and made deals to place my miniature signs in donut shops, beauty parlors where I go on a monthly basis. I worked with a couple of restaurants and beauty parlors by placing a small ad in their flyers and placing my ad in their stores. We complemented each other and seemed like a win-win situation.

STEP 11: ADVERTISE THE BUSINESS.

(Time line: 5 days)

- Produce flyers, business cards, and other hand-outs
- Promote the business by attending community events that promotes the interests of seniors.
- Senior Centers
- Distribute flyers in hot spots such as groceries, strip malls, gas stations, parking lots, etc...

- Advertise in local magazines and newspapers. Create an activity to sponsor local events and community gatherings
- Knock on doors and distribute flyers and mailers in your local community or neighbors
- Yellow Pages, Phone Books and Local Newspaper ads, clip ads

Remember that advertising is purely numbers game. The more frequent that your business name is out in the community, the higher your chance in securing local interest.

Making the whole world aware that you are in business is an important key to the success of the business. You can start with your family members by sending them a letter, email and come up with a birthday get-together party. Ask for a list of their friends and families with telephone numbers. Then expand from your neighborhood by distributing flyers, mailers and business cards, go to your local parish community, attend community gatherings, network with your community, go to shopping centers and strip malls to pass flyers and cards in the parking lots, businesses and to anyone you meet on the street. Come up with creative and inexpensive ideas to advertise the business. Call your local newspaper and place ads and ask for a deal. Partner with another company or individual who will split the cost of advertising. Look for every opportunity to drum up the community interest. You need to be out there soliciting the business in any way, manner or form that you can afford. "Reap what you sow". Continuously market and advertise your business regardless of the economic situation.

STEP 12: CREATE A STAFF DATABASE.

Always maintain a list of interested employees and applicants database. Replenish the database with fresh new names and prospects. Keep in touch and if possible, retain the part-timers and the on-calls for emergency purposes.

- Advertise regularly for job placements and employment opportunities to have a continuous database of available employees and interested applicants
- Categorize the job applicants by addresses to cover certain areas and communities, special assignments, etc…

Finished: You may now start the business.

CHAPTER TWELVE: ETHICS

As we wind down our discussion on the operation of the business and its profitability, we should not forget another essential part of our role as provider of care, and that is ethics. In this business, we are responsible for the care of people coming from different cultures, ages and disabilities. Some will be medically and physically fragile, others may be elderly, sick, dying and there will be those that will solely depend on us for care, companionship and support. These are the people, that in most times will challenge and test our patience, knowledge, and skills as we prove our worthiness and true intentions. This process may take a little bit of time and a ton of understanding on our part. There will be times when we will face the challenge to cross the grey line, to test our vulnerability, ignorance or even our trustworthiness. It will expose us to the unique side of caregiving that would confront our personal beliefs, self-respect, moral values and ethical standard in life. The business will bring out the best and perhaps the worse in our being, and that it is up to us to make the right decisions. The business will help us achieve our goal of financial independence or perhaps personal ruin.

Our mission statement needs to reflect the embodiment of goodness, respect, and dignity in the treatment of our clients. In order to achieve this goal, our agency will provide the best caregiving service at all times. In drawing a contract of employment, we will be fair and just to our clients, their families, the staff, and to our independent contractors. We will observe fair labor laws and practices, treat our staff accordingly, and provide adequate training and informative resources that could be very helpful in their daily responsibilities. As employers, we will provide strict oversight of their performance by conducting frequent unannounced client visits, monthly performance reviews of our staff, and most important of all, to enforce the policies and procedures accordingly. We will rotate the staffing schedule to reduce the possibility of developing a personal relationship or favoritism between clients and staff.

In dealing with the clients, we should teach our staff to constantly observe the mission statement of the business…

"ALWAYS TREAT CLIENTS WITH DIGNITY AND RESPECT".

As a business owner, we have the responsibility to remain in-sync with your clients and with your staff, to be involved not only in the operation of the business, but also to be in constant communication with the clients and their families to be aware of their needs.

There will be times when staff become comfortable with their relationship to the clients and will cross the grey line to find an opportunity to exploit our client's personal interests and properties, leading to abuse of fiduciary relationship. The clients' mental, medical and physical condition makes them vulnerable to all types of negligence including financial, verbal, physical and even sexual abuse.

To our competition, practice what is fair and do not undermine the service practices by providing labor and services that are inadequate and impractical which in result, lowers the over-all cost of the service.

Now, do what is right for you and the business.

Client Abuse and Neglect

Statistics show that every year, tens of thousands of elderly Americans are abused in the privacy of their own homes, in relatives' homes, and even in facilities that are responsible for their daily care. More than half a million reports of abuse reach authorities as millions more cases go unreported. The difficult part about it, is that every time an abuse incident is reported, the perpetrators are long gone or have left the country even during an investigation is in progress. This chapter aims to teach about abuse and its signs, and by learning the signs and symptoms, we may be able to prevent it at the initial state. We will not only be able to help someone feel safe and vindicated, but we are also strengthening our own defenses against elder abuse and future litigations within our agency by taking preventative measures to reduce the numbers of possible victims and discourage possible perpetrators. If you suspect that an elderly person you know or in your care is being harmed physically or emotionally by a neglectful or overwhelmed caregiver/staff or another person/relative, you must act immediately by reporting the incident to the local police and adult protective services.

What is elder abuse?

It is very important to you as an agency owner to keep a tab on your staff's roles by conducting a monthly performance evaluation and un-announced client visits to conduct a regular survey with your clients in a strictly confidential basis. When you conduct the visits, and observed that one of your clients (a frail and elderly) have bruising in her/his arms or legs, you need to ask her/him how she/he got them. If by her explanation, your own gut feeling tells you that it is quite odd, and she/he changes or tries to avoid the subject, do not let your common sense dictate. Sometimes, our common sense does not make sense at all. Our job is to protect our clients and their rights, not our staff nor the business. Oftentimes, our clients will tell the truth, but if something does not seem right, you need to do what is right. It does not matter even if it could jeopardize the status of your business. The elderly including those that are young, but unable to speak up and stand up for themselves, those that become more physically frail and medically fragile, or unable to think or defend themselves are vulnerable to unscrupulous people who will take advantage of them.

Types of elderly abuse:

    a. **Physical abuse**
    b. **Neglect or abandonment by caregivers**
    c. **Emotional abuse**

   d. Sexual abuse
   e. Healthcare fraud and abuse
   f. Financial exploitation

Physical abuse

Physical abuse is the intentional or non-accidental use of force against a person that results in physical pain, injury, or impairment. Such abuse includes physical assaults such as hitting or shoving, the inappropriate use of drugs, restraints, or confinement.

Neglect or abandonment by caregivers

Neglect is the failure of an individual providing the care to fulfill a caregiving responsibility or duty. It can be intentional (active participation), or unintentional (by passively ignoring the client's urgent needs or calls), based on factors including malicious intent, ignorance, or denial of the provision of a service that the client urgently needs as integral part of their care.

Emotional abuse

Emotional abuse may include psychological and verbal abuse and other ways of treatment of an individual in manners that may cause emotional pain, stress and psychological impact on the persona of the client.

Verbal abuse may include:

   a. Intimidation with the use of threatening words or actions
   b. Words and or actions that may cause to humiliate and ridicule others
   c. Inappropriate accusations and use of jokes that brings down others people's feelings and emotions
   d. Non-verbal psychological elder abuse can take the form of ignoring the elderly person
   e. Isolating an elder from friends or activities
   f. Terrorizing or menacing the elderly person

Sexual abuse

Sexual elder abuse is contact with an elderly person without the elder's consent.

Healthcare fraud and abuse

Carried out by unethical doctors, nurses, hospital personnel, and other professional care providers, examples of healthcare fraud and abuse regarding elders include:

   a. Not providing healthcare, but charging for it
   b. Overcharging or double-billing for medical care or services
   c. Getting kickbacks for referrals to other providers or for prescribing certain drugs
   d. Overmedicating or under-medicating
   e. Recommending fraudulent remedies for illnesses or other medical conditions
   f. Medicaid fraud

Financial exploitation

This involves the unauthorized use of an elderly person's funds or property, either by a caregiver or an outside opportunist. An unscrupulous caregiver might misuse an elder's personal checks, credit cards, or accounts, steal cash, income checks, or household goods, forge the elder's signature engage in identity theft.

Signs and symptoms of elder abuse

At first, you might not recognize or take seriously the signs of elder abuse. They may appear to be symptoms of dementia or signs of the elderly person's frailty — or caregivers may explain them to you in that form. In fact, many of the signs and symptoms of elder abuse do overlap with symptoms of mental deterioration, but that does not mean you should disregard them.

General signs of abuse:

The following are warning signs of possible elder abuse:

a. Frequent arguments or tension between the caregiver and the elderly person
b. Changes in personality or behavior in the elderly

If you suspect elderly abuse, but are not sure, look for clusters of the following physical and behavioral signs.

Signs and symptoms of specific types of abuse

1. Unexplained signs of injury such as bruises, welts, or scars, especially if they appear symmetrically on two side of the body
2. Broken bones, sprains, or dislocations
3. Report of drug overdose or apparent failure to take medication regularly (a prescription has more remaining than it should)
4. Broken eyeglasses or frames
5. Signs of being restrained, such as rope marks on wrist
6. Caregiver's refusal to allow you to see the elder alone

These are just a few of the reminders that we all need to consider seriously. Our business and its future survival depend on how we care for our clients. By taking these simple steps for prevention and proper care, we not only lay the foundation of our business, but also set our morals and ethics on solid ground.

EXHIBIT ONE:
Sample Business Plan

ANGELCARE , Incorporated.

A Business Plan to Establish A Personalized Caregiving Business in San Bernardino County AngelCare Caregivers

Business Plan
Research made exclusively for ANGEL CARE Company, Inc.
By: HealthCare Training and Staffing Services [®].
September 01, 2000

Table of Contents

Executive Summary:

ANGELCARE is a service-oriented type of business that will provide personalized care to serve the needs of seniors, adults and children living independently at home who by their medical condition and other disabilities require them to be bed-bound and in need of personalized care as an alternative to confinement in an institution or a group setting. **ANGELCARE** will meet the needs of individuals living within the counties of San Bernardino. The business is established as a result of an overwhelming demand for a unique type of individualized care that will provide respite to tired family members and friends caring for a loved one, home companionship, transportation, live-in assistance, caregiver, home-maker, vocational and habilitation activities and training, mentorship, behavioral modification and therapy; and to supply staffing services to residential care facilities and other institution all under one service objective. ANGELCARE will serve the needs of a wide range of disabled and aging clients mostly from the Inland Valleys and from the Department of Aging.

The individualized service plan shall take into consideration the specific client needs and services, their functional ability, the clients' challenges, their behaviors and their ability to retain and respond to given task.

It is a unique service in a sense that the goal is to provide the personalized care service to the clients in a supportive, individualized, recreational and leisurely manner to be able to attend to their variable needs from basic companionship, meal preparation, light housekeeping, medication reminders, assistance in hygiene and personal needs, transportation to their medical, dental and personal appointments and errands, and all other related services in assistance to their home-bound and yet basic needs.

As of this time, there is no existing service like it in a sense that the service encompasses a wide variety of individualized care service to assist the clients in attaining their objective to live comfortably at home while addressing their medical, psychological, therapeutic needs. **AngelCare's** role is to make sure the clients goals and needs are met accordingly. We will also cater to meet the issues and needs of under-staffed residential care facilities, hospitals, skilled nursing facilities, hospices and private care.

HIGHLIGHTS: Graph

Objectives:

The objectives of our business are as follows:
1. To provide a unique personalized care service that will serve the needs of seniors, adults and children with medical or behavioral issues living independently at home as an alternative to an institutional and group setting.
2. To provide an excellent quality service rendered by trained, courteous, caring, professional staff at a cost that is competitive and affordable.
3. To maintain our projected start-up cost of approximately less than $ 8,764.00.
4. To start our business operations with just less than $ 3,500.00 and increase our expenses on as needed basis.

5. Our Projected Sales of $ 100,000.00 on our first year of operation and exceeding $ 800,000.00 by our fifth year in business.

6. It is our goal to exceed our gross margin higher than 45% on our second year and reach our maximum projections by the fifth year.

7. A net income of more than 30% of sales by the third year and reach our net profit / sales by 53% by our third year in business.

Mission

Our mission is to meet and exceed the expectation of an overwhelming demand for personalized care services of individuals living in their private home setting, senior homes, assisted living; those that are confined in hospitals and institutions, hospice care and skilled nursing facilities and to provide staffing support in under-staffed residential care facilities, hospitals, hospice care, skilled nursing facilities.

There are approximately 87 million aging Americans and we aim to cater only to a small fraction of that population including those living in facilities and institutions. We are aware of this high demand not only from seniors but also from those that are bed-bound and lack support from families and friends due to other commitments and personal issues.

The service will not only meet the needs of the average clients but also those with developmental disabilities and those with mental health issues by focusing on the individual's needs and services, disabilities, potentials, learning curve, behaviors and most of all to enhance the clients' physical, social, vocational and recreational skills.

ANGELCARE will offer a variety of personalized care from respite care, home companionship, transportation, live-in assistance, caregiver, home-maker, vocational and habilitation activities and training, mentorship, behavioral modification and therapy all under one service objective.

Company Summary:

ANGELCARE COMPANY, INC. is a new company that will establish personalized care service and staffing in the Inland Empire area and its business title is **ANGELCARE**. This company is proud to be the first to introduce a revolutionary approach in individualized care where it shall rise above the standards of your average caregiver agency as it introduces a unique approach to private care, companionship, activities, therapy, community integration, socialization and to provide staffing support services to facilities and institutions on an as needed basis.

ANGELCARE Company, Inc. will provide the best quality personalized care service supported by a goal that is to maintain the highest standard in safety and quality, and person-centered approach to caregiving.

Company Ownership

ANGELCARE will be established by ANGELCARE Company, Inc., as part of its initial project in the health care field. **AngelCare**, Inc. is owned and operated by its board of directors and members as principal investors and principal operators. The initial business address of the company shall be located at 123 Main Street, No.4, Main City, Ca. 123456. Telephone (800) 456-7890. The initial board of directors are as follows:

Mr. Joe Sample, President
Ms. Mary Sample, V-President
Mrs. Onlee Sample, Secretary
Mrs. Onlee sample, Treasurer
Mr. Onlee Wan Sample, Chief Finance Officer

AngelCare shall be managed and administered by Mr. Joe Sample, acting as President/Manager/caregiver staff. As clientele continues to grow, so is the number of staff who shall work as **independent contractors** in the business.

Start-Up Summary

The total start up cost for AngelCare is approximately **$ 8,764.00.** However, we only need **$ 3,500.00** or less to start the business conservatively by initially purchasing following:

a. Register Corporation with the Secretary of State
b. Secure a Business License
c. Background check and fingerprinting
d. Business Telephone Contact Number
e. Secure a Business Address/P.O.Box
f. Business card and flyers
g. Policies and Procedures
h. Service Agreement
i. Business forms

Upon completion of the above-mentioned requirements, the company will officially operate its business.

During our initial operation, we shall utilize our available funds to rent a post office box (P.O. Box) after using our residence as our office address. Then, register our company with the Secretary of State. Our next step is to secure a business license, open a business checking account at a local bank, purchase a business telephone (cell phone), make a partial deposit to cover general and professional liability insurance, get fingerprinted from a local Police or Community Care licensing office and clearance from DOJ-FBI, produce business cards and flyers for distribution in public places and parking lot and the local neighborhood.

Our estimated total asset is at $ 5,000.00 in cash reserves and equipment. We shall expect our first batch of clients after three months of marketing our services and by the sixth month of the first year in operation, we project that our monthly expenses and obligations will be easily met after reaching our service population of at least four regular clients that will be using our service on a daily basis.

Our business will be operating on a "single staff" basis represented by the business owner as the person with many responsibilities from securing a business contact (cell phone), printing of flyers and business cards that reflects our service contact numbers and address; then the distribution of flyers, emails, business cards and other paraphernalia to the community by going to populated places such as the parking lot, strip malls, groceries, neighbors and local community, senior centers, etc...

The first thing on the agenda after attaining our official business status is to secure a dedicated business telephone in a form of a cell phone which has a message reminder capability to be able to return the call on a timely manner.

During our first three months in business, we will be operating on a single staff represented by the business owner/caregiver with another support staff that is on an "on-call" basis. We need to reach out to the community to let them know about our new business. We need to massively distribute the advertising information and since we are on a very tight budget, we have to apply creative ideas on how to do it using the world wide web through emails and texting. If we need to go from house to house, office to office and person by person, we have to do it to drum up the business.

6.0 START UP GRAPH
Table 6.1 Start-Up Cost

Services

ANGELCARE shall offer the highest quality in personalized care and staffing services to be able to capture at a minimum 10% of the existing market in the local area. The objective of the company is to be able to attract clients from the following potential areas:

a. Private residences **65%**
b. Skilled Nursing Facilities, Assisted Living, hospitals and retirement homes **15%**
c. Clients from residential Care facilities **10%**
f. Staffing Services for under-staffed Facilities **7%**
e. Others **3%**

The main bulk of our service which consists of 65% shall cater for the needs of individuals living in their private homes where our agency shall supply caregivers on a 1:1 basis to meet their individualized needs. Our marketing and advertising will target those that are about to be discharged from hospitals, hospice care and by their medical needs shall require personal supervision, therapy and assistance in their daily care and chores, those that are in assisted living facilities and retirement communities that are used to being independent and by their health and age would require companionship and assistance in their daily activities or chores. The second to the biggest bulk of projected clientele of our service remains at 15%. Meanwhile, the remainder of 20% of our business shall cater to those that lives in residential care facilities for the elderly and those facilities that are under-staffed and in need of "on-call" only part time and temporary staff/caregivers.

The goal is to offer a unique personal service to capture a need that is difficult to meet... an excellent quality care based on an individualized need provided by genuinely caring, well-trained and professional staff. The service is client- centered in its goals and orientation focused on their personalized needs and services, behavior and developmental capacity. The company believes in the approach... "that no client shall be left unsupervised, inactive and unmotivated for any reason, to participate in their care and active lifestyle unless medical, psychological and self choice" prevents them from being doing so. **AngelCare** shall attempt to accommodate every client needs regardless of the issue whether it be behavioral, emotional or psychological. A personalized plan shall be developed individually to accommodate their needs and to keep them active and motivated to learn and participate in the daily activities whether it be exercises, therapy session, home chores and self-development, outing in the community or anything that they enjoy doing on a regular basis.

AngelCare shall offer the following component services with emphasis on the clients' choice, rights and self-interest:

A. Personal Needs:

AngelCare shall initially assess the clients based on their personalized care needs from companionship, medical services such as therapy activities to support them with their available skills, medication reminders, feeding, bathing etc... The client's daily care shall be based on their evaluation, assessment and recommendations from healthcare professionals, physician, prior to initiating the service. The service shall be based on the following:

1. Home Companion.
2. Respite Care.
3. Live-In caregivers.
4. Hourly Rate Care.
5. Caregiver Support Staff.

The primary focus of our service is to provide personalized support geared towards the provision of services to lighten the burden on the client's challenge. To attain this, the client's individual need is the main goal of the service. However, there must be delineation as to what is covered in the service and what is not. Our staff are caregivers and not maids, gardeners, carpenters, electricians, cleaners, plumbers housekeepers etc... Their main role is to provide supervision, personal care and individualized duties that are targeting the personal needs of the clients and not on what is related thereto such as light-home chores to tidy up the home to keep it safe and orderly. Our staff is at the client's home to take care of the client's personalized needs and not to take care of the needs of the house whatever that may entail. We shall leave the responsibility of cleaning the house to the house maids, the leaking faucet to the plumbers, the lawn to the gardener, etc... and by that sample, our service is clearly drawn and defined and that is to focus on the client and not on their home. However, part of the responsibility of keeping the client safe and to meet their needs, the house needs to be kept in a safe and orderly environment for the benefit of the client. Our client may provide light-housekeeping and to provide chores to meet the client's standard of care.

In order to keep the environment safe and in order, the staff may provide light duties to make it possible but not to compromise the personal needs of the client.

Home-companion services may include the following services:

a. Light housekeeping
b. Meal preparation
c. Medication reminders

d. Provide transportation or assist in the transport of the clients to their medical, dental appointments and other errands including going to the groceries, malls, parks to keep the client active.
e. Feeding
f. Therapy
g. Interactive-Activities
h. Washing clothes and drying
i. And other client care related services that may be requested by the client and or family as long as it does not compromise 1:1 supervision and care of the client.

Service Rates:

1. Respite: Minimum 3 Hours
   * $ 15.00/hour.
2. Basic Home Companion:
   * $ 12.00 - $ 15.00/hour
3. Live-In Companionship:

   a) $ 150.00/day (weekdays)
   b) $ 180.00/day (week-ends)

4. Driver/Transport: $ 50.00/trip
5. House chores ONLY $ 50.00/3 hours

The rate varies from state to state, agency policy as well as the type of care provided including transport, mobilization, lifting or repositioning of the client (if required) may serve as a factor in the cost of the service. The staff's ability to physically handle the needs and lifting of the client are crucial factors to consider when assigning a particular staff to handle the responsibility to assure not only the safety of the client as well as the staff. The rate of companionship services varies from per hour or per day at an average of 8-hours per service per client depending on where the service is established and what state requires. The average rate for companionship service is $ 12.00 to $ 25.00 per hour depending mostly on what the special care requires such as heavy lifting for repositioning or bath. Lifting of the clients to maintain skin integrity may compromise their safety as well as the staff. There is a reason for the service cost to be variable and that remains to be optional and dependent from the agency and its policy. The payment for the services is paid directly to the main office that will handle payroll and other expenses to be accounted for. Should the service require 24-hour supervision, a dedicated staff will be assigned to stay on the premises. These are **live-ins** to stay on the premises for at least five straight days. Then, a two-day substitute staff shall cover the remainder of the week schedule to cover the labor requirement.

The staff's focus is primarily on providing the clients with basic care followed by creative and functional, educational entertaining activities that will help them nurture personal goals and skills and provide unrestricted environment of free choice for activities, learning and personal growth. The activities shall consist of **8.0 hours of personalized care**, light housekeeping, medication reminders, meal preparation, feeding, news and book reading, errands to groceries, medical-dental appointments, community activities including trips to the park, churches and recreation centers, movie theaters etc...

Although most of our clients are fragile and the aging they are encouraged to be active and to participate in the daily activities and not to become fully reliant on the caregiver. The caregiver shall provide supervised activities on the use of home equipments, cooking utensils etc... The goal is to familiarize the clients with the life of self-reliance and independence by learning to cook, food preparation, housekeeping and home maintenance.

Develop personal, social, recreational, tactile and other related skills.

AngelCare staff will promote individualized development of personal self-care, feeding, occupational and recreational skills by providing activities that stimulates the interest of the clients from story telling, news reading and other activities to enhance the client's individual personal capacity. The clients will be provided transportation to and from special places of interest such as museums, parks, trips to the casino and other interesting places that clients prefer in order to enhance their social and recreational skills.

Independent Living Program.

To promote self-reliance and confidence the clients are encouraged to participate in the community to enhance their personal experiences, provide positive interaction with others in the community. **AngelCare** shall provide training, assistance and support in various areas of community integration as part of the clients' learning expectations including safety at home and in public, fine motor skills, mobility training and other activities of interest to the client.

Physical, recreational, occupational and emotional therapy.

Providing clients with activities that will enhance their physical, recreational and emotional needs such as morning exercises, walks to the parks, aromatherapy, interactive-music,

Behavior modification.

In order to keep the client active on a daily basis, a psychologist/behaviorist will be consulted to draw up a treatment plan to address individual behaviors which will be implemented by a staff familiar with the client in particular.

Transportation.

Clients are assigned with a caregiver that can drive them to and from their homes and other places of interest to them and pertinent to their needs and services.

Market Analysis

The agency shall retain a business address utilizing a personal residence or a post office Box (P.O.Box) as its place of operation to be located somewhere in the City of Ontario, Fontana or Ranch Cucamonga between the 10 freeway and the 15 freeway to be able service the needs of the local clients as well as those in neighboring cities. Our target market area shall be clients living within the cities of Claremont, Upland, Chino, Pomona, Diamond Bar, Alta Loma, Rancho Cucamonga, San Dimas, Montclair, Corona, Fontana, Colton, Apple Valley, Temecula, Palmdale,

Victorville and other neighboring cities. All these cities are divided into areas one, two, three and four respectively.

Our most potential group of clienteles are those coming from local area within the 25-30 mile radius from our office.

Market Segmentation:

1. The largest group of clienteles are coming from the areas of Pomona, Diamond Bar, Chino, Chino hills, Claremont, Montclair, Upland, Ontario, Fontana, Rancho Cucamonga, Rialto, Temecula and Perris areas.
2. The second largest group of possible clients shall be coming from Rialto, Corona, Riverside and Norco areas.
3. And the third group of clients are from the upper desert region including Victorville, Apple Valley and neighboring dessert cities.

Graph 9.1: Area Segmentation
Table 9.1: Market Analysis

a. Target Market Segment Strategy:

The strategy behind our market segmentation is listening to the needs of the community and the clients. We will maintain flexibility, practicality and most of all adaptability to the clients' ever-changing needs.

Another focal point for our reference shall be the variety of services we will provide to our clients, the quality of our services which follows the highest standard of care and supervision, the consistency in our staffing ratio to clients which is an average of 1:1 to maintain high quality standard as well as continuous training of our staff and most of all our focus on safety and cleanliness.

Service Business Analysis

Between 2004 and 2030 there will be more than 87 Million Americans reaching the age of 65. A large portion of that population may be living independently at home or if they are having some medical issues that would limit their independence, perhaps some would be in homes with assisted living, hospice, skilled nursing facilities, hospitals or living with a family besides their own. A small portion of the same population may have save enough for a comfortable lifestyle or may be not. Our client base are those that can afford the use of our services regardless where they live or the lifestyle that they have. Some of them may be bed-bound or just simply in need of assistance in getting through the days in their life from simple chores to a more complex tasks that due to their current health condition they are limited by what they can physically do on their own.

Competition and Buying Patterns:

The important elements in our service is advertising and promotions, high quality of care, regular training of staff, background checking and most of all communication.

There are at least four major types of competitors for our business.

a. Caregiver Staffing Agencies (Licensed and the Unlicensed)
b. Family caregivers
c. Home Health agencies
d. Non-Profit Volunteer Organizations

There are more competitions than we need in this business. What makes our service stand out from the rest of the competition is the high quality of our service and its affordability. Our staff is our advocates and the representation of what our agency stand for. Their excellent relationship with the clients and the client's families draw a significant impact on our service. What makes us unique from the rest of our competition are the following:

a. The best quality service.
b. All our staff are thoroughly checked on their background, credit, history and personality,
c. We require staff to maintain annually 40-hours of training units to be in active work standing.
d. Focus on safety and client.

THE COMPETITION:

a. Caregiver Staffing Agencies (Licensed and the Unlicensed)
b. Family caregivers
c. Home Health agencies
d. Non-Profit Volunteer Organizations

a. Caregiver Staffing Agencies:

Just like **AngelCare**, these staffing agencies provide similar type of services. However, the prices of their service is lower than what we provide due to their hiring practices and the quality of their service. Most of their staff are undocumented aliens that require low minimum pay. Although, not all of our competition are illegal in their business practices, they try to cut their cost in their operations thereby resulting in the cut in the price of their service.

Our most common caregiving agencies that we will compete with are:

1. Homestead (Franchise)
2. Senior Care (SBO)
3. Visiting Angels
4. Caring hands

Strategy and Implementation

AngelCare will focus on various geographical markets namely:

1. **Area One:** Diamond Bar, Chino, Chino Hills, Claremont, Montclair,
2. **Area Two:** Upland, Rancho Cucamonga, Ontario, Etiwanda,
3. **Area Three:** Fontana, Rialto, Corona, Temecula, Perris,

4. **Area Four:** Victorville, Apple Valley and other neighboring Upper Dessert areas.

Our target clients are coming from private residences, assisted living communities, hospices, skilled nursing facilities, hospitals and residential care facilities for adults and seniors living within the abovementioned geographical areas.

With our target location which is strategically suitable for clients living within the 20-30 mile radius.

Sales Forecast

Based on our sales forecast, the months of January, February, March and April when we aim to start are good months right after the holidays and the winter-spring season when a lot of our target population easily get sick with simple cases of flu, colds and other illness that makes them bed-bound. Our first month of the year, we will be aggressively advertising for our services. We see our first client call coming in on the middle of January. By the month of February 2002, we expect to receive referrals of approximately five clients from the hospitals, nursing homes and from private individuals/family members that are unable to care for their aging or ill family member. By the succeeding months, we expect the referral to increase by as much as 5 to 12 clients from the first day of operation. We assume sales growth by as much as 10% during our first three quarters of our operation and projected attainment of a full time service capacity within less than 8 months from date of initial operation.

GRAPH: SALES MONTHLY
Table 3.0 Sales Forecast

Milestones:

For the purposes of our milestone, during the months of June, July and August, we expect to have a steady inflow of inquiry on our service at an average of three sign-ups per month. Within the said months, our advertising funds will continue aggressively and expect to submit more service contracts by April, May and June 2002. By the month of September 2002, we should have a total of 15 contracts signed and service should be on an ongoing basis.

Table 14.0 Milestones

Management Summary

Our initial management team shall compose of the following who receives mentoring from the Board of Directors:

Board of Directors:

Onlee Sample, President
Onlee Wan, Vice President
Sample, Secretary
Sample, Treasurer
Administrator: Onlee Sample

Personnel Plan

The initial set of staff shall consist of one caregiver/administrator and one support caregiver/ staff. On the first day of operation, the very first caregiver staff is the President/Administrator/ caregiver who shall distribute flyers and business cards to public places and clients are interested in using the service, he should also be the first person to draw and sign the service contract. When an inquiry call comes in, he shall answer all inquiries on the service. He shall also make the arrangement to meet the first client and his family. At this point, the administrator should have readily available waiting list of staff that have passed the interview process and had their backgrounds verified and checked prior to being sent to their respective service calls or assignments. As the population of clients increase, so is the number of staff to increase in proportion to the clients signed up for the service.

Table 16.1 Personnel Plan

17. Financial Plan

The plan is to initially operate the business in a cost effective manner. With the total projected initial operating cost of $ 8,764.00 we will only need $ 3,500.00 to actually get the business started.

The breakdown of our initial cost is as follows:

Reservation of Corporate Name	$ 10.00
Live-Scan Fingerprinting	$ 184.00
Articles of Incorporation	$ 100.00
Gas /Mileage	$ 80.00
Law and Business Software	$ 100.00
Hep/HIV Certification	($ 80.00)
Accounting Software	($ 80.00)
Fictitious Business Name/	$ 100.00
Business License/	
City Registration	$ 100.00
Business Insurance/Site Deposit	($ 300.00)
Automobile Insurance Deposit	$ 100.00
Professional/General Liability Insurance	($ 600.00)
Workers Comp. Deposit	($ 800.00)
Non-Hire Transport Insurance	$ (800.00)
Others	$ 200.00
Computer	$ (1,500.00)
P.O. Box /Address	$ (200.00)
Telephone-Fax	$ 150.00
10-Key calculator	$ (25.00)
Answering machine	$ 40.00
Software/Database	$ 65.00

Pens/pencils/Supplies	$ 50.00
Equipment and supplies cost	
Market Research and Consultation	
(Optional)	$ (3,000.00)
Others	$ 100.00
Total Start-Up Cost:	
Excluding Fixed and Variable Cost	**($ 8,764.00)**

Our monthly expenses are as follows:	
1. P.O. Box Rent:	$ 25.00
2. Telephone Bill	$ 145.00
3. Credit card payment	$ 50.00
4. Advertising cost	$ 100.00
5. Employee payroll (1 staff)	
@ $ 12.00/hour	$ 2,500.00
6. Administrator payroll	$ 3,000.00
7. Insurance	$ 145.00
	$ 5,965.00

Important Assumptions:

Our important assumptions are as follows:

1. That there is no delay in our projected operation timeline.
2. That we will be able to locate a post office box (P.O. Box) as our initial address for our business.
3. That during our first month in operation, we would be able to secure two service contracts at $ 15.00/hour for 25 days of service per month.
4. That we will be able to secure a commitment contract for a Live-In companionship is $ 150.00/day for a minimum of three clients per month.
5. And, if our service continues to secure an average of 1 additional contract per month to defray for our monthly expenses.

Table: 18.1 General Assumptions

Break Even Analysis:

Our break-even projection is at $ 5,965.00 per month to cover for our monthly fixed cost including the salary of administrator and one staff/caregiver. In order to attain this, we need to have at least three (3) service contracts per month to achieve our income potentials in excess of our minimum target range. With our low monthly operating cost, we have the flexibility to control our service cost at a range that would make our business affordable to the average individual in need of our service. We project that if we maintain our minimum average of three (3) service contracts per month, we will be able to survive and make a modest profit as a result thereof. If we can only exceed our minimum goal, we can stay in business for a very long time. We would like to make the assumption that we are capable of maintaining a Live-In companionship fee of $ 150.00/day per client with special needs and if we can retain at least one (1) client per month which is not difficult to achieve, then we shall exceed our monthly break even. With our aggressive marketing style of knocking on doors in communities and handing our flyers personally from person to person and home to home, it is not very difficult to attain our financial goal. All these objectives are easily attainable within a 12-month period.

Graph: 21.1 Break Even Analysis

Table: 21.1 Break Even Analysis

Projected Profit and Loss

Our projected profit and loss (as indicated on our table) shows that during our first six months of operation, we expect to accommodate our first batch of two (2) clients by the month of January-February, March and April after consistent guerilla marketing and advertising. On said months, we will be generating gross sales of approximately $ 6,825.00 each month. During the first two months in operation, we project a negative gross after paying our monthly expenses. With our projected two clients to serve on the second and third months, we project a break-even. However, if we are to combine a Live-In services which we project to acquire during the second and third month of operation, we project a positive cash flow. Our average monthly operating expenses are approximately $ 5,350.00. With at least three (3) clients including a Live-In service we project to exceed our break-even point and anything exceeding three (3) client services is positive to our revenue projections. We realize that in order to make a considerable profit in this business, we need to expand our services into staffing of residential care facilities and we must have at least 15 caregivers in our roster.

Table 22.1 Profit and Loss Statement

Projected Cash Flow

For our cash flow projections, aside from the $ 3,500 start up funds we will use in purchasing jumpstarting our business, we need to continuously advertise in local newspapers, telephone directory, church and community directory, senior centers etc... in order to attract more clients. On our first quarter in operation, we need to infuse additional capital to offset for our monthly expenses. For that, we need to inject at least an average of $ 1,500.00 from our cash reserves. During the difficult months of January, March until June and July where we will be expecting shortage on revenue. By maintaining positive cash flow position and increasing our advertising, we will be able to gradually increase our projected revenues at a consistent phase of 25% growth to 35% on a monthly basis.

Graph: 21.1: Cash Flow

22. Projected Balance Sheet

Projected Balance Sheet indicates that our starting balance is $ 5,000.00 which by the following year 2003, our cash balance is $ 190,381.00 and by our third year of operation, our cash balance is at $ 321,567.00. With that revenue projection, we expect to rent an office space at a cost less than $ 800.00/month. At the start of our operation, our monthly expenses is at a very minimum to give us an opportunity to save a huge portion of our revenue which in turn translates to a low and affordable savings we pass on to our clients. Since, the price of our service is lower than the competitors, more clients will prefer to use our service on a long term basis. Part of our goal is to expand the business by the fourth year and considering selling the concept of the business in a form of a franchise. By selling our franchise, we project a gross revenue of more than $ 1 Million dollars per year in total revenues.

Table 24.1: Balance Sheet

EXHIBIT TWO:
Sample BY-LAWS

BY LAWS
OF
UNCLE SAM CORPORATION
(A California Corporation)

ARTICLE I -- OFFICES

Section 1. The registered office of the corporation shall be at: _____,
City, Ca. _____
The registered agent in charge thereof shall be:
Mr. _____

Section 2. The corporation may also have offices at such other places as the Board of Directors may from time to time appoint or the business of the corporation may require.

ARTICLE II -- SEAL

Section 1. The corporate seal shall have inscribed thereon the name of the corporation, the year of its organization and the words "Corporate Seal, "State"".

ARTICLE III -- STOCKHOLDERS' MEETINGS

Section 1. Meetings of stockholders shall be held at the registered office of the corporation in this state or at such place, either within or without this state, as may be selected from time to time by the Board of Directors.

Section 2. Annual Meetings: The annual meeting of the stockholders shall be held on the 1st Wednesday of February in each year if not a legal holiday, and if a legal holiday, then on the next secular day following at 10:00 o'clock A.M., when they shall elect a Board of Directors and transact such other business as may properly be brought before the meeting. If the annual meeting for election of directors is not held on the date designated therefore, the directors shall cause the meeting to be held as soon thereafter as convenient.

Section 3. Election of Directors: Elections of the directors of the corporation shall be by written ballot.

Section 4. Special Meetings: Special meetings of the stockholders may be called at any time by the Chairman, or the Board of Directors, or stockholders entitled to cast at least one-fifth of the votes which all stockholders are entitled to cast at the particular meeting. At any time, upon written request of any person or persons who have duly called a special meeting, it shall be the duty of the Secretary to fix the date of the meeting, to be held not more than sixty days after receipt of the request, and to give due notice thereof. If the Secretary shall neglect or refuse to fix the date of the meeting and give notice thereof, the person or persons calling the meeting may do so.

Business transacted at all special meetings shall be confined to the objects stated in the call and matters germane thereto, unless all stockholders entitled to vote are present and consent.

Written notice of a special meeting of stockholders stating the time and place and object thereof, shall be given to each stockholder entitled to vote thereat at least 30 days before such meeting, unless a greater period of notice is required by statute in a particular case.

Section 5. Quorum: A majority of the outstanding shares of the corporation entitled to vote, represented in person or by proxy, shall constitute a quorum at a meeting of stockholders. If less than a majority of the outstanding shares entitled to vote is represented at a meeting, a majority of the shares so represented may adjourn the meeting from time to time without further notice. At such adjourned meeting at which a quorum shall be present or represented, any business may be transacted which might have been transacted at the meeting as originally noticed. The stockholders present at a duly organized meeting may continue to transact business until adjournment, notwithstanding the withdrawal of enough stockholders to leave less than a quorum.

Section 6. Proxies: Each stockholder entitled to vote at a meeting of stockholders or to express consent or dissent to corporate action In writing without a meeting may authorize another person or persons to act for him by proxy, but no such proxy shall be voted or acted upon after three years from its date, unless the proxy provides for a longer period. A duly executed proxy shall be irrevocable if it states that it is irrevocable and if, and only as long as, it is coupled with an interest sufficient in law to support an irrevocable power. A proxy may be made irrevocable regardless of whether the interest with which it is coupled is an interest in the stock itself or an interest in the corporation generally. All proxies shall be filed with the Secretary of the meeting before being voted upon.

Section 7. Notice of Meetings: Whenever stockholders are required or permitted to take any action at a meeting, a written notice of the meeting shall be given which shall state the place, date and hour of the meeting, and, in the case of a special meeting, the purpose or purposes for which the meeting is called. Unless otherwise provided by law, written notice of any meeting shall be given not less than ten nor more than sixty days before the date of the meeting to each stockholder entitled to vote at such meeting.

Section 8. Consent in Lieu of Meetings: Any action required to be taken at any annual or special meeting of stockholders or a corporation, or any action which may be taken at any annual or special meeting of such stockholders, may be taken without a meeting, without prior notice and without a vote, if a consent in writing, setting forth the action so taken, shall be signed by the holders of outstanding stock having not less than the minimum number of votes that would be necessary to authorize or take such action at a meeting at which all shares entitled to vote thereon were present and voted. Prompt notice of the taking of the corporate action without a meeting by less than unanimous written consent shall be given to those stockholders who have not consented in writing.

Section 9. List of Stockholders: The officer who has charge of the stock ledger of the corporation shall prepare and make, at least ten days before every meeting of stockholders, a complete list of the stockholders entitled to vote at the meeting, arranged in alphabetical order, and showing the address of each stockholder and the number of shares registered in the name of each stockholder. No share of stock upon which any installment is due and unpaid shall be voted at any meeting. The list shall be open to the examination of any stockholder, for any purpose germane to the meeting, during ordinary business hours, for a period of at least ten days prior to the meeting, either at a place within the city where the meeting is to be held, which place shall be specified in the notice of the meeting, or, if not so specified, at the place where the meeting is to be held. The list shall also be produced and kept at the time and place of the meeting during the whole time thereof, and may be inspected by any stockholder who is present.

ARTICLE IV -- DIRECTORS

Section 1. The business and affairs of this corporation shall be managed by its Board of Directors, _____ in number. The directors need not be clients of this state or stockholders in the corporation. They shall be elected by the stockholders at the annual meeting of stockholders of the corporation, and each director shall be elected for the term of ore year, and until his successor shall be elected and shall qualify or until his earlier resignation or removal.

Section 2. Regular Meetings: Regular meetings of the Board shall be held without notice, at least quarterly, at the registered office of the corporation, or at such other time and place as shall be determined by the Board.

Section 3. Special Meetings: Special Meetings of the Board may be called by the Chairman on 2 days notice to each director, either personally or by mail, fax or by telegram; special meetings shall be called by the President or Secretary in like manner and on like notice on the written request of a majority of the directors in office.

Section 4. Quorum: A majority of the total number of directors shall constitute a quorum for the transaction of business.

Section 5. Consent in Lieu of Meeting: Any action required or permitted to be taken at any meeting of the Board of Directors, or of any committee thereof, may be taken without a meeting if all members of the Board of committee, as the case may be, consent thereto in writing, and the writing or writings are filed with the minutes of proceedings of the Board or committee. The Board of Directors may hold its meetings, and have an office or offices, outside of this state.

Section 6. Conference Telephone: One or more directors may participate in a meeting of the Board, or a committee of the Board or of the stockholders, by means of conference telephone or similar communications equipment by means of which all persons participating in the meeting can hear each other; participation in this manner shall constitute presence in person at such meeting.

Section 7. Compensation Directors as such, shall not receive any stated salary for their services, but by resolution of the Board, a fixed sum and expenses of attendance at each regular or special meeting of the Board PROVIDED, that nothing herein contained shall be construed to preclude any director from serving the corporation in any other capacity and receiving compensation therefore.

Section 8. Removal: Any director or the entire Board of Directors may be removed, with or without cause, by the holders of a majority of the shares then entitled to vote at an election of directors, except that when cumulative voting is permitted, if less than the entire Board is to be removed, no director may be removed without cause if the votes cast against his removal would be sufficient to elect him if then cumulatively voted at an election of the entire Board of Directors, or, if there be classes of directors, at an election of the class of directors of which he is a part.

ARTICLE V -- OFFICERS

Section 1. The executive officers of the corporation shall be chosen by the directors and shall be a Chairman, President, Secretary and Chief Financial Officer. The Board of Directors may also choose a one or more Vice Presidents and such other officers as it shall deem necessary. Any number of offices may be held by the same person.

Section 2. Salaries: Salaries of all officers and agents of the corporation shall be fixed by the Board of Directors.

Section 3. Term of Office: The officers of the corporation shall hold office for one year and until their successors are chosen and have qualified. Any officer or agent elected or appointed by the Board may be removed by the Board of Directors whenever in its judgment the best interest of the corporation will be served thereby.

Section 4. Chairman: The Chairman shall preside at all meetings of the stockholders and directors; he shall see that all orders and resolutions of the Board are carried into effect, subject, however, to the right of the directors to delegate any specific powers, except such as may be by statute exclusively conferred on the Chairman, to any other officer or officers of the corporation. He shall execute bonds, mortgages and other contracts requiring a seal, under the seal of the corporation. He shall be EX-OFFICIO a member of all committees.

Section 5. President: The President shall attend all sessions of the Board. The President shall be the chief executive officer of the corporation; he shall have general and active management of the business of the corporation, subject, however, to the right of the directors to delegate any specific powers, except such as may be by statute exclusively conferred on the President, to any other officer or officers of the corporation. He shall have the general power and duties of supervision and management usually vested in the office of President of a corporation.

Section 6. Secretary: The Secretary shall attend all sessions of the Board and all meetings at the stockholders and act as clerk thereof, and record all the votes of the corporation and the minutes of all its transactions in a book to be kept for that purpose, and shall perform like duties for all committees of the Board of Directors when required. He shall give, or cause to be given, notice of all meetings of the stockholders and of the Board of Directors, and shall perform such other duties as may be prescribed by the Board of Directors or President, and under whose supervision he shall be. He shall keep in safe custody the corporate seal of the corporation, and when authorized by the Board, affix the same to any instrument requiring it.

Section 7. Chief Financial Officer: The Chief Financial Officer shall have custody of the corporate funds and securities and shall keep full and accurate accounts of receipts and disbursements in books belonging to the corporation, and shall keep the moneys of the corporation in separate account to the credit of the corporation. He shall disburse the funds of the corporation as may be ordered by the Board, taking proper vouchers for such disbursements, and shall render to the President and directors, at the regular meetings of the Board, or whenever they may require it, an account of all his transactions as Chief Financial Officer and of the financial condition of the corporation.

ARTICLE VI -- VACANCIES

Section 1. Any vacancy occurring in any office of the corporation by death, resignation, removal or otherwise, shall be filled by the Board of Directors. Vacancies and newly created directorships resulting from any increase in the authorized number of directors may be filled by a majority of the directors then in office, although not less than a quorum, or by a sole remaining director. If at any time, by reason of death or resignation or other cause, the corporation should have no directors in office, then any officer or any stockholder or an executor, administrator, trustee or guardian of a stockholder, or other fiduciary entrusted with like responsibility for the person or estate of stockholder, may call a special meeting of stockholders in accordance with the provisions of these By- Laws.

Section 2. Resignations Effective at Future Date: When one or more directors shall resign from the Board, effective at a future date, a majority of the directors then in office, including those who have so resigned, shall have power to fill such vacancy or vacancies, the vote thereon to take effect when such resignation or resignations shall become effective.

ARTICLE VII -- CORPORATE RECORDS

Section 1. Any stockholder of record, in person or by attorney other agent, shall, upon written demand under oath stating the purpose thereof, have the right during the usual hours for business to inspect for any proper purpose the corporation's stock ledger, a list of its stockholders, and its other books and records, and to make copies or extracts there from. A proper purpose shall mean a purpose reasonably related to such person's interest as a stockholder. In every instance where an attorney or other agent shall be the person who seeks the right to inspection, the demand under oath shall be accompanied by a power of attorney or such other writing which authorizes the attorney or other agent to so act on behalf of the stockholder. The demand under oath shall be directed to the corporation at its registered office in this state or at its principal place of business.

ARTICLE VIII -- STOCK CERTIFICATES, DIVIDENDS, ETC.

Section 1. The stock certificates of the corporation shall be numbered and registered in the share ledger and transfer books of the corporation as they are issued. They shall bear the corporate seal and shall be signed by the President.

Section 2. Transfers: Transfers of shares shall be made on the books of the corporation upon surrender of the certificates therefore, endorsed by the person named in the certificate or by attorney, lawfully constituted in writing. No transfer shall be made which is inconsistent with law.

Section 3. Lost Certificate: The corporation may issue a new certificate of stock in the place of any certificate theretofore signed by it, alleged to have been lost, stolen or destroyed, and the corporation may require the owner of the lost, stolen or destroyed certificate, or his legal representative to give the corporation a bond sufficient to indemnify it against any claim that may be made against it on account of the alleged loss, theft or destruction of any such certificate or the issuance of such new certificate.

Section 4. Record Date: In order that the corporation may determine the stockholders entitled to notice of or to vote at any meeting of stockholders or any adjournment thereof, or the express consent to corporate action in writing without a meeting, or entitled to receive payment of any dividend or other distribution or allotment of any rights, or entitled to exercise any rights in respect of any change, conversion or exchange of stock or for the purpose of any other lawful action, the Board of Directors may fix, in advance, a record date, which shall not be more than sixty nor less than ten days before the date of such meeting, nor more than sixty days prior to any other action.

If no record date is fixed:

(a) The record date for determining stockholders entitled to notice of or to vote at a meeting of stock- holders shall be at the close of business on the day next preceding the day on which notice is given,--or if notice is waived, at the close of business the day next preceding the day on which the meeting is held. (b) The record date for determining stockholders entitled to express consent to corporate action in writing without a meeting, when no prior action by the Board of Directors is necessary, shall be the day on which the first written consent is expressed. (c) The record date for determining stockholders for any other purpose shall be at the close of business on the day on which the Board of Directors adopts the resolution relating thereto. (d) A determination of stockholders of record entitled to notice of or to vote at a meeting of stockholders shall apply to any adjournment of the meeting; provided, however, that the Board of Directors may fix a new record date for the adjourned meeting.

Section 5. Dividends: The Board of Directors may declare and pay dividends upon the outstanding shares of the corporation from time to time and to such extent as they deem advisable, in the manner and upon the terms and conditions provided by the statute and the Certificate of Incorporation.

Section 6. Reserves: Before payment of any dividend there may be set aside out of the net profits of the corporation such sum or sums as the directors, from time to time, in their absolute discretion, think proper as a reserve fund to meet contingencies, or for equalizing dividends, or for repairing or maintaining any property of the corporation, or for such other purpose as the directors shall think conducive to the interests of the corporation, and the directors may abolish any such reserve in the manner in which it was created.

ARTICLE IX -- MISCELLANEOUS PROVISIONS

Section 1. Checks: All checks or demands for money and notes of the corporation shall be signed by such officer or officers as the Board of Directors may from time to time designate.

Section 2. Fiscal Year: The fiscal year shall begin on the first day of January.

Section 3. Notice: Whenever written notice is required to be given to any person, it may be given to such person, either personally or by sending a copy thereof through the mail, by fax, or by telegram, charges prepaid, to his address appearing on the books of the corporation, or supplied by him to the corporation for the purpose of notice. If the notice is sent by mail, fax or by telegraph, it shall be deemed to have been given to the person entitled thereto when deposited in the United States mail, faxed or with a telegraph office for transmission to such person. Such notice shall specify the place, day and hour of the meeting and, in the case of a special meeting of stockholders, the general nature of the business to be transacted.

Section 4. Waiver of Notice: Whenever any written notice is required by statute, or by the Certificate or the By-Laws of this corporation a waiver thereof in writing, signed by the person or persons entitled to such notice, whether before or after the time stated therein, shall be deemed equivalent to the giving of such notice. Except in the case of a special meeting of stockholders, neither the business to be transacted at nor the purpose of the meeting need be specified in the waiver of notice of such meeting. Attendance of a person either in person or by proxy, at any meeting shall constitute a waiver of notice of such meeting, except where a person attends a meeting for the express purpose of objecting to the transaction of any business because the meeting was not lawfully called or convened.

Section 5. Disallowed Compensation: Any payments made to an officer or employee of the corporation such as a salary, commission, bonus, interest, rent, travel or entertainment expense incurred by him, which shall be disallowed in whole or in part as a deductible expense by the Internal Revenue Service, shall be reimbursed by such officer or employee to the corporation to the full extent of such disallowance. It shall be the duty of the directors, as a Board, to enforce payment of each such amount disallowed. In lieu of payment by the officer or employee, subject to the determination of the directors, proportionate amounts may be withheld from his future compensation payments until the amount owed to the corporation has been recovered.

Section 6. Resignations: Any director or other officer may resign at anytime, such resignation to be in writing, and to take effect from the time of its receipt by the corporation, unless some time be fixed in the resignation and then from that date. The acceptance of a resignation shall not be required to make it effective.

ARTICLE X -- ANNUAL STATEMENT

Section 1. The President and Board of Directors shall present at each annual meeting a full and complete statement of the business and affairs of the corporation for the preceding year. Such statement shall be prepared and presented in whatever manner the Board of Directors shall deem advisable and need not be verified by a certified public accountant.

ARTICLE XI -- AMENDMENTS

Section 1. These By-Laws may be amended or repealed by the vote of stockholders entitled to cast at least a majority of the votes which all stockholders are entitled to cast thereon, at any regular or special meeting of the stockholders, duly convened after notice to the stockholders of that purpose.

USEFUL CONTACT INFORMATION

<u>Associations</u>
American Health Care Association
1201 L St, NW
Washington DC 20005
(202) 842-4444
American Society on Aging833 Market St, Ste 511
San Francisco, CA 94103
(415) 974-9600 *www.asaging.org*

California Association for Health Services at Home
723 S St., Sacramento, CA 95814
(916) 443-8055
www.cahsah.org

California Association of Adult Day Services
921 11th St, Ste 701
Sacramento, CA 95814(916) 552-7400
www.caads.org

California Association of Health Facilities
2201 K Street
Sacramento, CA 95816
(916) 441-6400 www.cahf.org

California Association of Homes and Services for the Aging , 7311 Greenhaven Dr, Ste 175Sacramento, CA 95831
(916) 392-5111 www.aging.org

California Association of Residential Care Homes
2380 Warren Road, Walnut Creek, CA 94595
(925) 937-3046

California Center for Assisted Living
2201 K Street, Sacramento, CA 95816
(916) 441-6400, www.ca-assistedliving.org
National Center for Assisted Living
1201 L St, NW
Washington DC 20005
(800) 434-0222; (202) 842-4444 www.ncal.org

State Government
California Department of Aging
16 K Street
Sacramento, CA 95814
(916) 322-3887
Office of State Ombudsman
(916) 323-6681
www.aging.state.ca.us

California Department of Health Services
P.O. Box 942732
Sacramento, CA 94234-7320
(916) 445-4171
www.dhs.ca.gov

California Department of Social Services
744 P Street
Sacramento, CA 95814
(916) 657-3661
www.dss.cahwnet.gov

California State Capitol
Governor's Office
(916) 445-2841 www.governor.ca.gov

State Government Information Line
(916) 322-9900 www.ca.gov

Federal Government
White House
(202) 456-1414 www.whitehouse.gov

Insurance Resources
California Partnership for Long Term Care
714 P Street, Room 616
Sacramento, CA 95814
(800) 434-0888
www.dhs.ca.gov/cpltc

Health Insurance Counseling and Advocacy Program
(800) 434-0222
www.aging.state.ca.us/html/programs/hicap.htm

Other Resources

Area Agencies on Aging (www.cahf.org/public/client/areaagcy.php)
The California Department of Aging contracts with a statewide network of 33 Area Agencies on Aging (AAAs) which are responsible for the planning and delivery of community services for older persons and persons with disabilities.
(800) 510-2020

Eldercare Locator (www.eldercare.gov/)
A nationwide toll-free information and referral service
(800) 677-1116

Regional Centers for Persons With Developmental Disabilities (www.cahf.org/public/client/ddregctr.php) Regional centers are responsible for coordination of services and case management for persons with developmental disabilities, as well as diagnosis and assessment, preventative services to parents and persons at risk of having developmental disabilities, individual program planning, advocacy, monitoring and evaluation.

Statewide Ombudsman (www.cahf.org/public/client/calombud.php)
Each county has a Long Term Care Ombudsman program, whose goal is to advocate for the rights of all clients of long-term care facilities and adult day health-care centers in the state.
(800) 231-4024

EXHIBIT THREE:
POLICIES AND PROCEDURES
(SAMPLE ONLY)

Table of Contents

POLICIES AND PROCEDURES
(Sample Only)
AngelCare Respite and
Home Support Services

Introduction

AngelCare will provide personalized "In Home" care services in a private residential setting for children, adults and seniors. It aims to provide comprehensive non-medical personalized care service design specifically to meet the needs of children, adults and seniors living independently at home with physical, social and/or developmental disability who need supervision and assistance on a 24 hour basis. It is a service developed to assist families and their loved ones in their temporary care and supervision as an alternative to an institutional setting such as a hospital or a nursing home. The service is focused on improving the quality of health care services geared towards safety, health, social and other supportive services in a protective, friendly and non-institutional setting.

AngelCare will provide personalized care services including nursing, rehabilitation, activities, counseling, exercise, socialization, nutritious meals and snacks, and arrangements for transportation to and from the school or day program and other places of interest to the clients including but not limited to their errands and medical-dental appointments. It is established as a result of an overwhelming demand for a unique type of personalized care service that will provide individualized care, vocational and habilitation therapy, behavioral modification and therapy all under one service objective.

The individualized program plan shall take into consideration the specific client's needs and services, functional ability, challenges, behaviors and ability to retain and respond to given task.

Sample Personnel Schedule:

AngelCare
Note: Staff No. represents the staff ID No.
(Sample Staff 0.1)

WKEnd	Day	Mon 7:00a 2:00p	Tue 7:00a 2:00p	Wed 7:00a 2:00p	Thu 7:00a 2:00p	Fri 7:00a 2:00p
	1	Staff 0.1	Staff 0.1	Staff 0.1	Staff 0.12	Staff 0.12
	2	Staff 0.12	Staff 0.12	Staff 0.12	Staff 0.12	Staff 0.12
	3	Staff 0.13	Staff 0.13	Staff 4	Staff 4	Staff 4
	4	Staff 4	Staff 0.13	Staff 4	Staff 0.12	Staff 0.12
	5	Staff 5	Staff 0.13	Staff 4	Staff 0.12	Staff 0.12
6		Staff 6	Staff 0.13	Staff 4	Staff 0.12	Staff 0.12
7		Staff 6	Staff 0.13	Staff 4	Staff 0.12	Staff 0.12
	8	Staff 8	Staff 8	Staff 7	Staff 8	Staff 8
	9	Staff 9	Staff 9	Staff 8	Staff 9	Staff 9

	10	Staff 10	Staff 10	Staff 9	Staff 10	Staff 10
	11	Staff 0.13	Staff 0.13	Staff 10	Staff 0.12	Staff 0.12
	12	Staff 10	Staff 10	Staff 9	Staff 10	Staff 10
13		Staff 7	Staff 7	Staff 4	Staff 7	Staff 7
14		Staff 7	Staff 7	Staff 4	Staff 7	Staff 7
	15	Staff 0.1	Staff 0.1	Staff 0.1	Staff 0.12	Staff 0.12
	16	Staff 0.12	Staff 0.12	Staff 0.12	Staff 0.12	Staff 0.12
	17	Staff 0.13	Staff 0.13	Staff 4	Staff 4	Staff 4
	18	Staff 0.13	Staff 4	Staff 0.12	Staff 0.12	Staff 0.13
	19	Staff 0.13	Staff 4	Staff 0.12	Staff 0.12	Staff 0.13
20		Staff 0.13	Staff 4	Staff 0.12	Staff 0.12	Staff 0.13
21		Staff 0.12	Staff 0.12	Staff 0.12	Staff 0.12	Staff 0.12
	22	Staff 0.13	Staff 0.13	Staff 4	Staff 4	Staff 4
	23	Staff 0.13	Staff 4	Staff 0.12	Staff 0.12	Staff 0.13
	24	Staff 0.13	Staff 4	Staff 0.12	Staff 0.12	Staff 0.13
	25	Staff 0.13	Staff 4	Staff 0.12	Staff 0.12	Staff 0.13
	26	Staff 0.12	Staff 0.12	Staff 0.12	Staff 0.12	Staff 0.12
27		Staff 4	Staff 0.13	Staff 4	Staff 0.12	Staff 0.12
28		Staff 5	Staff 0.13	Staff 4	Staff 0.12	Staff 0.12
	29	Staff 6	Staff 0.13	Staff 4	Staff 0.12	Staff 0.12
	30	Staff 6	Staff 0.13	Staff 4	Staff 0.12	Staff 0.12

NURSING AND SOCIAL WORK

AngelCare will provide a variety of non-medical, and social service needs. Medical and Mental/Behavioral issues are monitored by a registered nurse and a social worker on staff. Both should be knowledgeable and experienced in meeting the psychological and social needs of the clients. The Registered Nurse will be retained as a regular staff present at AngelCare while the clients are present. Staff is expected to provide medication monitoring and reminders. The staff is likewise trained on a regular basis to monitor the following client needs:

a. Medication administration and management.
b. Blood pressure/weight.
c. Bladder training and/or continence.
d. Nutrition instruction and special diet.
e. Specific nursing procedures .
f. Personal care services
g. Bathing, Hair care
h. Assistance with meals
i. Arrange for speech, physical, recreational and behavior therapy or counseling

There shall be a social worker on staff who will provide a therapeutic counseling, information, referral services, caregiver support groups, Individual, group, and/or family counseling.

Types of nursing services available:
1. Medication administration and management.
2. Blood pressure/weight
3. Bladder training and/or continence
4. Nutrition instruction and special diet
5. Stool monitoring

Personal care services
1. Bathing
2. Hair care
3. Assistance with meals
4. Assistance in Activities of Daily Living

Other Services:
1. Speech therapy
2. Recreation therapy
3. Physical therapy
4. Social work services
5. Information and referral
6. Individual and/or family counseling
7. Transportation places for appointments, shopping, etc…
8. Medical assessment
9. Medical Treatment
10. Podiatry care
11. Art therapy
12. Music therapy
13. Reality therapy
14. Exercises
15. Assistance dressing/grooming/using the toilet

Activities:

AngelCare will provide the clients with excellent personalized services and activities that is significant to their well being. The program of activities offered will be diverse, focusing on mental and physical stimulation, the strengths and interests of the clients.

The clients are encouraged to take part in activities on a regular basis.

Pottery making, gardening, arts and crafts, games, dancing, exercises, computer-Internet, participate in a play or stage presentation etc.…

Nutrition:

Proper nutrition plays an important role in preserving the health of our clients. AngelCare shall provide a minimum of healthy diet meals and snacks on a daily and as needed basis.

Special diets are often necessary for clients. Those meals, as well as the standard meals, will also be appetizing, tasty and attractively served as well as a regular meal. AngelCare shall also provide meals that are calorie controlled, kosher, vegetarian or meet the special requirements of diabetics, provide supplemental feedings or pureed foods provided when necessary.

Clients will be served with a well-balance diet consisting of the six basic food groups.

Sample meals: Menu will be available upon request and updated every month, one week in advance.

Transportation

AngelCare shall provide an experienced and safe driver on a regular and timely manner. There shall be an experienced and trained transporter and shall undergo regular safety training sponsored by AngelCare. The means of transportation will be safe and maintained in good working condition where a maintenance and mileage log shall be retained on a regular basis. There shall be safety equipment present and available at all times. Prior to transporting all belt will be fastened to secure the safety of the client and there will be a radio or cellular phone available for emergencies.

Admission Policies:

The admission policies must provide information relevant to the category and types of clients accepted for care, ages of the clients, rates and refund policies, acceptance and retention limitations, pre-admission appraisals, needs and services plans, medical assessments and an Admission Agreement which contains the typical information a client or his or her authorized representative would need to know prior to entering accepting the service . A description of the following items must be included in this section:

1. Persons accepted for care, including age range and compatibility with staff
2. Intake procedures
3. Criteria for determining appropriateness of he service and proposed activities (i.e. interviews, procedures for obtaining and developing the necessary paperwork)
4. Needs and Services Plan
5. Client's Rights/Personal Rights. (At a minimum there should be a statement that client/clients will be informed of their rights and that client/client's rights will not be violated)
6. Medical Assessment
7. Pre-Admission Appraisal Plan
8. Emergency Information
9. Sign-in and Sign-out Procedures
10. Immunization Requirements
11. Admission Agreement. The admission agreement is to include the following information:

- Description of basic services offered. (All basic services must be either offered or, if a client is currently obtaining specific services through other means, planned for in the event the service is needed at a future date)
- Description of optional services offered. (Reviewed to ensure that required "Basic Services" are not included in this description)
- Payment provisions, such as rates for basic & optional services, payor, due date, and frequency of payments.(Reviewed to ensure provisions are clear and rate charged to SSI/SSP recipients does not exceed the established maximum)
- Modification conditions. (Reviewed to ensure at least 30 day advanced notice for rate change)
- Refund Policy. (Reviewed to ensure that the policy is clear and is not in violation of licensing regulations)
- Reasons for termination
- Visiting policy
- House rules

Exercise

AngelCare will encourage client participation on all daily exercises

Occupational Therapy:

Equipment and supplies for creative skills such as leatherwork, needlework, ceramics, woodworking, painting, and graphic arts.

Massage/ YOGA / Music Therapy

Clients who are spastic and others that have muscle and joint issues will benefit from a therapeutic massage where a trained staff will provide muscle toning and water therapy. With the use of softened floor mats clients will be able to lay down and roll over on a therapeutic ball; soak their feet in a vibrating wash basin as they listen to a soft classical music to sooth their aching pains.

Music Therapy

1. Stereo/CD Player
2. Soft lights and inviting colorful room
3. Big pillows
4. Soft plastic floors
5. Natural sound tapes and audio visuals
6. Colorful soft tone pictures and posters.

AngelCare staff will be with a stethoscope, thermometer, blood sugar tester. There will be a designated Registered Nurse who will do the diagnosis and evaluation, and there will also be a physician who is on call and available when ever the need for consultation and evaluation is needed.

Therapeutic Recreation and Activities for Adults and Seniors

The main goal of therapeutic recreation is to increase self-esteem, and maintain a minimum function of the upper and lower extremities, which will help individuals adjust within a mainstream environment, where people interact and socialize to the best of their abilities. The key focus is on clients' morale and their enjoyment of life. Therefore, in order to achieve this, a good recreational activity program is essential.

AngelCare Home will provide daytime and mid-morning activities including evening activities that simulate the clients' physical, psychological and mental attributes.

Sensory activities are the essence, and the backbone of any therapeutic activity program. The goals are to maintain, and in most cases, to increase a person direct contact with self, client's immediate environment, and community. Our goal is to focus on the five senses that must be stimulated at all times to delay, and slow the inevitable degeneration of our brain cells, and motors skills and those senses are:

a. Sense of Touch (sewing, cooking, playing the piano, holding a book, etc...)
b. Sense of Smell (food, perfume, flower, chemicals, etc...)
c. Sense of Hearing (noise, singing, story, bitter)
d. Sense of Taste (sweet, sour, salty, bitter)
e. Sense of Visual (colors, lights, objects, self, others, etc...)

Part of the therapeutic activity involves sewing, knitting, and crocheting were always the pastime of the pastime of the young ladies centuries ago, and nothing has changed with our generation. Therefore, it is more than appropriate for a recreation department to provide adequate materials to help bring back not only the good old time in the life of the elderly, but also to bring a sense of high self-esteem to those who thought life was no longer worth it.

GAMES:

Bingo is one of the most popular games to date that enhances social interactions, and mainstreaming for the elderly. There are various forms of bingo games such as:
- Music bingo
- Math bingo

To better accommodate individuals with visual impairment, the bingo materials can be found in all kind of size ranging from small to jumbo. This game is played at the day program, in a proactive settings. The number of players can vary from two dozens of people. Bingo helps maintain the mental readiness, and the visual abilities of the players.

Table games such as:
a. Dominos
b. Cards
c. Monopoly, etc...
d. Chinese Checkers also called interactive games, are very appropriate for the independent individuals, and very sociable people as well.

Arts and crafts workshops must be prepared to accommodate the needs, and abilities of the elderly person. The activities must be creative and simple.

Tactile Stimulation and Sports Activities

a. Finger painting
b. Coloring and retraceable pictures
c. Cutting and pasting
d. Free expression drawing etc...

Bowling games are also popular for all ages. It is a special day or held on week-nights specially Saturday night for most children, adults, and elderly people. It is appropriate for people in wheelchair, and those who walk with a cane. Bowling gives a sense of physical and mental balance, because a straight line must be followed to complete the games successfully.

Adaptive sports are among the most popular events in people's life of all ages, since ancient time. These activities consist in promoting the use of lower and upper extremities. These activities are numerous, and the most accessible to the adults and the elderly on wheelchairs are:

a. Kick balls encourage the use of – knees, legs, and feet.   While sports like:
b. Volleyball
c. Tossing
d. Throwing darts
e. Basketball
f. Catching balls increase the use of- shoulders, arms, and hands.
g. Parachute is another exciting sport. It is suitable for small or large group. It consists in placing sponge and plastic balls are not too heavy on top of an open parachute, which is held by a certain number of people, seated in a circle like formation. At the signal of the group leader, everyone shakes his side of the parachute to prevent the bouncing balls to escape, and reach the floor on their side.

Exercise:

Daily exercises are very important in everyone's life to set an upbeat pace for the rest of the day. It is crucial for the adults and the elderly people who are in physical disadvantage due to sickness, and aging problems. It is one of the unique ways to stimulate the older people mentally, and physically.

Music therapy for the elderly is the essence of music in their life. A music therapist must be aware of the cultural background of the aged group he is serving to better reach the intended goals. It is within the national guidelines, and requirements for the music therapist to go back 30 to 40 years in the life of the aged individual to facilitate better responses. By so doing, the choice of repertoire will be appropriate to bring back reminiscing memories of their youth long gone. The following music activities are appropriate:

a. Sing along (gospel, spirituals, oldies, jazz, folks, etc...)
b. Rhythm band (drum, tambourine, stick, bells, maracas, etc...)
c. Name that tune
d. Musical Chair
e. Choir group (men's, ladies', mixed)

f. Entertainments (musical shows, holiday events, concert halls, etc...) The goals of therapeutic recreation in the day program are to replicate what the clients could do in the community, at home, in church in social club, including playing musical instruments such as drums, guitar, keyboard, violins, etc...

Hours Required: These activities shall be conducted with the supervision of a certified nursing assistant CNA, which must take at least 90 hours of recreational activity every three months.

GROUP ACTIVITIES / TABLE TOP / RECREATION / ADAPTIVE SPORTS COGNITIVE TRAINING:

VOCATIONAL SKILLS DEVELOPMENT WHICH INCLUDES ACADEMICS, BASIC LETTER WRITING & NAME IDENTIFICATION, AND CALENDAR RECOGNITION.

SKILLS: SENSORY MOTOR STIMULATION, BUILDING SOCIAL AND COMMUNICATION SKILLS. LEARNING ABOUT TEXTURES, SMELLS, COLORS, SAFETY, ETC., INFORMALLY LEARN TO PUT THINGS ON/IN TARGET, UTILIZE VARIETY OF ITEMS TO CREATE PROJECTS.

TABLE TOP GAMES: INTRO TO VARIOUS GAMES; INFORMALLY TEACH HOW TO TAKE TURNS, HOW TO MOVE OBJECTS, GAME PIECES AND COOPERATIVE, PLAY; AND COMMUNICATION SKILLS.

COOKING CLASS: INFORMAL TRAINING ON HOW TO READ A RECIPE, MEASURE INGREDIENTS, POUR, STIR AND MIX. PREPARATION FOR SNACK AT SNACK TIME AS APPROPRIATE.

DOMESTIC SKILLS: INFORMAL/FORMAL TRAINING TO SET TABLE AND PREPARE FOR MEAL PER ISP OBJ.

FOOD ART: MAKING CRAFT OBJECTS FROM THINGS FOUND IN THE KITCHEN, MAKING FOOD (JELLO JIGGLERS, ETC.) THAT CAN BE EATEN FOR SNACK ON FRIDAY, MAKING SENSORY PLAYDOUGH THAT HAS SMELL/TACTILE STIMULATION.

ART/PAINT PROJECT: MAKE A PAINTING WITH ASSORTED COLORS OF WTERCOLORS; FINGERPAINTS, WASHABLE PAINTS ON THE ARTBOARD PAPER USING FINGERS/BRUSHES/ROLLERS, ETC.

ART: INFORMAL TEACHING, CREATING CRAFT PROJECTS USING VARIETY OF ITEMS, PAPER, CHALK, MATERIALS, JEWELRY, FEATHERS, ETC.

TABLE TOP ART: INFORMAL TRAINING ON HOW TO MOLD AND SHAPE CLAY CREATE DIFFERENT OBJECTS. COLOR & TEXTURE AWARENESS.

GARDENING SKILLS: INFORMAL TEACHING ON HOW TO WATER THE YARD & PLANTS.

HOW TO CULTIVATE SOIL & PLANT SEEDS & PLANT CARE.

MUSICAL BAND: INFORMAL TARINING ON HOW TO HOLD AND MAKE SOUNDS WITH VARIOUS MUSICAL INRUMENTS, OFFERING OPPORTUNITY FOR CHOICES.

MUSIC EXERCISE: SENSORY MOTOR STIMULATION, INTRODUCTION TO VARIOUS EXERCISE TECHNIQUES, ROM TRAINING TO DIFFERENT SOUNDS AND RYTHMS OF MUSIC, FOLLOWING PHYSICAL THERAPISTS RECOMMENDATION FOR INDIVIDUAL. ROM TO MUSIC VIDEO.

MOBILITY TRAINING: TO DEVELOP ECH CLIENTS INDEPENDENCE TO BE MOBILE WITHIN THEIR ENVIRONMENT, BOTH IN THE COMMUNITY AND AT HOME.

ADAPTIVE SPORTS: INFORMAL TRAINING ON HOW TO THROW/ROLL/CATCH/PASS A BALL OR OTHER OBJECT, BASKETBALL, BOWLING, VELCRO DARTS, ETC.

COMMUNITY OUTING: INFORMALLY WORK ON APPROPRIATE SOCIAL BEHAVIOR, COMMUNICATION SKILLS AND PURCHASING SKILLS.

COMMUNITY AWARENESS: TRAINING IN LOCATION IDENTIFICATION, OBJECT IDENTIFICATION (FLOWER, TREE, COLOR, CAR, NEIGHBORS, ETC.) COLLECT ITEMS SUCH AS LEAVES, FLOWERS, ACORNS, ETC FOR ART/CRAFT PROJECT FOR THURSDAY OR FRIDAY. (NATURE WALKS, PICNICS).

COMMUNICATION SKILL: INFORMAL/FORMAL TRAINING COORDINATED THROUGHOUT THA DAY WITHIN ALL ACTIVITIES, TO DEVELOP RECEPTIVE AND EXPRESSIVE COMMUNICATION.

DISCUSSION OF CURRENT EVENTS: INFORMAL TRAINING TO DEVELOP SOCIAL SKILLS, AWARENESS OF DAILY EVENTS IN THEIR PERSONAL LIVES.

REST & RELAXATION PERIOD:

CLIENTS RELAX AND LISTEN TO MUSIC ON RADIO OR TAPES & SOCIAIZE WITH PEERS.

Story Time

BOOKS ON TAPE, BOOKS READ ALOUD, CORRESPONDING PUPPETRY SKILL: COMMUNICATION, CORRELATION OF COLOR TO PICTURE OF COLOR, SENSORU TOUCH BOOKS TO FEELING, ETC.

GAMES AND PHYSICAL ACTIVITIES CLIENTS

BALL AND BEAN BAG TOSS:
Toss around in a circle
Toss under or overhand
Toss, bounce, roll, kick to a target

CHASE THE BALL:
EQUIPMENT: Two rubber balls that are different colors.
DESCRIPTION: Players from a circle sitting down. The colored balls are given to Players on opposite sides of the circle. The two balls are passed around the circle, one ball trying to catch the other one.

BEAN BAG CLEAN UP:
EQUIPMENT: half as many bean bags as players.
DESCRIPTION: Arrange two teams one on each side of the dividing line. Divide bean bags. On the first signal have the players throw the bean bags to the other side. Continue to throw bean bags back till the second signal. The side with the fewest bags win.

BEAN BAG IN CIRCLE:
EQUIPMENT; One bean bag for each player.
PLAYING AREA: Any smooth hard surface; marked as shown.
DESCRITPION: The players stand 4-8 feet away from a double circle target drawn on the play area and toss bean bags at the target. A bean bag landing in the outer circle scores one point while one landing in the inner circle scores two points. The player with the most points win. It can be played in teams.

BALL PASSING RELAY:
EQUIPMENT: One ball per team.
DESCRIPTION: Divide the group into equal teams arranged one behind the other. Sitting down or side by side. The first player of each team holds the ball and on the signal GO passes the ball to the next player and on the end of the Line to win.

CIRCLE STRIDE BALL;
EQUIPMENT: A Ball
DESCRIPTION: Players form s circle sitting down; legs are stride and the feet touch those of their adjoining players. The ball is put into play by hitting it by Hand to go trough the other players legs. This player is then eliminated, returning when the next player is eliminated.

CLOTHES RELAY:
EQUIPMENT: Two grocery sacks, each with a set of large old clothes: simple Items that can be put on while sitting down for each team. Or one bag for each player.
DESCRIPTION: To be the first team to dress and undress.

SODA CRACKER RELAY:
EQUIPMENT: Two soda crackers per player.
DESCRIPTION: The players are divided into teams. Each players is given two Soda crackers. The first player on each team eats his crackers. As soon as he is able, he tries to whistle. When the first player of the team has whistled, the second player may begin eating his crackers. The game continues until the last person has whistled.

SPOON OUT
EQUIPMENT: 2 blindfolds, cotton balls, 2 large spoons, 2 large bowls, and clock or watch with second hand.
DESCRIPTION: All the cotton balls are placed in one bowl. The full bowl and the empty bowl placed side by side on the table. A player is Seated at the table, then blind folded. He is al-

lowed to feel where the bowls are in front of him one time, then he is given a spoon, and must try to move as many cotton balls as possible from the full bowl, within a time limit. Each player takes a turn. The player who gets the most cotton balls into the bowl wins.

COTTON THROW
DESCRIPTION: make a mark, and see who can throw the ball of cotton the farthest.

MUSICAL BALLOONS
EQUIPMENT: Balloons, enough for all but one player. A record player.
DESCRIPTION: The players sit in a circle, all but one holding a balloon, another balloon, another person is in charge of the music. When the music starts the balloons are passed in the same direction. When the music stops the player without a balloon in his hand is out of the game.
Musical hats: Same as above.

APPLAUSE
DESCRIPTION: While one person is out of the room, the others decide what he should do when he returns. Ex. Scratch his head, shake someone's hand. When the person returns, the others begin to clap slowly. As the person gets closer to the accomplishment they clap faster, or slower if they .Are not close.

GUESS THE SPICE
EQUIPMENT: Eight or more spices, paper cups, paper, pencil a sample of each Spice is placed in an open, unmarked container. Each container is marked with a number. A master list is made of the numbers and their corresponding spices. Each spice is passed around for each client to examine by sight and smell only no tasting allowed. They then write on their papers the numbers of the spice containers and what spice they think each one is. The correct answers are read from the master list and the players correct their own papers. The winner is the player with the most correct answers.

WHAT IS IN THE BAG
EQUIPMENT: At least 10 paper bags, a kitchen utensil for each bag. Paper and Pencil for each player. In advance place each utensil in a separate, numbered bag and seal.
DESCRIPTION: Each bag is passed around the circle. After feeling the outside of the bag, each player writes down the number of the bag and his corresponding guess as to what is inside. The winner is the player with the most correct guesses.

Balloon game
EQUIPMENT: Balloons, about 15-20 a person.
DESCRIPTION: To see how many balloons one person can hold using his arms, Legs, chin, etc. in a given amount of time.

JIGSAW

EQUIPMENT: One simple puzzle for teams of 2-4 players. A shallow box to fit each puzzle for moving. DESCRIPTION: Each group is allowed 10 minutes to work the puzzle, it is then. Passed on the next group. The first group to finish a puzzle wins.

DON'T CROSS YOUR LEGS

DESCRIPTION; During an activity or party as each player is caught crossing Legs they are out. The last to not cross their legs wins.

SOAP BUBBLES

EQUIPMENT: Soap bubbles and blowers for two or three

DESCRIPTION: To see who can blow bubbles the greatest distance down a table.

YESTERDAYS PICTURES

EQUIPMENT: An old photograph of each player.

DESCRIPTION: Who can match up the most correct pictures.

PERSONAL TRIVIA

EQUIPMENT: Paper and pencils, small bag or bowls.

DESCRIPTION: Each player briefly writes down three facts events, experiences from his life that he hopes are unknown to anyone else in the group. The papers are folded and collected in the bowl. One person reaches in for a paper and reads the three facts. The player to the readers right begins guessing and it continues until everyone has named someone he think .it. The correct person reveals himself and then has the option to elaborate on his facts. The person who guessed correctly picks the next player.

CARD GAMES	RUMMY
HEARTS	Five Hundred Rummy
Black Jack Hearts	Wild Cat Rummy
Red Heart Jacks	Gin Rummy
Spot Hearts	
OLD MAID	SLAP JACK
ANIMALS	SOLITAIRE
CRIBBAGE	POKER
DICE GAMES	ROUND THE SPOT
COOTIE	UNDER AND OVER SEVEN
ACES IN THE POT	CARGO
EVEREST	NEEDLE WORK
SEWING	QUILTING
CROHET	KNITTING
LATCH WORK RUGS	NEEDLEPOINT

MISCELLANEOUS ACTIVITIES

SING A LONGS

PROJECTS
NAIL CARE
PAINTING
PET VISIT
CERAMICS
FLOWER ARRANGING
FIELD TRIPS
BIRDWATCHING

SOCIAL ACTIVITIES
BIBLE STUDY
TEA TIME
CURRENT EVENTS
PIN PALS
COFFE SOCIAL
ARTS AND CRAFTS
PAPIER MACHE
SOAP CRAVING
STENCILS
MOSAICS
MOBILES
& BOXES
POPSICLE CRAFTS
FELT CRAFTS
CRAYON ON CLOTH
PICTURES
CHARCOAL DRAWING
INDIAN CRAFTS
STRING ART
TOY MAKING

PARTY AND HOLIDAY IDEAS
BACKWARD PARTY
CLOWN PARTY
WESTERN PARTY
INDOOR BEACH PARTY
NEWPAPER PARTY
PUZZLE PARTY

BINGO
TABLE GAMES
POTPOURRI

MOVIE AND POPCORN
COOKING
WOOD PROJECTS
GARDENING
MODELING
PUZZLES
WHITTLING

CHURCH
GOOD HUMOR LADIES
GROUP DISCUSSIONS
STORY TIME
MONTHLY NEWSLETTER

CLAY
SPONGE ANIMALS
COLLAGES
YARN CRAFTS
DECORATED BOTTLES

BOOK ENDS
CRAYON DRAWING
TEXTURED CRAYON

NATURE CRAFTS
LEATHER WORK
TIN CAN CRAFT
DOOR STOPS

BALLOON PARTY
COUNTY FAIR
CIRCUS PARTY
NAUTICAL PARTY
PIONEER PARTY
SCAVENGER HUNT

PARTY

HILLBILLY BASH	WINTER WONDERLAND
A MAGIC BANQUET	BREAKFAST IN THE YARD
SUPER BOWL PARTY	BARNYARD BASH
CANDY PULL	FASHION SHOW
HAWAIIAN HOLIDAY	HOLLYWOOD PARTY
MUSIC PARTY	PUPPET SHOW
PIRATE PARTY	GRANDPARENT PARTY
NEW YEARS EVE PARTY	ARBOR DAY PARTY
VALENTINE'S DAY PARTY	CUPID'S CARNIVAL OF HEARTS
GROUND HOG DAY	SADIE HAWKINS DAY PARTY
SAINT PATRICK'S DAY PARTY	SPRING PARTY
APRIL FOOL'S DAY PARTY	EASTER PARTY
MAY DAY PARTY	MOTHER'S DAY PARTY
MEMORIAL DAY	4TH OF JULY
FATHER'S DAY	PATRIOTIIC PARTY
GYPSY PARTY	COLUMBUS DAY PARTY
HALOWEEN PARTY	HALOWEEN CARNIVAL
THANKSGIVING PARTY VETERAN;S DAY PARTY	
CHRISTMAS DAY PARTY	CHRISTMAS CONCERT
CHRISTMAS PARADE	CHRISTMAS EVE

MONEY RAISING ACTIVITIES

APRON BAZAAR	CHRISTMAS BOTIQUE
WHITE ELEPHANT AUCTION	GARAGE SALE
RUMMAGE SALE	FAVORITE RECIPE BOOK
BAKE SALE	CHILI SUPPER
PANCAKE BREAKFAST	PIE SOCIAL
SPAGHETTI BREAKFAST	HOT DOG STAND

Mission Statement:

The key element in our care is our excellent relationship between staff and the clients and their families.

The following factors are our asset:

1. Quality of care and supervision which upholds the highest standards
2. Safety and cleanliness
3. Staffing that adheres to utmost courtesy, respect, freedom from abuse and neglect, experience and education maintained by the staff in general
4. Continuous staff training and in-services / certification on medication monitoring, risk and safety management and proper client care and supervision
5. Program variety, practical application and consistency.
6. Consistency in programming and follow-up on client's progress and development

7. How the clients will be able to learn and enjoy their activities that address their needs and services

ADMISSION CRITERIA

1. Clients who are in need of our services, use of wheelchairs, needing assistance with hygiene, transferring and other personal needs.
2. Must be free of behavioral conditions which pose a hazard to self and to staff.
3. Will accept individuals with health conditions that require incidental medical services, clients with medical condition(s) that are chronic and stable, temporary in nature and are expected to return to a condition normal for that individual and is under the medical care of a licensed professional.
4. Will accept both ambulatory and non-ambulatory clients.
5. Must be in the process of acquiring self-help skills.
6. Will provide feeding assistance to those clients in need.
7. Will provide transfer assistance to clients in wheelchairs. If a lift device is required, this must be provided by another entity.
8. Will accept clients who wear adult briefs.
9. Will accept ensure that incontinent clients are checked at regular intervals and are kept clean.
10. Will accept clients who require scheduled toileting at regular intervals.
11. Will provide assistance to clients who can benefit from scheduled toileting by assisting or reminding them to go to the bathroom at regular intervals.
12. Will accept clients who require assistance in hygiene and self-care tasks.
13. Will provide all necessary assistance to clients in need.
14. Will not accept individuals who require health services or have a prohibited health condition(s) including:
    1. Naso-gastric and naso-duodenal tubes.
    2. Staph infection or other serious infection.
    3. Active, communicable TB.
    4. Conditions which require 24 hour nursing care or oversight.
    5. Stage 3 or 4 decubitus ulcers.
    6. Any other condition or care requirements which would require the Association to be licensed as a health .

CLIENT TRAINING TOPICS:

- Recreation/Leisure
- Travel Training
- Personal Care
- Health and Safety Awareness
- Medication Management
- Nutrition & Meal Preparation
- Self-Identity, Personal Adjustment, Communication, Civic Awareness & Responsibility

- Vocational Development
- Functional Academics
- Client Skills
- Behavior Management
- Other Supports As Needed

A. Recreation/Leisure: Staff will instruct the clients in choosing appropriate leisure time activities. Staff will emphasize the benefits of community-based recreation and leisure activities.

- Helps client unwind and relax
- Opportunities to meet new people
- Exposure to different social situations and use of skills, such as communication skills, proper dress and appropriate grooming
- Exposure to different cultures
- Exercise through sports
- Learning about surroundings
- Increasing knowledge (Example: Museums, Lectures)

Clients will also receive instructions on how to choose a recreational activity, including: Client interest:

- o Budget – What you can afford
- o Availability
- o Choose of recreational activities
- o Different types of parties: Selecting an appropriate party for holidays, birthdays and different occasions, formal to informal, dinner to movies
- o The different occasions
- o The type of entertainment
- o Clients will learn to use natural resources in making arrangements for recreation and leisure; such s, newspapers, phone books, etc.
- o Planning a menu for appropriate number of people
- o Invitations

Planning a Trip:
- o Deciding where to go
- o Amount of money needed
- o Food arrangements
- o Attractions or tours, cost, times

Making Reservations:
- o Decide location and motel
- o Stay in motel or with friends
- o Calling ahead for cost and information

B. Travel Training: Clients will receive training to ride public transportation for community integration activities. Training will include actual travel to/from the program to the following possible locations:

- Shopping Centers
- Recreational Events
- Restaurants
- Employment Sites

Training will be given on:
- Locating bus stops
- Selecting the proper bus
- Transferring buses
- Paying bus fares
- Debarking the bus
- Pedestrian laws
- Bus schedules

C. Personal Self-Care & Hygiene: Staff will assist clients in presenting themselves to the public in an acceptable manner. Modern, age appropriate clothing, coupled with a clean body and attractive hair style will be the focus to establish self-esteem, as well as, presenting a well groomed image to the public. For those clients who are in need of assistance with their self-care tasks, staff will provide all necessary supports.

The focus will be on the following areas:
- Discuss and role play how to recognize when a bath or shower is necessary
- Discuss and demonstrate how to maintain their own hair
- Discuss and demonstrate proper way to brush teeth and gums
- Discuss and play with female clients how to take the proper care needed during her menstrual cycle
- Discuss and demonstrate how to present a neat appearance
- Discuss and demonstrate how to care for their shaving needs, including the use of various related appliances and toilet articles
- Discuss and demonstrate how to care for their clothes properly
- Discuss and demonstrate how to properly care for nails

D. Health & Safety Awareness; Medication Management: Clients will learn, in a group as well as on an individual basis, Emergency Procedures:
  o What to do in case of fire
  o What to do in case of a disaster
  o What to do in case of an accident
  o What to do in case of illness
  o How to use basic first aid techniques in treating minor injuries
  o What to do if someone is having a seizure

- o What to do if someone is choking
- o When calling a police, what information do you need to tell them
- o The identification and safe storage of poisons
- o Keeping floors and walkway areas clear of hazardous objects
- o How to obtain hard to reach items and how to lift heavy items
- o Safe use of electrical outlets and appliances
- o How to operate a flashlight and understand its value as an emergency appliance
- o Use of fire extinguisher
- o Discussion of awareness of medications taken, their need, and dosages
- o Teach proper use of over-the-counter drugs and medicines not requiring a prescription
- o Emergency phone numbers: Police, Fire, Doctor, Pharmacy, Etc.
- o Discussion of services provided by medical care facilities

Disaster and Fire Drills will be conducted at random every month. Staff will time the clients and note in a Disaster/Fire Log the time and any concerns. The staff will also discuss the drill with the clients. Both the clients and staff will discuss any concerns they may have.

E. Nutrition & Meal Preparation: Staff will instruct client on Nutrition & Basic Cooking & Meal Preparation Tasks on an individual basis. Staff will train client to prepare their morning snacks, as well as, provide training in lunch preparation skills. (Example: Use of microwave, cutting sandwiches, pouring beverages). Training will also be provided in preparing simple food items.

The clients will learn & shall also demonstrate the use of:

- o Pots & pans for cooking purposes
- o Safe use of knife
- o Measurements
- o Kitchen techniques such as chopping, paring, grating, baking, broiling, boiling, frying
- o The proper food storage
- o Safe use of stove & oven
- o Proper & safe use of kitchen appliances (Example: garbage disposal, toaster, coffee pot, electric mixer, microwave oven)

F. Self-Advocacy, Self-Identity, Personal Adjustment, Interpersonal Relations & Communication: AngelCare will focus on each individual's needs in learning Self-Advocacy Skills. The focus will be, but not limited to, the following areas:

- o Knowing their rights
- o Learning to say no
- o Obtaining & requesting assistance
- o Learning to express their own view point
- o Speaking out in an appropriate manner
- o Making informed choices

Self-Identity, Personal Adjustment, Interpersonal Relations & Communication Skills include:

    o   Use of personal identification
    o   Discussion of wishes 7 desires
    o   Development of goals
    o   Discussion & demonstration of getting along with others
    o   Discussion of issue of privacy, respecting others & appropriate social behavior
    o   Discussion & demonstration of basic communication skills

G. Client Skills: Client will learn shopping / client skills in the natural environment. Staff will train clients in the following areas:

    o   To buy simple items
    o   To request assistance from salesperson when needed
    o   To shop for bargains
    o   To verbalize information about types of stores
    o   To exchange items
    o   To exhibit appropriate behavior in stores
    o   To locate products in different areas of stores
    o   To purchase items appropriate to need
    o   To purchase food in a restaurant or take-out shop
    o   To purchase items from vending machines & other coin-operated machines

H. Functional Academics: Staff will instruct clients in Functional Academic Skills in small group settings and on an individual basis. Functional Academic Skills Training will include: Functional Reading

    o   Functional Writing
    o   Functional Academics
    o   Functional Client Skills

Training will be provided in the natural environment and will include:

- Identification of important personal data
- Responding appropriately to written information on watches, clocks & other dials & gauges
- Responding appropriately to written information found on safety signs, size labels, price tags & other signs & labels
- Locating needed information from simple charts, diagrams, maps & menus
- Carrying out simple directions written on packages, machinery, equipment & items that are assembled
- Responding appropriately to key words found on employment forms & other simple blanks & forms
- Identifying help wanted ads, printed advertizements, correspondence & other written materials & will seek the assistance of a responsible person to decode written & printed material that he/she is unable to read
- Carrying out transactions involving money (Example: pay telephone, bus fare, vending machines)

- Identifying situations involving time (Example: day of week, month of the year, seasons, major holidays, arriving on time to scheduled activities & events)

HEALTH CONDITIONS: Restricted Health Conditions of Clients that AngelCare will not be able to accept unless proper training and experienced staff are available:
- Use of inhalation-assistive devices
- Colostomy/ileostomy
- Need for fecal impaction removal, enemas, or suppositories
- Use of indwelling urinary catheters
- Staph or other serious, communicable infections
- Insulin-dependent diabetes
- Wounds (Stage 1 or 2 dermal ulcer or an unhealed, surgically closed incision or wound)
- Gastronomy (feeding, hydration, and care)
- Tracheostomies
- Clients with metered-dose inhalers and dry powder inhalers
- Clients who require oxygen
- Clients who rely upon others to perform all activities of daily living (ADL's)
  Bathing
  Dressing
  Toiletiing
  Transferring
  Eating
  Continence
- Clients with incontinence
- Clients with contractures
- Naso-gastric and naso-duodenal tubes
- Active, communicable TB
- Conditions that require 24-hour nursing care and monitoring
- Any other condition or care requirements which would require the to be licensed as a health as defined by Sections 1202 and 1250 of the Health and Safety Code

Universal Precaution

PROCEDURE	WASH	WEAR
DAY TO DAY INTERACTIONS	X	X
SHOWERINNG/BATHING, TOOTH BRUSHING, MISCELLANEOUS ORAL HYGIENE	X	X
MENSTRUAL CARE	X	X
FIRST AID	X	X
CHANGING LINENS/LAUNDRY	X	X
CLEANING UP TOILETING ACCIDENTS/VOMIT	X	X

TAKING RECTAL TEMPERATURE OR ADMINISTERING ENEMAS/SUPPOSITORIES	X	X
SHAVING WITH DISPOSABLE BLADE RAZORS	X	X
APPLYING TOPICAL MEDICATIONS	X	X
DISPENSING ORAL MEDICATIONS X	X	
COLLECTING URINE OR BM SPECIMENS	X	X

UNIVERSAL PRECAUTIONS

TO PREVENT TRANSMISSION OF BLOOD BORNE DISEASE

General Information

Many potentially communicable diseases go unrecognized so universal precautions (barrier precautions) should be taken routinely regardless of the known or unknown diagnosis of an individual when contact with blood or body fluids is anticipated.

All direct care staff (persons whose activities hands on contact with clients) should routinely use appropriate barrier precautions to prevent skin and mucous membrane exposure when contact with blood or other body fluids of any client is anticipated. Disposable gloves should be worn for touching blood and body fluids, mucous membranes or non-intact skin of all clients, for handling items or surfaces soiled with blood or body fluids. Staff should be aware of the potential for transmission of disease to client, client staff and client to client.

Techniques

Hand washing before and after contact with each client is the most effective way or preventing and controlling the spread of infection.

Hand washing should be done when:
- Arriving and leaving work;
- Between each direct contact with a client;
- Before and after use of disposable gloves;
- When hands are dirty;
- After handling soiled equipment and soiled linens;
- Preparing or serving meals;
- Preparing and dispensing medications;
- After using the bathroom for self and or client.

Essential of hand washing:
- Running water;
- Rub/scrub hands together;
- Cleansing agent such as soap or detergent (liquid soap preferred);
- Paper towels that are conveniently available.

Hand washing procedures:
- Remove watch and jewelry;
- Expose the forearms;
- Turn on water to a comfortable temperature;
- Scrub vigorously with soap and running water for at least 30 seconds, with special care to areas between fingers, around nails and forearms;
- Rinse thoroughly with water;
- Dry hands thoroughly with paper towels and discard paper towels in covered, lined trash container.

Gloves should be worn when assisting client with:
- Bathing or cleaning the rectal or genital areas;
- Giving mouth care;
- Shaving with a disposable blade razor;
- Cleaning toilets;
- Cleaning up urine, stool or vomit
- Menstrual care and disposal of sanitary pads;
- Performing wound care.

Gloves should be changed after direct contact with each client. Hands should be washed immediately after gloves are removed. If a glove is torn during use, remove glove and replace with a new glove. Gloves should always be worn when staff have open wounds or rashes on their hands.

General purpose utility gloves (rubber household gloves) may be used for housekeeping chores involving potential contact with blood, utility gloves may be decontaminated and reused by should be discarded if they are peeling, cracked or discolored, or if they have punctures, tears, or other evidence of deterioration. Disposable gloves should be not reused.

Daily Reminders of Universal Precautions

Bathroom:
Bathrooms should be cleaned and disinfected routinely with disinfectant diluted with water. Wash tubs/showers with spray bottle of disinfectant diluted with water. Gloves should be used when cleaning bathrooms. Toilet brushes should be soaked in disinfectant between uses and be replaced as needed. Dispose of urine, stool, vomit, dirty water used not to be used on Kitchen floors. Dirty water used for mopping up the floor should not be disposed of in the sink where food is prepared.

Laundry:
All soiled linen should be handled as little as possible. Clothing or bed covers soiled with fecal matter, urine or blood should be washed separately and staff should wear gloves when handling these contaminated linens.

Personal Care:

Each clients needs own hygiene items: toot brush, brush comb, and razor (if used). These items are not to be shared and need to be stored separately. Tooth brushes need to be changed frequently. Disposable gloves must be worn for all mouth care. Staff should change gloves after each client.

A   Staff Requirements:

ADMINISTRATOR: JOB DESCRIPTION

The Administrator has full of responsibility of the supervising caregivers'/staff assigned in private homes or in facilities. Responsibilities include the following:

1. To supervise all care and services rendered to the clients.
2. Be on call and must be available when needed during the day and be capable of filling in for any position on any shift if staff person is not available for duty.
3. To handle all daily transactions with the client and their families, physician, therapists and relay health condition in a timely manner and log on to the client record, changes and progress notes.
4. Recruit, evaluate and employ staff. Handle all reprimands or terminations.
5. Complete all client assessments, and maintain client records. To monitor client vital signs and physical conditions, regularly converse with client and families to establish their needs.
6. To provide physical check on the client's state if an incident or unusual occurrence happens.
7. Establish policies and procedures, programs and budgets.
8. Oversee all the financial records and the office related business.
9. Be the community contact and public relations.
10. Provide In-service training for staff and all new staff orientation/training. Attend to all meetings including staff, client's consultants and their families.
11. Medication monthly review–audit and review with clients if needed. Regularly go over with the clients records, drug profile and appraisal needs and assessment plan.

JOB DESCRIPTION: OFFICE MANAGER:

Educational Requirements: High School Graduation
Experience: 1 year experience performing the duties of secretary/office manager including computer literacy.
1. Maintain all files and records (general, clients, personnel).
2. Answer telephones courteously and politely, and to relay messages to appropriate parties in a timely manner.
3. Interface with caregiving staff and clients/families and their physician. Computer input, including the storage and retrieval of generated reports and correspondence.
4. Maintain and distribute office supplies.
5. Correspondences (incoming, outgoing and fax).
6. Distribution of administration mail.

7. Any other duties as requested by administration.

STAFF Caregiver/Direct Care Staff
Educational Requirements: High School Graduate
Experience: Preferred 1 year direct care experience in a Residential setting.
The duties of all STAFF will be:

1. To supervise protect and care for client's needs at all times.
2. To consistently interact with the client.
3. To be able to hear and help resolve the needs of the client.
4. To identify possible needs of the client for professional services and communicate findings to professional staff.
5. To maintain daily records :
   5.a. Client's progress.
   5.b. Client's behavior and problems.
   5.c. Medication.
   5.d. Progress.
6. To assist client and provide daily household chores.
7. To transport client to medical and dental appointments and other scheduled activities.

NIGHT WORKER:
Educational Requirements: High School Graduate
Experience: 1-year caregiving experience in a residential setting.
The duties of the Night Worker shall be:

1. Required to remain awake through the night shift for the safety of the client.
2. Perform any and all duties required of the Staff Caregiver.
3. Check on client hourly or every thirty minutes.
4. Record in log.
5. Meet needs of client during night hours.
6. Clean the house and laundry clothes.
7. Empty all trash cans.
8. Maintain house standards including rules, discipline, cleanliness etc.
9. Awaken client at designated hours.
10. Prepare meals and snacks for clients.
12. Perform other duties as required by the Administrator.

Sample Employment Agreement

AGREEMENT

This Agreement for Employment is made on this _____ day of _____, 200___, by and between_____ (hereinafter referred to as "Employer") and _____ (hereinafter referred to as "Employee").

The Employer shall employ Employee subject to the following terms and conditions.

1. Employment for the above Employee shall commence on _____, 20___ .
2. The following duties and responsibilities shall be strictly observed by the Employee:
a. To supervise, protect and care for client's needs at all times.
b. To consistently interact with the client.
c. To be able to hear and help resolve the needs of the client.
d. To identify possible needs of the client and to provide a nurturing and caring environment, and to communicate all observations, concerns and issues of the client to the attending staff and the health care professionals.
e. To maintain daily records :
    1.a. Client's progress.
    1.b. Client's behavior and problems.
    1.c. Medication.
    1.d. Progress.
f. To assist client and provide daily household chores.
g. To transport client to medical and dental appointments and other scheduled activities.

NIGHT WORKER:
i. Required to remain awake throughout the night shift for the safety of the client.
j. Perform any and all duties required of the Staff Caregiver.
k. Check on client hourly or over 15-30 minutes.
l. Record in log.
m. Meet needs of client during night hours.
n. Clean the house and laundry clothes.
o. Empty all trash cans.
p. Maintain house standards including rules, cleanliness etc.
q. Awaken client at designated hours.
r. Prepare morning meal for clients.
s. Perform other duties as required by the Administrator.

In addition to the duties stated above, the Employee shall perform such further and other duties required by the Employer.

3. The Employee shall work _____ through _____ from _____ A.M. to _____P.M. and such additional hours as are required by the Employer for the Employee to competently perform the duties of his position.

The Employee shall use his or her best efforts on behalf of the Employer.

4. The Employee shall comply with all stated standards of performance, policies, rules, and regulations. A copy of policies and procedures manual containing a more complete explanation of many of these standards has been given to the Employee. At this time, Employee acknowledges receipt of this manual. The Employee shall also comply with such future Employer policies, rules, regulations, performance standards and manuals as may be published or amended from time to time.

5. Employment under this Agreement shall commence on_____, 20____ and shall terminate on _____, 20__, unless terminated prior to such time for cause.

6. The Employer shall make payment to the Employee a set amount as compensation for services rendered. The Employee agrees to accept the sum of $ _____ per hour, (Minimum: 3 hours) payable [choose one] (weekly, bi-weekly, monthly, bi-monthly) in the amount of $ _____.

    For Live-in staff, employee shall receive $ _____/ day.

    In addition to the above compensation, the Employee will not be entitled to any "fringe benefits":

7. This contract of employment may terminate upon the occurrence of any of the following events:

    (a). The death of the Employee; (b). The failure of the Employee to perform his duties satisfactorily after notice or warning thereof; (c). For just cause based upon non-performance of duties by Employee; (d). Economic reasons of the Employer which may arise during the term of this Agreement and which may be beyond the control of the Employer.

8. The Employee shall not, at any time during the period hereof, and for 10 years from the date of termination of this Agreement, directly or indirectly, within geographic area of 20 miles, engage in, or become involved in, any business competitive or similar to that of the Employer.

9. This Agreement may not be assigned without prior notice by either party. Such assignment is subject to the mutual consent and approval of any such assignment.

10. This Agreement constitutes the complete understanding between the parties, unless amended by a subsequent written instrument signed by the employer and employee. Any dispute under this contract shall be required to be resolved by binding arbitration of the parties hereto. Each party shall select one arbitrator and both arbitrators shall select a third party. The arbitration shall be governed by the rules of the American Arbitration Association then in force and effect.

Signed this _____ day of _____, 20____

_____   _____
         Employee   Employer

SAMPLE DAILY STAFF SCHEDULE

6:00	Prepare meals
7:00	Wake up Client
7:15	Meal time
7:35	Make sure transportation is on time.
7:40	Meal / Pass meds
7:50	Meal
8:00	Transport Client to appointment
8:30	
9:00	Clean house/ Update records
11:00	Prepare lunch meal
12:00	Lunch time
12:30	
1:00	Community activity
1:30	
2:00	Client free time/Movies/News
3:00	Snacks
3:30	
4:00	Interaction/Communication/Exercise
4:30	Shower time
5:00	Dinner
5:30	Clean up
6:00	TV / reading/ interaction
6:30	Reading and interaction
7:00	Neighborhood Walks
7:30	Back from walk
8:00	Snack
8:30	Brush teeth
9:00	Sleep
9:30	Lights Out
10:00pm	Sleep

STAFF QUIZ

1. Mrs. Smith has fallen, and is complaining of pain in her ribs. What should you do?
2. Mr. Hath has fainted and is barely breathing, has bluish fingers and face. What will you do?
3. Mrs. C has taken the wrong medication. What should you do?
4. P. M. shift person has not shown up for her shift. What you should do?
5. The Administrator is not available to answer your question, and you think someone should be sent to the hospital to be checked out. Who will you call?

   First: _____

   Second : _____

6. Mr. Johnson is complaining of severe chest pain; something is terribly wrong. What number will you call?

7. Food found in the refrigerator is over three days old. Should you throw it out?

8. Relatives came into the middle of the night, what do you need to do?

9. Mrs. Lapp doesn't like her sleeping pills taken at 9:00 p.m. wants you to call the doctor and get something else. What will you do?

10. Toilet is plugged and water is overflowing. How are you going to handle it?

11. What is the location of the following?

> Water main shut off
> Electrical shut off
> Propane shut off
> Emergency exit
> Medication cabinet

12. In case of an extreme emergency, you have to evacuate the clients. Where will you make arrangements to take them and what will you take with you?

13. It's 11 a. m. Saturday and you are out of a medication for Mr. X. Should you give him someone else's that is the same thing?

14. On Sunday p.m., Mr. Z wants you to give him an enema; he has been constipated for 5 days. What will you do?

15. Mrs. Tapp falls, is able to get up on her own, but is really very confused and blood her pressure is up. What will you do?

16. What numbers indicate a high blood pressure?

> Systolic_____ Diastolic_____

17. Mrs. Ferr, who never complains, says she is not feeling well and has pain in her arm but has never fallen. What will you do, if anything?

18. Mrs. Jean refuses to take her medications. What should you do?

> 1. _____
> 2. _____
> 3. _____

19. Mr. Pete comes down with a cold on Tuesday night. Is there anything you should do?

20. Mr. John became very agitated and hit Mrs. Cat. She wasn't hurt enough to warrant medical attention, but Mr. John remains verbally and physically abusive. What do you think you should do?

21. Your family calls and you have an extreme emergency at home and are needed at once. What will you do?

22. Your pay check is not correct. What will you do?

23. Mrs. Smith is upset with you over her laundry and she keeps insisting she's right. How should you handle the situation?

24. Mr. Pete is gone and you cannot find him anywhere. What steps, other than searching the area, should you do?

25. Mrs. Cathy wants an aspirin. Can you give her one?

SAMPLE EMPLOYEE MANUAL

This manual contains policies that are expected to be strictly observed by caregiver/staff at all times. It should serve to answer most of the questions that would normally arise. Our primary and outmost concern is taking good care of our clients and ASSURE THEIR SAFETY AT ALL TIMES. This is, after all, their home and they deserve respect, courtesy and to be treated with dignity at all times. It is essential that all information about the client remain confidential unless revealed to authorized representatives and consultants.

It is important to know your responsibilities to the best of your ability and to maintain rapport and a cooperative spirit with your clients and fellow employees, regardless of race, color, religion, sex, or national origin. Staff employees must maintain a neat and clean appearance and to have courteous attitude towards the people who we come in contact with at the client's home at all times.

Each person in this is under the direction of the Administrator, who is responsible for your performance and well being.

This is endeavored to employ only people that are best qualified for the position, and upon commencement of employment, ensure that they are properly oriented. We will not discriminate against any employee because of sex, age, religion, creed, color or national origin. Working conditions shall be maintained in a manner that is fair and free of bias and discrimination. The employee understands that employment is AT-WILL. The employer or employee may terminate employment at anytime, for any reason or for no reason at all.

To help the employees know what is expected from them, the following personnel policies have been established:

1. **Absence, Leave of:** All leaves of absence must be approved by the Administrator. This can cause an adjustment in the anniversary date of employment.

   _____ Employee Initial

2. **Absence, Notification of:** Employees must notify their shift supervisor or the Administrator when unable to report to work for any reason. This notice shall be as early as 24 hours if possible, but no later than (3) hours before scheduled work time.

   _____ Employee Initial

3. **Abuse of Clients:** Zero Tolerance to Abuse and Neglect of Clients. This agency will not tolerate any form of abuse and neglect. Any employee who has been alleged and is suspected of abusing any of the clients physically, emotionally, financially or mentally, will be immediately suspended and at the option of the administrator may be terminated and the local authorities notified pending investigation. Immediate termination will be required upon completion of the investigation and conclusion that indeed such allegation is founded/substantiated.

   _____ Employee Initial

4. **Accidents, Employees and Clients:** All accidents, however slight, must be reported to the Administrator as soon as possible. If an employee is injured, the appropriate Worker's Compensation forms must be filled out and given to the Administrator or Manager.

_____ Employee Initial

5. **Addresses:** It is the responsibility of the employee to keep the office informed any change of address, marital status, number of dependents and phone number. It is imperative to our operation that we able to contact each employee by telephone.

_____ Employee Initial

6. **Benefits:** We do pay into the federal social security program, unemployment insurance, and worker's compensation programs. However, we do not provide dental and medical insurance, and other benefits to our employees.

_____ Employee Initial

7. **Breaks:** An employee working a full 8-hour shift shall take a 30-minute lunch break after the first four hours. An employee is to take a 30-minute lunch break after 5 hours of work, if working less than 8 hours. If the employee is on duty (example: Night Shift Supervisor), he shall be paid regular time for the on-duty meal period; employee is to have undisturbed lunch break. Each employee is entitled to take a 10 minute break for every two hours worked.

_____ Employee Initial

8. **Bulletin Board:** Information of importance to employees can be found on the bulletin board in the employee lounge. Scheduled in-services and employee activities of the month will also be posted there.

_____ Employee Initial

9. **Canvassing and soliciting:** Canvassing, of any type, is prohibited. Any soliciting or collection for any purpose, or the sale of any tickets or merchandise by employees or outsiders, must the approval of the Administrator; eg. Avon, Mason Shoes, Fuller Brush, etc.

_____ Employee Initial

10. **Conduct:** We have high standards of conduct to maintain. Kindness and friendliness towards fellow staff, clients and their visitors are expected. Employees will refrain from gossiping, loud talking (especially at night), Unnecessary noise, and any other activities disturbing to clients. Information concerning clients are strictly confidential and will not be transmitted to unauthorized persons.

_____ Employee Initial

11. **Eating and drinking:** There will be no eating or drinking in other than the designated areas, and only during scheduled lunch or breaks.

_____ Employee Initial

12. **Employee Credit References:** No misleading information will be given to creditors requesting verification of employment and salary. Only factual information regarding position and date of employment will be given.

_____ Employee Initial

13. **Employee, full-time/part-time:** A full time employee is an individual that works a minimum of 32 hours a week; a part-time employee is one who is regularly scheduled to work less than 32 hours in a week.

_____ Employee Initial

14. **Evaluations:** Employees will be evaluated semi-annually and annually on their work performance.

_____ Employee Initial

15. **Fingerprints:** Regulations require that all employees undergo fingerprinting and criminal records clearance prior to initial contacts with the clients. Employees shall reimburse the employer for the.

_____ Employee Initial

16. **Fire prevention:** Fire rules and regulations must be posted on the bulletin board and updated annually. All employees must become familiar with the fire and disaster plan and understand the role they play in an emergency. Smoking is prohibited in any part of the client's home unless permitted by the client and only in designated smoking areas. Smoking is permitted only during regular breaks. Cigarette butts are not to be thrown on the ground and must be disposed in a fire safe manner.

_____ Employee Initial

17. **Garnishment of wages:** Employees must understand the importance of careful planning in their credit purchases to prevent assignments of wages and garnishments must be honored.

_____ Employee Initial

18. **Gifts: All** employees will not accept gifts, tips or gratuities of any kind from the clients, their families and guests, nor will they be designated representative of the client in any trust, wills, power of attorneys or any public document involving the client property or interest. This will be a ground for immediate termination of employment.

_____ Employee Initial

19. **Health of employees:** Each employee will be required to have a pre-employment physical examination and a T.B. skin test, paid for by the employee. Chest x-ray, if needed, is at the employee's own expense. Employees are also required to have a current first aid CPR card.

_____ Employee Initial

20. **Holidays:** Full-time and part-time employees will be paid time-and-a-half for working a holiday. In order to receive the above benefits, the employee must have been employed for at least 30 days.

_____ Employee Initial

The following are considered holidays:

New Years Day
Easter
July 4th
Labor Day
Thanksgiving
Christmas Day

21. **Information about Clients:** All inquiries concerning a client's personal affairs or condition will be referred to the Administrator. Un-authorized release of information may be grounds for dismissal. In addition, all inquiries about possible client services must be referred immediately to the administrator/manager; please take a name and phone number and note date and time.

_____ Employee Initial

22. **Jury Duty:** Any person asked to serve on jury duty shall notify the Administrator as soon as possible.

_____ Employee Initial

23. **Mail:** All mail will be delivered unopened to the administrator's desk. Employees should have their mail addressed to their homes. Client's mail must remain private and unopened when handed to them by staff. Staff are never allowed to open, meddle nor interfere with clients' correspondence and mail.

_____ Employee Initial

24. **Overtime:** Time and a half will be paid for the sixth consecutive day WITHIN the same work-week (Monday through Sunday). Double time will be paid for the seventh consecutive day within the same week. This only applies to hourly employees.

_____ Employee Initial

25. **Payroll Period:** Paydays are on the 15th and 30th of each month, after 10 AM. If the payday falls on a Saturday, the checks will be issued on Friday. If the payday falls on a Sunday, the checks will be issued on Monday.

_____ Employee Initial

26. **Promotions:** When opportunities for promotion become available, first consideration will be given to present employees, taking into account performance records, ability, loyalty, seniority and anticipated length of future service under our employment.

_____ Employee Initial

27. **Properties:** Employees will be held responsible for negligent and willful destruction of client and agency properties. Any employee found removing the client's and the agency's property will be prosecuted and terminated.

_____ Employee Initial

28. **Schedules:** Work schedules are prepared every other week and posted on the bulletin board. No changes are to be made requested prior to the scheduled posting. Employees will be scheduled to work holidays on a rotating basis. If you need some special time off, contact the Administrator.

_____ Employee Initial

29. **Sick leave:** The agency does not provide sick leave benefits.

_____ Employee Initial

30. **Telephone:** Every employee must answer the phone calls with utmost courtesy at all times. Employees will refrain from using the phone for personal matters except for emergency use only. Long distance collect calls for other than the business will not be accepted. All telephone bills incurred by the employee that are not business related will be deducted from the paycheck.

_____ Employee Initial

31. **Training:** All new employees will be required 8-Hour Introductory Staff Training prior to assigned projects. In order to continue their employment with this agency, all employees shall receive 40 hours of training annually. All employees will be required to attend a minimum of at least 20-hours of continuing education in-service-training courses on a yearly basis. These in-services will be posted on the bulletin board. All employees must attend all training services.

_____ Employee Initial

32. **Employment is "AT-WILL":** Employment has no specific duration and may be terminated by either the employer or the employee at any time, with or without reason or cause.

_____ Employee Initial

33. **Uniforms:** The employees will provide for their own uniform tops and pants. Neatness, cleanliness, good personal hygiene and good housekeeping habits are required for all employees. Employees may wear pants or skirts of their choice but they must be in clean, appropriate and presentable condition at all times.

_____ Employee Initial

34. **Visiting Hours:** Established hours for visiting requests is 7:00 a.m. to 5:00 p.m., after which time remaining visitors will be asked to leave with a diplomatic approach. Employees are discouraged from having any visitors during working hours. Children may only be brought to work in case of emergency and only with the permission from the Administrator.

_____ Employee Initial

35. **Work Time Recording:** All employees are to keep their own time sheets current. Record the start and end time. No one shall clock in (sign-in) for other staff. Doing so will be a ground for termination.

_____ Employee Initial

36. **Intoxicating Liquors/Alcoholic Beverages or Drugs:** Any employee drinking on the premises or coming to work intoxicated or under the influence of any prohibited substance/drugs/alcohol will be terminated immediately. Staff are not allowed to drink on the job. Drug testing will be required for all employees prior to employment and during employment at a random basis. Refusal to undergo testing is a ground for possible termination of employment or hiring.

_____ Employee Initial

37. **Vacation:** We have no paid vacation at this time. Employees desiring time off must give 20 days notice.

_____ Employee Initial

38. **Suspension:** The policy of this agency is a two-day suspension for non-completion of job duties. These two days will be without pay.

_____ Employee Initial

39. **Work schedules:** All employees must follow their work schedule at all times. They are responsible for making sure that work assignments are completed on a weekly basis. We realize interruptions happen, but the work should be done within that work-week period.

_____ Employee Initial

FINAL NOTE: This policy manual does not contain a complete listing of all factors of employment. We have provided this as a guide, written additions will be posted on the employee bulletin board. If there are any questions, please feel free to ask.

All employees will be asked to sign a statement acknowledging the fact that they have read and understand the policies of this manual.

Staff will receive a Job Description at time of employment. The administrator/manager shall maintain the right to add to or interchange job duties, as circumstances warrant.

_____ Employee Initial

EMERGENCY PROCEDURES

EXTREME EMERGENCY

Examples:
A. A client shows signs of a heart attack stroke
B. A client has fallen and fallen is bleeding or is unconscious
C. A client is choking
D. Any life-threatening situation

PLAN OF ACTION

IF YOU ARE ALONE, CALL 911.

The staff is to remain with the client and shall administer first aid while the other staff person calls 911 for help. Take vital signs, if possible, and write on the emergency info sheet. When client needs to go to the hospital, staff must complete and send the "Emergency Info Sheet" with the extra copy of the "Medication Sheet" (located in the front of his/her record) with him/her. Staff must document every person, place and thing (what happened, where it happened, who was involved, what time did it happen, what did you do to resolve the emergency, who did you call and notify) that relates to the event in the client's record.

URGENT CARE:

This is when a client is not in need of immediate attention but may need to see a doctor within a few hours.

Mild fever of 101, severe migraine, small cuts or injuries that don't need emergency care, rashes, etc.

PLAN OF ACTION

1. Take vital signs; write them down.
2. Call administrator or manager; at this point, he/she may take over and handle the next steps described.
3. Call the doctor. Make sure you report to him/her the vital signs, symptoms and the sequence of events or occurrences, (ie) when it started, how often, etc. (some of the doctors will see the client).
4. Do as the doctor directs, unless it is not allowed by our nursing consultant. We are a non-medical staffing agency and do not provide nursing care unless that staff person is licensed or registered to do so within regulations.
5. Call family and give a report of the situation. If necessary, transport, or make arrangements to transport, to urgent care or the preferred hospital.
6. Complete the "Emergency Info Sheet" and get the client and the "Medication Sheet" ready at the time of transport. Document, in the chart, your actions and results, then complete an Unusual Occurrence/ Special Incident Report.

OUTLINE OF ILLNESS PROCEDURES

1. Any change in a client's physical condition must be reported to the manager/administrator. Do not assume someone else has already reported the condition to the administrator; failure to report an occurrence or incident may result in a write up or possible termination of work.
2. Make sure you log the change in the client's record, and report it to the oncoming staff and other appropriate staff person is notified on a timely manner and accordingly. The assigned manager should inform the client's doctor and family.
3. Isolate a client who has a cold, flu, or other communicable disease etc., by keeping him/her in the room even when taking meals.

4. If client is sick in bed, keep him/her inside the room. If his/her condition will be long term, he must be transferred to an appropriate facility with the approval and recommendation of the family physician.

VIOLENT OR UNCONTROLLABLE CLIENTS

IF PHYSICAL VIOLENCE HAS OCCURRED, CALL 911 AND REQUEST POLICE AND AMBULANCE SERVICES.

If a client becomes unmanageable, violent, destructive, berserk, completely demented, etc.

PLAN OF ACTION

- Do not leave the client unattended, call 911.
- Keep other clients away from the uncontrollable client. Try to keep him/her a separated area; do not leave this person alone.
- Call administrator; if unobtainable, call in additional help.
- Call the client's doctor, if unavailable, call one of the doctors on duty and ask if they will come over and treat the client.
- The local ambulance service can assist you; call them if you feel that the client will most likely be transferred to a hospital.

CLIENT FUNCTIONAL ASSESSMENT

Client Name_____ DOB:_____

Soc. Sec. No: _____

(Client)_____ is 85 years of age, Caucasian

male, diagnosed with severe Dementia, seizure disorder. He has no apparent hearing or vision loss. He does not have the ability to communicate/express his wants and needs verbally or by hand gestures. He is non-ambulatory due to cerebral palsy.

Client will require lifting. Client is _____ :ht _____ wt.

(Client)_____is unable to perform any self help skills, including bathing, dressing, hygiene, toileting or feeding. He is unable to reposition himself or sit up without support. He is unable to properly operate his wheelchair.

Medications:

Currently takes Neurontin 300 mg two times per day; Dilantin 50mg in a. m. and 100 mg. In p. m.; and Reglan 20 mg in p.m.

He has no known mental health deficits. His socialization skills are limited due to mental retardation. This also affects his cognitive functioning skills which are extremely limited. He has no self-abusive behaviors. He does not have the ability to manage his own hygiene and self-care.

Client was referred by: _____

Emergency contacts: _____

SAMPLE: INDIVIDUAL HEALTH CARE PLAN NOTE (Form)

(Client)_____ will be fed via his g-tube. His needs will be met according to acceptable guidelines. He will fed three times per day at home with the following diet:_____

He will wear attends and must be changed three times per day (he is incontinent). While client is unable to effectively communicate his wants and needs utilizing conventional methods (verbalization/expressions), agency will ensure that all staff are trained to identify needs/wants through observation and familiarization with clients current methods of communications as reported by staff.

(Client)_____will frown and/or cry when uncomfortable. When all efforts to make comfortable are unsuccessful, contact numbers will be called.

Emergency numbers are listed on the vital sheet kept in his chart. The emergency numbers will be contacted for medical and non-medical emergencies should the need arise.

(client)_____will be repositioned in his wheelchair every _____ while at home. Feeding and changing will occur at _____ by staff members. His feeding and all medical needs will be handled by the LVN and emergency contacts.

FUNCTIONAL CAPABILITIES ASSESSMENT

NAME:

BATHING:

   A. Does not bathe or shower self
   B. Performs some bathing or showering tasks
   C. Bathe or showers self independently

CONTINENCE:

   A. No bowel and/or bladder control
   B   Some bowel and/or bladder control
   C. Use of assertive devices, such as catheter
       Comments:_____
   D. Complete bowel and/or bladder control

DRESSING:

   A. Does not dress self
   B. Puts on some clothing by self
   C. Dresses self completely
       Comments:_____

EATING:

   A. Does not feed self.
   B. Feeds self with assistance from another person
   C. Feeds self completely
       Comments:_____

GROOMING:

    A. Does not tend to own personal hygiene
    B. Tends to some personal hygiene tasks
    C. Tends to own personal hygiene
    Comments:_____

VISION:

    A. Severe/profound impairment
    B. Mild/moderate impairment
    C. No vision impairment
    Comments:_____

TOILETING:

    A. Not toilet trained
    B. Does not toilet self
    C. Goes to toilet by self
    Comments:_____

HEARING:

    A. Severe/profound loss
    B. Mild/moderate impairment
    C. No hearing loss
    Comments: _____

TRANSFERRING:

    A. Unable to move in and out of a bed or chair
    B. Needs assistance to transfer
    C. Is able to move in and out of a bed or chair
    Comments: _____

COMMUNICATION:

    A. Does not express nonverbally
    B. Does not express verbally
    C. No hearing loss
    Comments:_____

REPOSITIONING:

    A. Unable to reposition
    B. Repositions from side to side
    C. Repositions from front to back and back to front
    Comments: _____

MEDICAL HISTORY AND CONDITIONS:

WHEELCHAIR:

A. Unable to sit without support
B. Sits without support
C. Needs assistance moving wheelchair
D. Moves wheelchair independently
E. Does not use wheelchair
MEDICATIONS: _____

_____

MENTAL AND/OR EMOTIONAL STATUS:

Comments:_____

WALKING:

A. Does not walk
B. Walks with support
C. Walks well alone

SOCIALIZATION AND COGNITIVE STATUS:

_____

_____

Comments:_____

Medical assessment shall clearly and thoroughly include:

(1). Assessment shall be performed by a licensed physician, or designee, who is also licensed professional, and the assessment shall not be more than one year old when obtained.

(2). Examination for communicable tuberculosis and other contagious/infectious diseases.

(3). Identification of the client's special problems and needs.

(4). Identification of any prescribed medications.

(5). Client's ambulatory status

(6). Physical restrictions, including any medically necessary diet restrictions'

(7). Primary diagnosis and secondary diagnosis.

(8). Other medical conditions.

(9). Prior medical services and history.

(10). Current medical services and history.

(11). Identification of the client's needs as a result of any medical information contained in the report.

CARE FOR CLIENT'S WHO RELY UPON OTHERS TO PERFORM ALL ACTIVITIES OF DAILY LIVING (TOTAL CARE) Prior to accepting a client into care, the agency Intake manager shall complete the following:

1. An approved plan of operation demonstrating the staff's ability to care for client's as specified in the care plan.
2. A Needs and Services Plan that includes all of the following:
    a. A plan to monitor the client's skin condition
    b. Specific guidelines for turning the client (time, method, acceptable positions).
    c. Objective symptoms indicating when a licensed professional must be contacted.
    d. A method for feeding.
    e. A method for determining the client's needs.
    f. A method for communicating with the client.
3. A list of emergency contacts and a list of readily observable conditions that indicate when emergency intervention is necessary.
4. A list of persons to contact in the event of non-emergency client distress or discomfort and a list of readily observable conditions that indicate when the administrator is to contact those persons.
5. A description of the client-specific training that staff will receive. The training must be provided by the client's health care provider (physician or nurse).

In order to determine the agency's ability to provide the services needed by a client with mental health issues, the family member shall ensure that a written intake assessment is prepared. A written intake assessment is prepared by a licensed mental health professional prior to acceptance of the client. This assessment may be provided by a physician if the work is supervised by a properly licensed mental health professional. Administrator shall utilize placement agencies, including, but not limited to, county clinics for referrals and assessments.

CLIENT ASSESSMENT FORM
A. MENTAL STATUS   YES   NO

1. Mental disorder
2. Developmental disability
3. Dual diagnosis – Drug/Alcohol/

Substance Abuse/MH or Regional Center
If any of the condition exists, please describe:
The condition:_____
Severity of the disorder: _____
Current or previous treatment: _____

BEHAVIOR ASSESSMENT:
Does the client have a history of any of the following:

                                                                    YES / NO

1. Physical assaultive
2. Verbal assaultive

3. Sexual assaultive or molestation
4. Violence to self or others
5. Cruelty to others
6. Attempts to poison others
7. Use of weapons
8. Cruelty to animals
9. Destruction of property
10. Stealing
11. Arson

B. HEALTH HISTORY

Client's primary physician name: _____
Phone:_____

YES / NO

Does the client use any prescription medications?
If yes, please list non-prescription:

_____
_____
_____

Does the client use any non-prescription medications? If yes, please list non-prescription:

YES / NO

_____
_____
_____

Does the client have any of the following:

YES / NO

1. Asthma
2. Epilepsy
3. Allergies
4. Diabetes
5. Eating disorders
6. Visual impairment
7. Physical impairment
8. Infectious disease
9. Special diet
10. Pregnancy
11. Chronic medical condition
12. Incontinence

If the answer to any of the above is yes, please describe:

The type and severity of the condition:

_____

_____

The treatment the client is receiving for the condition:

_____

Names and dosages of medications the client receives:

_____

Any limitations due to the condition:

_____

Any special services required due to the conditions:

_____

Does the client use any prescription medication?

YES / NO

If yes, list prescription

_____

Does the client use any non-prescriptions?

YES / NO

BEHAVIORAL ASSESSMENT
If the answer to any of the above is yes, please describe:
The behaviors:

_____

Frequency and duration of the behaviors:

_____

Approximate date of the last occurrence of the behaviors:

_____

_____

Anything that seems to trigger the behavior:

_____

_____

_____

How behavior is controlled:

_____

_____

Does the client have a history of any of the following:

YES / NO

1. Depression or withdrawal
2. Anxiety
3. Mood Swings
4. Suicide attempts
5. Suicide attempts

6. Paranoia
7. Hallucinations
8. Restlessness or hyperactivity
9. Inappropriate sexual activity
10. Confusion with sexual identity
11. Refusal to attend therapy
12. Disruptiveness
13. Tantrums
14. Wandering
15. AWOL
16. Substance abuse
17. Ingestion of toxic
18. Refusal of medications
19. Refusal of medical treatment
20. Refusal to bathe or wear clean clothes
21. Resistance to authority
22. Careless disposal of smoking materials

If the answer to any of the above is yes, please describe:

_____

_____

The behaviors:

_____

_____

Frequency and duration of the behavior:

_____

_____

Medical Assessment:

Is the client being treated for, or have been told by a doctor in the past that he/she has any of the following?

(Please check all that apply):

Heart disease   _____
Chronic Long Disease   _____
Kidney disease   _____
Asthma   _____
Hepatitis C   _____
Diabetes   _____
Aneurysm   _____
Stroke   _____
Liver Disease   _____
Seizures   _____
Melanoma, Breast   _____
AIDS   _____
Prostate or Bladder Cancer   _____

Other Serious Medical Problems   _____

Skin Cancer   _____

None of the above   _____

Other Cancers   _____

High Blood Pressure   _____

Do you take, or have you been advised to take, prescription medications regularly for (please check all that apply):

High Blood Pressure   _____

Heart Disease   _____

High Cholesterol   _____

Chest Pain/Angina   _____

Stomach or Intestinal Problems   _____

Lungs or Breathing   _____

Kidney or Incontinence   _____

Abdominal pain   _____

Unexplained weight loss   _____

Fever   _____

Do you have unexplained and/or undiagnosed symptoms such as:

Swollen glands   _____

Loss of Consciousness   _____

Rectal bleeding   _____

Loss of Appetite   _____

Do you currently use tobacco?   _____

What is your average usage?   _____

Have you been advised in the last 3 years to undergo surgery, testing, treatment, or consultation for any medical condition that you have not undergone?

Do any of the following conditions apply to the client:

1. Non-Ambulatory   _____
2. Bedridden/bedfast   _____
3. Paralysis   _____
4. Contracture   _____
5. Inability to transfer to and from bed   _____
6. Needs assistance with eating,   _____
   bathing, dressing, grooming or toileting

If the answer to any of the above is yes, please describe:

_____

The type of limitation and its severity:

_____

Any assistive devices used by the client:

_____

Any treatment of therapy needed by the client as a result of the condition:

_____

In Case of an Emergency:

Client's primary physician: **Family:**

Name: _____ _____

Phone:_____   _____

Pager:_____   _____

Applicant/Authorized

Representative:_____

Date: _____

Representative: _____

Date: _____

Training Provided for Care Clients (Evaluation Form)

Client Name:_____

Staff will be trained to care for (Client) in the following manner by LVN:

1. Staff will be trained to lift and transfer him to and from bed and changing table.
2. Staff will be trained to wash hands and face, brush teeth and hair according to (Client) preference.
3. Staff will be trained how to communicate with Client), using his method of communications (smiles/frowns).
4. Staff will be trained to observe (Client) for signs and symptoms of distress using his method of communication discomfort (crying, squirming in chair).
5. Instructors will be trained as to what activities (Client) prefers to participate in and how to ascertain what activity he wishes to participate in.

As soon as the Intake Manager determines that the agency is able to meet the client's needs, it is time to draw a service agreement. Based on what is stated on the service agreement, the agency shall require at least three working days for the agency to provide the service or staff. The three days will also give enough time for the agency to look on its data base for available staffing to cover the shift. For the mean time, the agency may also brief the staff on the client who about to receive the service.

Caregiving Service Contract (SAMPLE)

This service contract is entered into between Angel's Personalized Care Services herein known as "Caregiver" whose business is located at _____, _____,Ca._____, and Mr. _____ of 12345 A Street, Pomona, Ca. 91764 herein known as the client.

IN CONSIDERATION OF the amount of

_____$ 15.00 per hour Home companion

_____$ 150.00 per day for whole day of service

Which amount shall be paid by the Client to the "Caregiver" in consideration of the following:

1. *Lite Housekeeping.*
2. *Medication reminders.*
3. *Driving/transporting to medical/dental appointments.*
4. *Cooking, meal preparation*
5. *Lite gardening with the client as part of the activity*
6. *Lite lifting.*
7. *Laundry.*
8. *Assistance in all activities of daily living such as hygiene, bathing, toileting, repositioning,*
9. *Reading newspaper and story telling.*
10. *Grocery*
11. *Bill payments*
12. *Errands*
13. *Community walks.*
14. *Daily exercises.*

The payment for the service shall be paid at the end of the service.
Signed

_____   Date:

Representative   (Signature)

_____   Date:

Client   (Signature)

DEATH POLICY

If a client is found deceased, call 911 and notify the administrator or manager immediately. The administrator or manager is to notify the client's responsible party immediately.

EMERGENCY PROCEDURES

EXTREME EMERGENCY
Examples:
A. A client shows signs of a heart attack stroke
B. A client has fallen and fallen is bleeding or is unconscious
C. A client is choking
D. Any life-threatening situation

SAMPLE PLAN OF ACTION
IF YOU ARE ALONE, CALL 911. IF THERE IS MORE THAN ONE STAFF PERSON:
The supervisor is to remain with the client and shall administer first aid while the other staff person calls 911 for help. Take vital signs, if possible, and write on the emergency info sheet. Always when you are sending a client to the hospital, complete and send the "Emergency Info Sheet" with the extra copy of the "Medication Sheet" (located in the front of his/her record) with him/her. Be sure you document every person, place and thing that relates to the event in the client's record.

URGENT CARE:

This is when a client is not in need of immediate attention but may need to see a doctor within a few hours.

EXAMPLES: Mild fever of 101, severe migraine, small cuts or injuries that don't need emergency care, rashes, etc.

SAMPLE PLAN OF ACTION

1. Take vital signs; write them down.
2. Call administrator or manager; at this point, he/she may take over and handle the next steps described.
3. Call the doctor. Make sure you report to him/her the vital signs, symptoms and the sequence of events or occurrences, I.E. when it started, how often, etc. (some of the doctors will see the client at the)
4. Do as the doctor directs. Call family and give a report of the situation. If necessary, transport, or make arrangements to transport, to urgent care or the preferred hospital.
5. Complete the " Emergency Info Sheet" and get the client and the "Medication Sheet" ready to be transported. Document, in the chart, your actions and results, then complete an Unusual Occurrence/Incident Report (Lic. #624), if required for that particular problem.

SAMPLE OUTLINE OF ILLNESS PROCEDURES

1. Any change in a client's physical reported to the designated family representative and the administrator. Failure to report an occurrence or indent may result in a reprimand or dismissal.
2. Make sure you log the change in the client's record, and report it to the oncoming staff and make sure that other, appropriate staff persons are notified. The assigned supervisor should inform the client's doctor and family.
3. Isolate a client that has a cold, flu, etc., by keeping him in his room and having him eat all meals there.

What is a LOW SODIUM DIET ?

Most of us think of "salt" when we hear the word "sodium". But table salt and sodium is not the same thing. Table salt is a chemical combination of 40% sodium and 60% chlorine. It is the sodium salt, which we try to reduce on a "low salt" diet.

People with high blood pressure and certain types or heart disease may be advised by their doctors to reduce the amount of sodium in their diet. Sodium is a necessary mineral for maintaining good health. About 1100-1300 milligram (mg.) of Sodium daily is considered a safe and adequate amount. But most of us eat up to 7,000 mg. a day!

There are four sources of sodium in our diet. One major source of sodium is table salt. Many people salt their food without realizing it! Sodium also comes into our diet from salt added during cooking. Sodium occurs naturally in some foods, like milk, or celery.

Another source is processed food. Sodium is added for preservation, flavor or to retain color. Reading the labels on canned and bottled food is the best way to learn about the sodium in prepared foods. Sodium may appear as sodium bicarbonate, monosodium, glutamate, and sodium products. These can be found in your supermarket labeled "sodium free" "reduced sodium" and "unsalted". Many products now specify the amount of sodium in milligrams in a serving on the nutrition label.

As of 1985, federal regulations define sodium labeling as the following:

"Sodium Free" - less than 5 milligrams per serving

"Very Low Sodium" - 35 milligrams or less per serving

"Low Sodium"- 140 milligrams or per serving

"Reduced Sodium"- processed to reduce the level of sodium by 75%

"Unsalted" - processed without salt, where the food normally is processed with salt.

Low Calorie Diet A "calorie" is a measure of the energy or fuel value in foods. The number of calories we need depends on the activity and body size. Our bodies need less calories with age, especially if we are less active. Just to maintain and not gain weight, we may need to eat less. Being overweight can be a hazard to good health. Obesity is associated with high blood pressure increased levels of blood fats and cholesterol, and the most common types of diabetics. All of these, in turn, are associated with increased risks of heart attacks and strokes.

If weight loss is desired the amount of calories must be reduced. This will allow the body to use up the extra fat which it has stored. The goal can be met by either eating foods with fewer calories or by increasing activity.

Weight Loss Tips:
- Check with the attending physician, he must order the special diet
- Cut back on sweets, fried and other fatty foods. Eat a variety of foods including vegetables, fruits and whole grain products
- Set a goal. Plan to lose no more than 1 to 2 pounds a week.
- Don't cut back calories too far. It is usually not safe to go below 800 calories a day.
- Moderately increase physical activity
- Eat slowly, and chew each bite thoroughly
- Keep track of what is consumed

Low Fat – Low Cholesterol

Many people are concerned about the amount of fat and cholesterol in their diet. Saturated fat and cholesterol have been linked with atherosclerosis, which is a major cause of heart disease. Persons with high cholesterol levels, or with a history of heart or blood vessel diseases may be advised by their doctor to reduce fat and cholesterol in their diet.

Fat is needed in our diet in moderate amounts. Some fatty acids are essential for proper growth and healthy skin. However, fat is concentrated form of food energy or calories, and many clients eat more in the form of fat than they should. Many health experts recommend cutting back on the total amount of fats and fatty foods in the diet.

In doing so, be aware that there are different types of fats, and try to eat less saturated fats. Saturated fats are usually solid at room temperature, and occur in large amounts in food from animal sources such as meat, poultry and dairy products. Unsaturated fats are usually solid at room temperature, and are found in larger amounts in vegetable oils and fish.

Cholesterol is fatty substance found only in animal products. It is especially abundant in eggs and organ meats such as liver. This doesn't mean you can't eat a specific food you like. For example eggs and liver contain cholesterol but they also contain may essential vitamins and minerals. Most foods can be eaten in moderate amounts, provided your overall fat and cholesterol intake are not excessive.

To avoid too much fat, saturated fat, and cholesterol:
* Choose lean meat, fish, poultry, dry beans and peas as your protein sources, trim off fats.
* Moderate use of eggs and organ meats
* Limit intake of butter, cream, hydrogenated margarine, shortenings, palm and coconut oil, and foods made from such products.
* Broil, bake or boil rather than fry
* Read labels to determine type and amount of fat content

How to Increase Dietary Fiber
1. Use whole wheat bread instead of white. For a variety choose from pumpernickel, whole wheat, oatmeal, and bran breads, muffins, rolls and crackers.
2. Dry or cooked breakfast cereals made from wheat, bran and oats contain a good amount of fiber. Examples: All Bran, Shredded Wheat, What Bran Flakes and oatmeal are higher in fiber than puffed wheat, corn flakes and cream of rice.
3. Fresh fruits and vegetables provide excellent fiber. Clean them and leave on the skins and peels, which are a roughage type of fiber. Frozen or canned fruit and vegetables are good fiber sources.
4. Use legumes in your menu. Lentils, beans, and peas are a low cost, high protein source. You can use them in soup, salads, side or main dishes.
5. Encourage fiber found in snacks like popcorn and nuts.

SNACK SCHEDULE

	3:00 pm	7:00 pm
MONDAY	ICE CRAM CUP/ APPLE JUICE	FRESH FRUIT JUICE PUNCH
TUESDAY	HOMEMADE COOKIES/ CRANBERRY JUICE	FRESH FRUIT/ LEMONADE
WEDNESDAY	FRESH FRUIT/ ORANGE JUICE	CRACKERS/ GRAPE JUICE
THURSDAY	ICE CREAM CUPS PUNCH	LEMONADE/BANANAS LEMONADE

FRIDAY	CRACKERS AND CHEESE APPLE JUICE	ICE CREAM BARS JUICE PUNCH
SATURDAY	FRESH FRUIT/ ORANGE JUICE	CUSTARD/ GRAPE JUICE
SUNDAY	CUPCAKES/ Apple Juice	FRESH FRUIT/ CRANBERRY APPLE JUICE

WEEKLY CLEAN UP SCHEDULE

Daily: Cook meals.
Monday: Soak and scrub burner and grills. Clean kitchen cobwebs.
Tuesday: Clean out refrigerator, shelf by shelf, taking the shelf out and washing it in the sink.
Wednesday: Clean out and organize pantry. Put away stock.
Thursday: Straighten out drawers.
Friday: Clean dishwasher thoroughly.
Saturday: Clean out microwave completely.
Sunday: Clean out refrigerator and clean coffee maker.

CHRONIC ILLNESS

The best description of chronic illness is a disease that persists for a long time. A disease may be considered chronic if it has lasted for over 6 months. Symptoms of the chronic disease may "flare up" or lessen during the duration of the illness.

There are times when care providers will observe the flow of care being interrupted by specific behaviors that a chronically ill person will manifest. These behaviors may seem illogical and inappropriate unless the care providers understand them.

It is proven fact that, when a person continually suffers from an illness over a long period of time, some type of change in his/her behavior will occur. Even a young person might change his/her social behavior to avoid embarrassment because of an illness. It is a cause-and-effect situation. Depression is one of the most well-known reactions to chronic illness.

Clients will often only deal with that which they feel the can handle. The chronically ill often are in a state of denial. They may block information that is too threatening or stressful to deal with. They may present that the illness or a situation just doesn't exist. They may present that the illness or a situation just doesn't exist. They may rationalize or make excuses as to why certain things happen. Things are more acceptable when an explanation is given, even if it's not a true explanation. They may even begin to believe it is the truth.

Another type of blocking is regression. If a situation is too difficult to deal with, a person may withdraw and daydream about better things or happier times. Eventually a person can do this to the point where he/she is in a daydream state-permanently. He/she will not be able to function in the realities and activities of daily living. One theory relates this type of regression to why people believe they are thirty again or play with dolls as if they were real babies.

The changes in lifestyle that may result give understandable reasons for feelings of bitterness and anger. We have all heard of an elderly person being described as a "crabby old person", but is he/she normally "crabby" or is it a result of his/her illness? If you can ascertain the reason behind the bitterness or anger, it will help you to better understand and counteract the reaction. It is not unusual for this anger, exhibited by sharp criticism or hostile outbursts, to be directed towards the care provider, family members or fellow clients.

When a elderly person suffers from chronic illness, he/she have to rely on others to assist him/her with their daily living. For some clients, there is need for a bond of security. This is sought from the care providers, family, and friends.

They will flatter, give gifts or try to play on a person's ego or emotions to gain the attention and security they want. Those clients will often use statements like, "I don't know what I'd do without you", or "You are the only one who loves me," which are examples of manipulation. Once you are aware that they are trying to manipulate you, then you can better handle the situation. Set your boundaries and limitations and be consistent in asserting yourself.

Sometimes a person will say one thing and mean another. We, as care providers, need to be aware of the underlying message. A chronically ill person may say, " I can deal with the pain in my back but my friend thinks I have a broken vertebrae". The person could be projecting his/her own concerns about the illness. He/she may indeed have a fracture in his/her vertebrae but really does not want to complain about how bad the pain is.

A good rule to follow is, "WHEN IN DOUBT, SEND THEM OUT". Get him/her to the doctor or a hospital, if you feel that there is the possibility of a more serious condition. He/She may just be voicing insecurity and need to talk it out, but it is better to be safe than sorry.

A Care provider can do something to lessen these symptoms or reactions.

The following are examples:

1. Encourage participation in recreational and social activities.
2. Encourage exercise (after consulting with attending physician for precautions)
3. Have a " Grump Support Group", letting him/her talk about his/hers feelings with others who are experiencing the same type of things.
4. Make sure he/she eats a balanced diet and get enough rest
5. Make a overall plan and have a "Team" approach, i. e. use the family, friends, clergy and staff to support the plan and carry it through.
6. Try to get him/her involved in a cause; the cause can distract him/her from his/her own problems.
7. Make him/her feel useful; even doing small jobs like folding towels will help a person know that there are still some things they can do. These type of activities will improve their self esteem.

This may be a helpful tool to share with the family of a client who has a difficult personality.

DEPRESSION

Many different factors can contribute or lead to depression. About 10 – 15 % of the elderly population suffers, at one time or another, from either chronic or acute depression. Symptoms usually manifest themselves as mood disturbances and vary in degree of severity. Many times depression is mistaken for dementia.

Depression can be brought on by diseases or impairments. If the persons learns to successfully accept/adapt to that disease or impairment, the depression can subside. Because diagnosis is so difficult, doctors may try a therapeutic trial of antidepressants to help distinguish between dementia and depression. However, dementia and depression can co-exist, making it difficult to diagnose. Often, the dementia is dominant over depression. Person having both depression and dementia are often difficult to care for, and may not be appropriate for Residential care.

Person who suffer with chronic disease, and those who have suffered multiple losses like financial, physical, social, or psychological, are more likely to suffer with depression. Many of our elderly are grieving. They are suffering losses. We need to be sensitive to those losses and help them through those times as best we can.

The symptoms of depression are different from other types of mental illness. Persons with depression show visible signs of one or more symptoms. The physician can diagnose depression by looking for both physical and mental signs.

THE ART OF LISTENING
1. Stop talking – you can't listen while you are talking
2. Don't interrupt – give the speaker time to say what he has to say. THEN, and NOT BEFORE, ask your questions or reply to what has been said.
3. Single conversation – don't try to engage in two conversations at once. You may HEAR two people at one time, but you can not EFFECTIVELY listen to two conversations at once.
4. Ask questions – when you don't understand or when you need further clarification, ask questions.
5. Empathize with the other person – try to put yourself in his place so that you can see what he is trying to say.
6. Show interest – make eye contact.
7. Concentrate – actively focus your attention on the speaker's words, ideas, and feelings related to the subject.
8. React to the subject, not the speaker – don't allow your reactions to the speaker influence your interpretations of what he says. His ideas may be good even if you don't like him as a person or like the way he looks speaks or moves.
9. Control your anger – try not to get angry at what he is saying. Your anger will most likely prevent you from understanding what he is REALLY saying.
10. Listen for what is NOT said. Sometimes you can learn just as much by determining what the other person leaves out or avoids saying as you can by listening to what he actually says.

Dealing with Grief, Losses, Death, and Dying

Task of Mourning

"Grief work" is the term used to describe the tremendous amount of energy a person expends completing the tasks of mourning. Grief work is accomplished as the old bonds with the physical person or object are gradually released. and a new bond of memory is established. Four tasks of mourning must be accomplished to work through grief. These tasks occur concurrently with the phases of grief.

Accepting The Reality Of The Loss
Experiencing The Pain Of Grief
Adjusting To An Environment In Which The Deceased Is Missing
Withdrawing Emotional Energy And Reinvesting It In Another Relationship

COPING WITH GRIEF

All clients entering into long term care are suffering from loss; loss of their home and possessions, spouse, ability to drive, deterioration or loss of physical and mental abilities. The impact of these losses will vary with each individual. Some people feel intense stress while others adjust to these losses more readily.

SIGNS AND SYMPTOMS OF GRIEF:

EMOTIONAL:	PHYSICAL:
Crying, sighing	lack of energy
Anxiety, fear	sleepiness
Anger, guilt	gastrointestinal problems
Withdrawal	aches, pains and weakness
Irritability	weight loss or gain
Constant complaining	hypochondria
Doubtfulness	confusion

HOW TO ASSIST A PERSON WITH GRIEF & LOSS
1. Listen; let the person talk about the loss.
2. Allow the person to cry and weep.
3. Ask questions and bring the subject out; the person's feelings need to be articulated. Repetitive expressions of the person's feelings will help him/her get over to the loss.
4. Encourage the person to keep a journal or log, writing out his/her feelings.
5. Allow the person as much control over his/her living environment as possible; often, the client feels he/she has lost control of his/her life.
6. Physical contact such as gentle touch, a hug or holding the person's hand can have a comforting effect.
7. Encourage the person to exercise regularly as allowed by physician

DEALING WITH BEHAVIOR PROBLEMS

Behavior: Clients who disagree or argue with most things.

How to handle: Don't support the negative feelings. Call attention instead to his or her knowledge and creative thinking: "It sounds like you have some interesting ideas; will you elaborate on them?"

Confront the negativism: "You sound irritated to me. Is something bothering you?" If negative feelings are expressed, thank the member for telling you; don't begin an argument about what was said.

Behavior: Clients who are know-it-alls and experts on everything.

How to handle: Don't get into discussions that promote a winner or loser: "I appreciate your knowledge on the subject; let see what others think." Or, "Thank you for your point of view."

"You are a good resource. Who else would like to comment on this issue/idea?"

Remember to documents on the client's records any behavior problems. Indicate:

a. Date, time, duration
b. Preceding events
c. Result or consequence
d. Specifics
e. Your plan of action

ANXIETY DISORDERS

Anxiety is a state of uneasiness, fear, apprehension and impatience. The body gets ready for action and sets up a front line to protect us from danger.

Everyone experiences anxiety to some degree. Butterflies in your stomach before a test? Did you ever have pre-wedding jitters? Anxiety and fear are not normal when person dwells constantly on the impending event.

Symptoms can be so severe that person is too terrified to leave their home, attend social events, take care of financial business or even to shop for food.

Anxiety causes mental tension that has no apparent identifiable cause. Fear, due to specific reasons, causes mental tension. When we are anxious, our body processes speed up causing physical symptoms like sweating and muscle tension.

Usually when the event, impending subject, or occurrence has disappeared, the anxiety will dissipate. But, if the client continues to suffer with anxiety or fear, then medical help should be sought immediately.

SIGNS AND SYMPTOMS OF ANXIETY DISORDERS

EMOTIONAL:	PHYSICAL:
Uneasiness	Trembling
Jitteriness	Insomnia
Apprehension	Dry mouth
Intense fear	Hyperventilation
Intense stress	Irregular heart beats
Panic	Sweating
Tension	Twitching
Emotional numbing	Upset stomach – diarrhea
Guilt	Dizziness–faintness
Compulsive behavior	Fatigue

Obsessive behavior

Tips on assisting a client with anxiety:

a.   Seek medical help – medication or psychotherapy may be needed. The client needs to relax – seek relaxation therapy
b.   Warm baths and exercising may be helpful
c.   Reduce stress environment

REMINISCENCE

Reminiscence is the review of past experiences. It is natural process in which we all engage in at times. Reminiscence can bring peace and resolution to older people as they find meaning in their memories. Volunteer visitors, including family members, nurse, and health care professionals, can communicate a powerful unspoken message to the person who reminisces……………

"Who you are, what you have done, and the things you care about are very important to me. I believe in you. I accept you, I want to know your story. And, even more, I receive what you have to offer as a gift."

BENEFITS

Promotes mental and emotional well-being
Combats isolation, loneliness, and depression
Reflects on and reassesses life achievements
Communicates family folklore and heritage
Encourages social interaction
Resolves conflicts, fears
Builds self-esteem
Create a sense of continuity, linking accomplishments of the past to the present
Offers interesting things about each other or a period of history

STEPS

1.   Approach prospective group members individually. It is essential that group members be compatible. Five or six clients are generally considered an ideal size. Small groups give more time for each to express themselves.
2.   Begin and end with a reading, musical selection, game or anecdote.
3.   State the session's goals at the beginning
4.   Provide time for questions at the end of each session
5.   Restate goals and summarize key points at the end of each session
6.   Give a brief homework assignment

In Cases of Illness including CHRONIC ILLNESS

The best description of chronic illness is a disease that persists for a long time. A disease may be considered chronic if it has lasted for over 6 months. Symptoms of the chronic disease may "flare up" or lessen during the duration of the illness. There are times when staff will observe the flow of care being interrupted by specific behaviors that a chronically ill person will manifest. These behaviors may seem illogical and inappropriate unless the care providers understand them.

It is proven fact that, when a person continually suffers from an illness over a long period of time, some type of change in his/her behavior will occur. Even a young person might change his/her social behavior to avoid embarrassment because of an illness. It is a cause-and-effect situation. Depression is one of the most well-known reactions to chronic illness.

People will often only deal with that which they feel the can handle. The chronically ill often are in a state of denial. They may block information that is too threatening or stressful to deal with. They may present that the illness or a situation just doesn't exist. They may present that the illness or a situation just doesn't exist. They may rationalize or make excuses as to why certain things happen. Things are more acceptable when an explanation is given, even if it's not a true explanation. They may even begin to believe it is the truth.

Another type of blocking is regression. If a situation is too difficult to deal with, a person may withdraw and daydream about better things or happier times. Eventually a person can do this to the point where he/she is in a daydream state-permanently. He/she will not be able to function in the realities and activities of daily living. One theory relates this type of regression to why people believe they are thirty again or play with dolls as if they were real babies.

The changes in lifestyle that may result give understandable reasons for feelings of bitterness and anger. We have all heard of an elderly person being described as a "crabby old person", but is he/she normally "crabby" or is it a result of his/her illness? If you can ascertain the reason behind the bitterness or anger, it help you to better understand and counteract the reaction. It is not unusual for this anger, exhibited by sharp criticism or hostile outbursts, to be directed towards the care provider, family members or fellow clients.

When an adult or an elderly person suffers from chronic illness, he/she have to rely on others to assist him/her with their daily living. For some clients, there is need for a bond of security. This is sought from the staff/care providers, family, and friends. They will flatter, give gifts or try to play on a person's ego or emotions to gain the attention and security they want. Those clients will often use statements like, "I don't know what I'd do without you", or "You are the only one who loves me," which are examples of manipulation. Once staff is aware that they are trying to manipulate them, then staff can better handle the situation. Staff will set boundaries and limitations and be consistent in asserting staff.

Sometimes a client will say one thing and mean another. Staff/care providers, need to be aware of the underlying message. A chronically ill person may say, " I can deal with the pain in my back but my friend thinks I have a broken vertebrae". The person could be projecting his/her own concerns about the illness. He/she may indeed have a fracture in his/her vertebrae but really does not want to complain about how bad the pain is.

A good rule to follow is, "WHEN IN DOUBT, SEND THEM OUT". Get him/her to the doctor or a hospital, if you feel that there is the possibility of a more serious condition. He/She may just be voicing insecurity and need to talk it out, but it is better to be safe than sorry.

Staff/Care provider can do something to lessen these symptoms or reactions.

The following are examples:

Encourage participation in recreational and social activities.

Encourage exercise (after consulting with attending physician for precautions)

Have a "Grump Support Group", letting him/her talk about his/hers feelings with others who are experiencing the same type of things.

Make sure he/she eats a balanced diet and get enough rest

Make a overall plan and have a "Team" approach, i. e. use the family, friends, clergy and staff to support the plan and carry it through.

Try to get him/her involved in a cause; the cause can distract him/her from his/her own problems.

Make him/her feel useful; even doing small jobs like folding towels will help a person know that there are still some things they can do. These type of activities will improve their self esteem.

This may be a helpful tool to share with the family of a client who has a difficult personality.

EXERCISE

GOALS AND OBJECTIVES OF EXERCISE FOR THE ELDERLY

Even moderate, but consistent, exercise, begun late in life, can extend the client's life span. When a client does not get adequate exercise, all his body processes may slow down and muscles can grow weak from inactivity.

The instructions given must be clear, simple, and brief. Personnel must speak very clearly, because elderly clients easily misunderstand or may not hear well. Some techniques may need to be demonstrated.

The important thing is to stimulate clients to keep the physical capabilities they still have. The elderly can obtain much useful exercise by doing as much for themselves as they possibly can. Every time something is done for a client that he could have done himself, he is made that much more dependent.

Clients usually do what we expect them to do, but too often we do not expect enough of them, because of their apparent disabilities.

PLANNING AN EXERCISE PROGRAM

In planning an exercise program for the elderly, there are three kinds of groups to consider:

1. THOSE WHO HAVE HAD A STROKE OR OTHER PHYSICAL DIFFICULTY RESULTING IN PARALYSIS OR OTHRE INJURY.
2. THOSE WHO NOT BEEN EXERCISING AND ARE ONLY OLD OR OUT OF SHAPE, NOT INCAPACITATED OTHERWISE.
3. THOSE WHO, REGARDLESS OF AGE, EXERCISE IN SOME MANNER REGULARLY.

Certain physical problem must be taken into consideration when deciding what can realistically be expected to be accomplished.

PHYSICAL CONDITIONS TO CONSIDER
A. HEART & LUNG CONDITIONS
B. HIGH BLOOD PRESSURE
C. WEIGHT PROBLEM
D. INOPERATIVE LIMB
E. ARTHRITIS
F. EMPHYSEMA

The doctor may be able to tell you what exercise to do or to eliminate.

OTHER FACTORS TO BE CONSIDERED:

1. WHAT PRECAUTIONS WOULD YOU HAVE TO TAKE WITH EACH INDIVIDUAL?
2. HOW CAN YOU MOTIVATE CLIENTS TO TAKE PART IN THE EXERCISE?
3. WHAT TYPE OF EXERCISE DO YOU THINK EACH PERSON COULD DO TO BENEFIT HIS/HER PARTICULAR PROBLEM?
4. WOULD HE/SHE BENEFIT MOST FROM AN INDIVIDUAL PROGRAM OR GROUP PROGRAM OR BOTH?
5. THE NUMBER OF EXERCISES, AND THE NUMBER OF TIMES HE/SHE IS TO DO THEM?

Whatever exercise program is decided upon, no matter how small, is a beginning. It will establish a good base upon which to build.

THE BENEFITS OF EXERCISE:

- IMPROVES CIRCULATION
- STRENGTHEN THE HEART
- INCREASE OXYGEN INTAKE
- STIMULATES THE BRAIN
- AIDS DIGESTION
- AIDS ELIMINATION AND AVOIDS CONSTIPATION
- TONES MUSCLES
- RETARDS BONE LOSS
- REDUCES PAIN
- ENHANCES RELAXATION AND MAKES FOR BETTER SLEEP
- INCREASES SELF-ESTEEM
- HELPS MAINTAIN A POSITIVE ATTITUDE
- DISCOURAGES DEPRESSION

SAFETY SUGGESTIONS

1. GET APPROVAL FROM CLIENT'S DOCTOR BEFORE STARTING EXERCISE PROGRAM; EXPLAIN TO DOCTOR THE TYPE OF EXERCISES YOU PLAN TO INITIATE.
2. IF YOUR CLIENT IS SEEING A PHYSICAL THERAPIST, CONSULT THE THERAPIST FOR SPECIAL INSTRUCTIONS.
3. HAVE CLIENTS WEAR COMFORTABLE, LOOSE CLOTHING AND FLAT SHOES.
4. START SLOWLY.
5. INFLAMED JOINTS SHOULD NOT BE EXERCISED; HAVE CLIENT EXERCISE OTHER PARTS OF THE BODY.
6. IF ONE EXERCISE CAUSES PAIN, HAVE PERSON STOP AND TRY A DIFFERENT EXERCISE.

7. STRENGHT SLOWLY. DO NOT BOUNCE; BOUNCING CAN TEAR LIG-
AMENTS.
8. IF CLIENTS BECOME FATIGUED, STOP. EACH DAY THEY SHOULD BE
ABLE TO DO MORE.
9. EXERCISES SHOULD INVOLVE LARGE MUSCLES; AVOID ISOMETRIC
EXERCERSISE.
10. BE AWARE OF POTENTIAL HAZARDS IN THE ENVIRONMENT.

WARM UP ROUTINE

Warm muscles are less subject to injury than cold muscles. Therefore, warm-up exercises should be conducted before any exercise begin. The warm-up period should last about ten minutes; deep breathing, gentle, swaying movements and gentle, easy stretching. Soft music is best for this. Have clients remain in their chairs but make sure they have lots of large room. As you do the stretching exercises, you need to make sure you are stretching all of your tendons and ligaments. Movements should be slow. Don't stretch "until it hurts" or to the point of pain. And don't use bouncing or jerking movements as they can tear ligaments not used to stretching.

EYE EXERCISES

Eyes to the left, right, up, down and all around. Large flash cards of letters, numbers and pictures.

BREATHING

Sitting or standing, take a deep breath through the nose and then exhale slowly. Shrug both shoulders to starting position.

HEAD EXERCISES

Touch your right ear to your right shoulder. Move slowly. Hold the stretch for the count of five. Now the left side. Five repetitions. Move your chin toward your right shoulder, hold for 5 sec.; repeat on left side. Five repetitions. Lift your chin to the ceiling, hold for 5 sec. Put chin on chest, hold 5 sec. Five repetitions. Squeeze your face up, real hard. Now relax. Five repetitions. Just out your lower jaw. Pull back in. Five repetitions.

HANDS

Take your right hand and move each finger of your left hand open and closed several times. Repeat with other hand. Intertwine your fingers and move your hands left and right. Move them in circles to the right and to the left. This will limber your wrists. Hold your hands outstretched at shoulder level. Open your hands and stretch out your fingers as far as possible. Hold for 5 sec., then make a fist and squeeze it as hard as you can. Three repetitions. Rotate wrists out left 5 times.

ARMS AND SHOULDERS

Clasp your hand behind your head. Keep your hands there while moving your elbows forward and back. Five repetitions.

Shrug shoulder up to ears. Hold tight for count of five. Five repetitions.

Roll shoulders back 5 times; roll shoulders forward 5 times.

Bend palms toward wrist. Hold to count of five. Extend hands up, arms straight. Hold to count of 5. Alternate up and down five times.

Lateral Arm Lifts. Start with arms at sides, lift both arms out to sides and over head. Repeat 5 times.

Hold your arms straight out in front, parallel to the floor, with your palms together. Now move them straight out to the side, keeping then parallel to thee floor and then move them back to the front position. Clap your hands as you return. Repeat five times.

Put your hands on your hips. Move your elbows forward and back. Do five times.

Reach up with one arm as high over your head as you're able. Bring this arm down and raise the other arm over your head. Repeat 5 times.

Reach out in front of you, as though swimming, first with one arm and then the other. Repeat 5 times.

Totally relax your left arm. Put right hand under your left elbow and lift the relaxed left arm. Let your right arm do all the work. Repeat 5 times. Repeat, using left hand to lift right arm.

Lift right hand over your head and stretch to your left. Repeat for left side. Five repetitions.

Put arms over head; clasp hands. Slowly pull arms to right. Don't bounce.

Then pull arms to left. Repeat five times.

Put arms over head. First, reach as high as you can with one arm and then the other, like you were climbing ladder. Repeat five times.

Hold your arms, with elbows straight down at sides. Move your arms with elbows locked, up and straight out to the side. Move them up to at least the shoulder height. Repeat five times.

ROCK-A BYE-BABY: Grasp both elbows, or as close as you can, with both hands and move your arms left and right, moving your elbows out to the side as far as possible. Sing the song five times while making rocking motion.

TRUNK

TWISTING: Stand or sit with hands behind head, turn trunk slowly from side to side. Five repetitions.

SIDE BENDS: With both hands behind head, smoothly and slowly bend from side to side. Repeat five times.

HIP BEND: Put your hands on your hips, lean forward and then back to an upright position. Repeat five times.

HIP TWIST: Put your hands on your hips. Twist your body to the right and then the left. When you twist, move your arms and head as well. Repeat five times.

LEGS AND FEET

Sit still and bounce your feet on the floor, first one foot, then the other. Repeat as long and fast and hard as you are able.

Sit with your feet flat on the floor. First raise your heels off the floor, but keep your toes down and then raise your toes off the floor, keeping your heels on the floor. Repeat ten times, then do again in a rocking motion.

Extend legs; pull toes toward you. Hold 5 sec. Point toes. Hold 5 sec. Five repetitions.

RELAXATION TECNIQUES

PROGRESSIVE RELAXATION

Lie comfortably on your back in a quiet environment. Allow yourself to become passive. Begin by taking a few deep breaths and then relaxing into your natural breathing rhythm. Tense and release groups of muscles one at a time, including your hands; arms; head and face, including jaw, mouth, eyes and forehead; shoulders, chest and neck; abdomen and buttocks; upper legs and feet. Notice what the tension feels like as you contract each muscle group. Then focus on the experience of letting go of this tension as you progressively relax parts of your body. Allow the tension to float out of your muscles as you let them go as limp as you can.

COUNTING BREATHS

First, make yourself comfortable in your chair. Keep your back straight. Try not to move during the exercise. Place your hands on your thighs or in your lap with your thumbs together, providing some tension at that spot so you won't go to sleep. Close your eyes. Now, take a deep, slow breath., As you inhale, count one to yourself.

Then, slowly, exhale all the way out, counting two to yourself silently. Another inhale is three, out is four. Quiet, slow breaths (your breathing will gradually become more swallow). In on five, out on six. In, seven, out, eight. In on nine, out on ten. Keep counting. When you get to ten, start over at one. Slow, natural breaths.

If you lose count, start over at one. Just count your breaths. If a thought comes, don't let it take hold. Let pass on through as if it were a gentle breeze passing through your hair. Just count your breaths. Begin practicing this technique five to ten minutes a day and gradually increase the time to suit your needs. When you finish this exercise, ask yourself, "How do I feel?"

Hold your legs off the floor and straight out in front. Point your toes out away from you like a dancer and move your feet up and down in a walking movement. Raise one thigh off the chair as high as you can then put it back down on the chair. Repeat five times.

Extend one leg and rotate it five times in one direction and then five times in the other direction. Leg lifts-raise the right one up and down five times then five times in the other direction. Hold your legs at the ankles. Totally relax the top leg and lift with the bottom leg. Repeat five times. Knee lifts-Raise each knee five times toward chest.

Heel Raises-Raise heels up and down five times each.

Ankle twist-Holding legs out, rotate ankles first one direction to the count of 5, then the other. Five repetitions.

NOW BEND FORWARD LIKE A RAG DOLL. LET YOUR ARMS HANG.

ASSESSMENT/EVALUATION

The Administrator together with the Nurse shall have primary responsibility for evaluation of planned activities.

1. Shall keep on file an activity interest assessment form for each client.
2. Shall keep on file an individual client activity plan.

3. Shall keep on file document forms for activity schedules, clients participation and evaluations.
4. Shall have a client/family suggestion box.

ARTHRITIS

Arthritis is an inflammation or swelling of a joint. In most case, it occurs gradually. Most forms are chronic, lasting for years. In seniors, the two most common forms are Osteoarthritis and Rheumatoid. The underlying cause of Arthritis is not known, but the effect on the joints and pain can be substantial.

The client might complain about aching, swelling, stiffness (especially in the morning or after a nap), and pain of various degrees. Medical science has developed some good medications to combat Arthritis. The success of these medications varies from client to client. It is imperative to keep the weight. Exercise, diet, and adequate rest can help in keeping the symptoms at a minimum.

OSTEOARTHRITIS

The Most common form of Arthritis is Osteoarthritis. "Osteo" means bone, and "itis" means inflammation. This is a degenerative joint disease that produces stiffness or pain in the fingers or in weight bearing joints, such as knees, hips and the spine. Over 75 % of the Seniors in America are affected in one form or another by this disease.

RHEUMATOID ARTHRITIS

Rheumatoid Arthritis can affect almost all of the joints. Chronic inflammation will deform a joint by causing sticky adhesions. These adhesions will become scar tissue and eventually harden. The sufferer will go through periods of "flair ups", leaving more and more damage each time, if not arrested. Women are affected three times more frequently than men. The onset of the disease usually begins in the small joints in the hands and the feet.

ARTHRITTIS AND RELATED DISEASE
Chief Complaints:
Physical:
ACHING PAIN IN JOINTS
USE IS LIMITEDINFLAMED TISSUES AROUND JOINTS
TIREDNESS   REDNESS
STIFFNESS   HEAT IN JOINT AREAS
SEVERE "FLAIR UPS" SHOULD ALWAYS BE REPORTED
TO THE PHYSICIAN
EMOTIONAL: Because this is usually a chronic disease, sufferers can display emotional symptoms such as depression, irritability, and helplessness. (See chronic Illness for more examples)

TIPS TO ASSIST A PERSON WITH ARTHRITIS AND RELATED DISEASES:

a. Have the attending physician diagnose the problem and follow-up. Make sure the client follows prescribed medication regimen.

b. Make sure the client is getting the proper diet, exercise and, and sleep. Encourage Range of Motion exercises.

c. Adapt the living necessities so that the client can cope as much for self as possible.

d. Make sure clothing is easily managed. Velcro can be put on instead of buttons. Make sure shoes and slippers fit properly and give adequate support. Adaptive eating equipment (WITH LARGE HANDLE OR PLATE GUARDS) can be utilized. Cut the client's meat in small bite size pieces.

Physical therapy as prescribed by the physician. The therapist can administer a heat treatment that can be helpful.

HOT SHOWERS OR BATHS CAN BE HELPFUL.

GOUT

Gout is caused by a defect in the uric acid. The body does not eliminate this waste product from the urine. Currently, the cause for this is unknown. Too much alcohol or Vitamin C can cause more acid in the urine; they should be avoided. Gout can cause pain and swelling in the joints and has periods of "flair ups" which cause a great deal of pain. Medications for prevention and acute attacks are often prescribed.

HIP FRACTURES AND REPLACEMENTS

Hip fractures are one of the most common type of fractures occurring in the elderly. The hip is a ball and socket joint. The fracture usually results from a fall. The fall may caused by tripping or misplaced footing but can occur, for example, from stepping off a curb or stair.

Osteoarthritis and Rheumatoid Arthritis can be extremely painful and severely affect the physical abilities of the sufferer. In these types of cases many times a hip replacement is performed.

If a hip is indicated, often the physician will recommend the person have physiotherapy treatment. The stronger the muscles and joint surrounding the hip are, the better the result will be from the surgery. The surgeon can replace the hip but not the muscles, tendons and ligaments.

Artificial components, a socket, ball and shaft make up the prostheses to replace the defected parts. The success is very high and the recovery rate is usually very good.

Physical and Occupational therapy can assist the client in returning to a normal level of functioning. Often, adaptive devices can help ease activities of daily living.

It is important for the client to understand they may not walk as well as they had expected to. The hip area will be sore. It will take time to establish strength in the hip. The Physician and Physical Therapist will determine whether a person will use a walker or crutches. Crutches are usually preferred when there are no other medical problems to consider because they allow for a normal walking pattern to be established.

At any time, even years later, a hip prosthesis can displace or become defective in some manner. It rarely happens, but it can occur. If a client complains about pain in the area, seek medical attention.

GASTROINTESTINAL DISORDERS

Gastrointestinal disorders are those illness or disease related to the digestive system. The most common examples affecting the elderly are as follows:

Constipation	Diarrhea
Peptic Ulcers	Heartburn and Indigestion
Diverticulitis	Hiatus Hernia
Irritable Bowel Syndrome	Colitis
Hemorrhoids	

CONSTIPATION

Many seniors suffer from constipation due to their use of prescription medications like pain killers and over-the-counter medications such as constipation.

Constipation can be described as the inability and/or difficulty of passing a stool. The stool is usually hard and dry. Medication is usually tried to assist in the elimination process. If the stool is not successfully eliminated, an impaction can occur. Impaction is defined as a large amount of hard or soft stool usually in the large intestine, that the person is unable to pass. This can lead to a life threatening situation in which surgery may be required. An ASP (Appropriately Skilled Professional) can perform a rectal exam and contact the attending physician for orders to try an enema(s) or to physically remove the impaction.

SIGNS AND SYMPTOMS:

Physical Signs:	Symptoms:
Leaking grainy stool	Unable to eliminate and have constant urge
Distended	Pain in abdomen and rectum
Firm & tender abdomen	Nausea and loss of appetite
Low grade fever	Emotional distress

TIPS ON PREVENTION:

1. Have the client keep track daily of bowel activity
2. Proper Diet and exercise
3. Regular elimination schedule (45 minutes after a meal works well)

Fiber can help in the prevention of constipation. Whole grain cereals, fresh fruits and vegetables, fruit juices and whole wheat bread are good sources of fiber. Prunes and prune juice are healthy – natural laxatives. Many people testify to hot or warm prune juice being extremely effective. Other types of laxatives such as Castor Oil, Bisacodyl, Ducolax, Milk of Magnesia and Cascara.

DIARRHEA

Certain medications can cause diarrhea, but diarrhea is most often caused by an infection or food allergies. Diarrhea is frequent elimination of watery stools. Stress can also be prime factor in causing diarrhea. Rigorous cramping can occur before and during a diarrhea attack.

If food is not properly stored, prepared or handled, food poisoning can occur. This is easily prevented by proper training of the dietary staff, posted policies and procedures regarding sanitation, cooking, storage and handling of food items.

If food allergy is suspected, the attending physician can perform tests to investigate further and advice to proper dieting.

SIGNS AND SYMPTOMS
Physical:

Cramping	Urgency
Watery stool	Frequency
Flatulence	

HOW TO ASSIST:

Clear liquid diet (if you can't see through it, it's not clear liquid). As person improves, add: Rice Water, ripe banana, cream of wheat or rice, avoid fats & spicy foods, or over-the counter remedies.

If the problem persists seek advise from the attending physician.

TAKE STEPS TO PREVENT DEHYDRATION. IF DEHYDRATION DOES OCCUR, CONTACT THE PHYSICIAN IMMEDIATELY OR SEEK IMMEDIATE MEDICAL ATTENTION.

PEPTIC ULCERS

Peptic ulcers are open areas in the lining of the upper intestines, stomach or esophagus. Due to an imbalance of the body's natural digestive aids, increased acids and enzymes can cause ulcers to develop. The pain can be severe and/or belching can occur. There are now several medications that can heal and improve an ulcer condition. Proper diet, reduced stress levels, and avoiding smoking can help prevent ulcers or reoccurrence.

BEWARE: SOME MEDICATIONS CAN CAUSE PEPTIC ULCERS

HEARTBURN AND INDIGESTION

Heartburn and indigestion occur when the stomach acids back up to the esophagus. Regurgitation can occur. If this is a chronic problem the client should be seen by the attending physician. Antacids should only be give per doctor's orders.

PREVENTIONS OF HEARTBURN AND INDIGESTION
1. Avoid acid and fatty foods.
2. Avoid carbonated and caffeinated drinks
3. Quit smoking
4. Cook fruits and vegetables
5. Reduce stress

DIVERTICULITIS

Diverticuli are small sac-like pockets formed on the large intestine wall. This is an exceedingly common disease in the elderly. Many persons with diverticuli do not have any symptoms. Others, unfortunately, have many. Diverticulitis is the inflammation of the diverticuli. This occurs when the sac-like pockets are filled with feces, seeds or nuts. The symptoms are pain, diarrhea and/or constipation, vomiting and nausea. If a client is suffering from these symptoms, he should see his physician. As an ongoing treatment for diverticulitis, high fiber diets are often recommended.

HERNIA

A hernia is defined as an abnormal protrusion of an organ through a weak wall in the body cavity. The most common type of hernia occurs in the groin area.

A hiatus hernia is the stomach protruding partially into the chest cavity because of the hiatus (the opening in the diaphragm) being too wide. This condition can cause heartburn, indigestion and regurgitation.

PRECAUTIONS FOR HERNIA SUFFERS:

1. Eat slowly and chew food completely
2. Drink liquids apart from mealtimes
3. Avoid carbonated drinks
4. Avoid over-eating
5. Don't lay down immediately after a meal; it is best to wait two hours before retiring. Keep the head of the bed slightly elevated.
6. Don't wear items too tight in the stomach area.

IRRITABLE BOWEL SYNDROME

Irritable Bowel Syndrome is one of the "Twentieth Century" disease. Sufferers have symptoms of cramps and diarrhea caused by spasms in the large intestines. This is also termed spastic colon, and nervous bowel. Inflammation of the colon (colitis) can occur.

When this illness becomes chronic, ulcers can occur and complicate the condition. Stress, diet, and food allergy may cause or contribute to irritable bowel syndrome.

However, there is no concrete proof as to the actual cause. In severe case, anticholinergic and sedative types of medications may be prescribed.

HEMORRHOIDS

Hemorrhoids may occur internally or externally in the rectum/anus area. Pain, burning, itching, and a small amount of bleeding can occur. Chronic constipation or pressure on the veins of the rectum cavity will create hemorrhoids. A good way or pressure to describe hemorrhoids is varicose veins of the rectum. Other contributing causes are excessive use of laxatives, obesity, liver disorders, and rectal tumors.

High fiber diets will make the elimination process easier, thus relieving pressure on the rectum. In severe cases, surgery may be necessary. The attending physician may prescribe sits baths, suppositories or topical ointments. If suppositories are needed and the client is unable to do self care an ASP (Approximately Skilled Professional). Can assist.

RESPIRATORY DISEASES
EMPHYSEMA

Cigarette smoking is the number one cause of emphysema. Seldom is emphysema inherited. It's development begins early in life, but the symptoms will appear in the later years. Emphysema is a lung disease in which the alveoli (air sacks in the lungs) become damaged to the point where they can no longer hold air. The emphysema sufferer will be short of breath.

Edema and chronic bronchitis will often accompany emphysema. A person with this disorder may develop a persistent chronic cough and a wheeze.

There is no cure for Emphysema; treatments only help relieve some of the symptoms. The damaged lung tissue cannot be replaced. Treatment includes restricting the sodium intake in the diet. As the condition becomes more severe, the person will have to use a canula and oxygen equipment.

ASTHMA

Asthma is an illness that usually begins in early childhood, but can occur at any age. It has a tendency to clear up by the early adult years. The most familiar kind of Asthma is Bronchial Asthma. There are two basic types of Bronchial Asthma. Extrinsic, is the type that is brought on by an allergic reaction like hay fever. Intrinsic is the second type and usually comes later in life and is often brought only by a respiratory tract infection, emotional problems stress, anxiety, and the like.

Asthma attacks can vary from mild discomfort to respiratory failure. The main symptoms are wheezing, shortness of breath, a dry cough, and a tight feeling in the chest. Preventive measures can be taken will good results; however, there is no cure for Asthma at this time. Immunotherapy can be performed but its success is limited. The most commonly used drugs on the market today are prophylactic (preventive) drugs and inhaled corticosteroid drugs.

PLEURISY

Pleurisy is an inflammation of the membrane lining in the lungs. Viral Pneumonia is one possible cause. Pleurisy causes sharp pains to occur with every breath. Pleurisy can usually be effectively treated with antibiotics.

PNEUMONIA

Pneumonia is an infection caused by viruses and/or bacteria, involving the membrane lining. The two main kinds are Lobar Pneumonia and Bronchopneumonia. The inflammation in bronchopneumonia takes hold in the bronchi and bronchiolus (air passages into the lungs) but then spreads and may eventually involve both lungs.

The symptoms include fever, chills, shortness of breath, chest pains when breathing, an increased amount of sputum that is usually green or yellow-green in color, and pleurisy. Tylenol or Aspirin (if allowed) will help reduce the fever. Antibiotics and/or antifungal will usually care Pneumonia.

PULMONARY OBSTRUCTION

The common type of pulmonary obstruction is pulmonary embolism (clot). The embolism is a blood clot that has broken free from its place of origin, usually from inside a leg. The embolism will travel through the bloodstream until it encounters an area narrower than itself. Most often, this will be in the heart or lungs.

The symptoms include dizziness, sharp chest pains when breathing, rapid pulse shortness of breath, and coughing up blood.

The use of thrombolytic drugs can be an effective treatment. If the embolism is small enough in size, then anticoagulants can be used to dissolve it. Surgery may be needed if the embolus (clot) is very large.

DIABETES

There are two types of diabetes. Type 1 is insulin-dependent and Type 2 is non-insulin-dependent. Often, they are referred to as "juvenile-onset", insulin-dependent, or "adult-onset", non-insulin-dependent. Both types of diabetes can occur at any time, but usually begin at the age associated it.

Diabetes is a result of a defect in the metabolism of sugar (glucose). Sugar and starches (carbohydrates) are changed into glucose and enter the bloodstream. Once a person develops diabetes, it is usually a chronic disease, lasting for the rest of his life.

Type 1, insulin-dependent diabetes, usually starts during childhood and is caused by an insufficient production of, or a complete failure to produce insulin. Insulin is normally produced by the pancreas. It is a hormone which regulates the body's use of glucose. If the person's body produces too little, or none at all, they must have insulin daily (sometimes several times a day). If they do not get the insulin, the body becomes hyperglycemic – TOO MUCH SUGAR! This can be extremely dangerous, possibly fatal.

Type 2, non-insulin-dependent diabetes, is usually controlled by diet and/or oral medication. The onset is usually during middle age. It is more common in women than in men. About a third of Type 2 diabetics can be successfully treated by diet without any medication. If the person follows the diet prescribed by the physician, gets rest, and gets plenty of exercise, they may be able to live medication "free".

With both types of diabetics, monitoring should be done. An ASP (Appropriately Skilled Professional) from local home health service can monitor the client and Medi-Care usually pays for it. Routine doctor visits should be attended. Always remember that the client needs to give himself the insulin injection, or it can be done by an SP. If the ASP performs the service, make sure you keep the ASP's name, plan, and services accurately documented.

HYPERGLYCEMIA

Hyperglycemia will occur when there is too much sugar (glucose) in the blood stream. The accumulation is usually a gradual process. Often you can observe signs or symptoms which indicate the sugar is on the rise.

Signs and symptoms:

Excessive Hunger

Frequent Urination
Weakness
Muscle Pain
Abdominal Pain or Vomiting
Deep Rapid Breathing
Confusion
Emotional Changes
Prevention:
Proper Diet
Exercise
Routine blood tests for glucose level

HYPOGLYCEMIA

This is the term used for low blood sugar. This can rapidly lead to a critical condition or death. It is caused primarily by either too much insulin, infection, a lack of food or excessive exercise.

Symptoms:

- Weakness
- Sweaty
- Tremors & Shaking
- Headaches
- Hunger
- Personality Changes

Hypoglycemia can result in seizure or coma.

IF UNCONSCIOUS, CALL 911

If conscious, seek immediate medical attention. The ASP or client should check blood sugar level. If the sugar level is 40 or lower, have the client consume one of the following:

4oz to 6oz	Apple juice
4oz to 6oz	Orange juice
4oz to 6oz	Soft Drink (not diet)
1 Tablespoon	Grape Jelly
1 Tablespoon	Corn Syrup

RE-CHECK BLOOD SUGAR LEVEL AFTER 5 MINUTES; IF STILL LOW, REPEAT WITH A SECOND DOSE.

CALL ATTENDING PHYSICIAN WITH REPORT AND RESULTS.

INCONTINENCE

Incontinence can be contributed to illness, a physical problem or medication. Many seniors have a minor incontinence problem of leakage. This is easily managed by a disposable undergarment like Depends, Attends, incontinent pad or generic equivalent.

Incontinence is humiliating for most seniors. Often, they may withdraw from social interaction to avoid embarrassment. Wetting of clothing and hiding of undergarments may occur as the client may be too disconcerted to let the care provider know.

About 1 in 10 persons over the age of 65 has a problem with some degree of urinary incontinence. Coughing or laughing can put pressure on the bladder and cause leakage.

It is essential that a record of when, how long, how much and other pertinent information be kept to establish a pattern, if any, and to provide the Appropriately Skilled Professional (ASP) a basis for diagnosis.

Some clients can be retrained by the ASP to control their bladders. Being sure the client urinates every 2 hours is usually the first step in establishing a routine. The client might be instructed to do some exercises to improve muscle tone. Occasionally, a doctor may prescribe a medication to help control incontinency.

TIPS ON INCONTINENCY
1. Visit a doctor make sure the client does not have an infection.
2. Make sure the toilet is easily accessible and nearby. Commodes may be used at night if cleaned promptly and stored away during the day.
3. Encourage the intake of fluids, especially clear ones like water.
4. Remind the client to go to the restroom.
5. Make sure garments are easily removed.

PROSTATE DISEASE
Elderly men should be checked annually for prostate disease. A rectal exam can be done in the physician's office during a routine visit. The prostate is a small organ about the size of a walnut. It is located next to the bladder (where urine is stored) and surrounds the urethra (the canal through which urine passes out of the body). Because of the close proximity to the urethra, an enlarged prostate can make urination difficult.

Acute prostatitis is the inflammation of the prostate resulting from a bacterial infection. It can usually be treated successfully with antibiotics. When the infection reoccurs continuously, antibiotics may be used for 3 months. Often the condition clears up by itself, but symptoms may last a long time.

Benign prostatic hypertrophy (BPH) is an enlargement of the prostate. It is caused by small noncancerous tumors that grow inside the prostate. It is not known what causes these growths, but they may be related to hormone changes with aging.

An enlarged prostate may, eventually, obstruct the urethra and cause difficulty urinating. Dribbling after urination and the urge to urinate frequently are common symptoms. In rare cases, the client may be unable to urinate. In severe cases, surgery may be necessary to remove the overgrown or tumor areas of the prostate.

URINARY TRACT INFECTIONS
Urinary tract infections usually effect the kidney, bladder or prostate organs. Symptoms like painful urination, burning or frequent urination, fever and groin pain occur. Incontinence can be a sign urinary tract infection. A urine analysis is usually performed to detect the infection and cause.

In cystitis, the bladder is inflamed from bacterial causes. Obstruction, mostly in men, can also lead to cystitis. The onset is often sudden. The physician will usually prescribe an antibiotic and a lot of fluids. After about 10 days the infection has typically abated.

Other problems like a defective ureter or pyelitis are causes of urinary tract infection. Medical attention should always be sought.

Urinary tract infections are treatable disorders; however, if left untreated, chronic infections can lead to permanent damage. Usually surgery or other extreme medical procedures can help to successfully overcome the problem.

It is important to follow up with a repeat Urinary Analysis to ensure the infection is gone.

HEART DISEASE

There are many types of cardiovascular diseases. About half of all Americans develop some form of heart disease. Heart disease can be hereditary. The age and sex of a person can increase the chances of heart disease. These include reducing high blood pressure, avoiding or quitting smoking, and lowering blood cholesterol.

ANGINA

This is the most common form of heart disease in adults and seniors. There are two basic types of angina. Classic angina results from arteriosclerosis (hardening of the arteries). Arterioclerosis occurs as fatty deposits develop and clogging transpires. This may develop over many years. When the artery is clogged, "angina", a temporary plain in the chest occurs. Variant angina can strike from a spasm or constriction of the coronary artery. When the blood flow is cut off as a result of the spasm or constriction, "angina", a pain very similar to that of classic angina occurs.

Unstable angina is term used to describe the angina resulting from both types of angina, separately occurring at various times. If the client uses nitroglycerine, the standard is 1 every 5 minutes up to 3 doses. If no relief occurs, call an ambulance.

ARRHYTHMIAS

Impulse beats of the heart occur 60 to 100 times a minute. The number of beats per minute is called the heart rate. The heart rate can increase with exercise or stressful situations and decrease with sleep and relaxation. Arrhythmias are distinctive irregular beats of the heart rate, originating from the heart. Many people experience minor irregular beats from time to time but distinctive arrhythmias should be taken seriously.

HYPERTENSION

Hypertension can be defined as too much tension on the blood vessel walls. The primary cause of hypertension is unknown, yet many factors can increase the chance of developing it. Medical sciences has sufficiently proven that smoking, obesity, and excessive salt usage can increase the chance of developing high blood pressure. Many medications are successful in keeping the blood pressure within normal limits; these include Diuretics, Vasodialators, and Beta Blockers.

CONGESTIVE HEART FAILURE

Congestive heart failure (CHF) is caused from the heart's failure to pump blood. CHF typically develops gradually over a period of time. There are many treatments that can reduce the painful and disabling affects, but it left untreated, death can occur. When the pumping of the blood by the heart is reduced, the blood and oxygen supply to other parts of the body is decreased. The body functions will begin malfunctioning. Many symptoms can occur such as shortness of breath, swelling or water retention (edema) and rapid heart beat. Anemia, serious Vitamin B deficiency, Hyperactive Thyroid, and Bacterial Infections can also cause CHF.

Mediation can successfully treat the symptoms of CHF and the person can live a relatively normal life, but should maintain routine visits to the attending physician for monitoring.

It is further recommended that the client's weight be checked once a week. Specifically watch for the feet and ankles swelling. If the client has gained more than 5 pounds, the physician should be notified. It is important for the client to take the prescribed medication properly and follow a low sodium diet.

Other types of heart disease include the following:

ASHD

Heart Valve Disorders	Rheumatic Fever
Congenital Heart Defects	Mitral Valve Prolapse
Bradycardia	Pericarditis

STROKE

The American Heart Association offers the following statistics about stroke:

- Stroke is the third leading cause of death in the United Sates.
- There are approximately half a million new stroke cases each year.
- Of these, nearly 75% occur in persons 65 years or older.
- Strokes occur more frequently in men than in women.
- Most stroke victims survive.
- Twenty percent of stroke victims develop aphasia.

Stroke is a general term used to describe the interruption of blood flow to the brain. The amount of damage caused by the stroke will depend on the severity and the area affected. Most strokes are caused by a blood clot or hemorrhage. There are two common types of strokes: CVA Cerebral Vascular Accident and TIA Transient Ischemic Attack.

CVA – CEREBRAL VASCULAR ACCIDENT

When a cerebral vascular attack occurs, the damage is permanent. However, in time, some recovery may occur. Many older persons have hardening or narrowing of the arteries in the brain to one degree or another. This condition is called arteriosclerosis. High blood pressure is a prime factor in the development of arteriosclerosis. When the hardening or narrowing is substantial this can lead to the forming of clot. When this clot occurs the functions control by that area are partially or completely hindered. This type of stroke is called cerebral thrombosis and typically occurs during sleep.

Another type of clot is called an embolism. This usually is formed in the large arteries of the neck. When it breaks off, it is carried by the blood stream to the brain, causing a stroke termed cerebral embolism. This is common in persons suffering from a heart attack and most often happens when a person is awake.

CEREBRAL HEMORRHAGE
The most serious kind of stroke is called cerebral hemorrhage. This type kills approximately 75 to 90 percent of its victims.

Hemorrhage is bleeding, cerebral is brain, cerebral hemorrhage is bleeding in the brain. The bleeding results when an aneurysm bursts, interrupts the blood flow and spills out onto the surrounding blood cells causing even more damage. This type usually occurs during the waking hours and has other symptoms like headache, vomiting and loss of consciousness.

TIA's - TRANSIENT ISCHEMIC ATTACK
This type of stroke is commonly called a mini-stroke. It can cause permanent damage with chronic reoccurrences. TIA's are a definite warning sign that something is amiss. Blood thinning and anti-clothing medications are often prescribed to prevent a stroke. TIA's symptoms include temporarily blurred vision, difficulties in verbal communication (speech, reading and writing), motor coordination, and dizzy spells.

PREVENTION SUGGESTION:
1. Reduce high blood pressure, and monitor regularly.
2. Eat a proper diet, avoid obesity.
3. Regularly exercise.
4. Medication therapy, if needed, as prescribed by the doctor.

UNDERSTANDING APHASIA
Understanding the aphasic person is the key to providing proper care. Sometimes the aphasic person is thought to be confused, but that is not the case. Aphasia is the most common type of language disorder in adults. It is usually caused by a cerebrovascular accident (CVA, or stroke). A stroke is an interruption in the flow of blood to the brain. In aphasia, this interruption happens in the area of the brain that control speech. Over half of the persons suffering from a stroke have a degree of this speech disorder. Head injury or trauma can also cause aphasia.

The brain is separate into two large globes. The right and left cerebral hemisphere comprise the "thinking" areas of the brain. The cerebral hemispheres sit on top of the cerebellum, a smaller globe that extends to form the spinal cord.

Speech is controlled by the left hemisphere of the brain, and injury to this area results in aphasia. Between one-third and one-half off all left-brain will produce some degree of aphasia.

TIPS ON COMMUNICATING WITH A PERSON WITH APHASIA:
1. Never rush the person, try to communicate in a calm atmosphere.
2. Use simple words and directions.
3. Give him/her plenty of time to talk and encourage him/her to talk.

4. Use eyes and no questions.
5. Give positive reinforcement.
6. Establish routines and consistency in activities of daily living.
7. If necessary, use a word or alphabet board.

Speech therapy may be covered under MEDI-CARE for up to a one-year period of time. Some home health services can provide speech therapy in client care.

DEALING WITH MEMORY PROBLEMS
1. Establish a fixed routine, whenever possible.
2. Keep messages short and clearly stated.
3. Give directions one step at a time.
4. Repeat training as often as necessary.
5. Use memory aides, like posters, with important information.
6. To help him/her remember his/her room, use familiar objects from his/hers home.
7. Have all staff, family, and friends repeat the same directions when training someone for a specific problem.

HEARING LOSS AND DEAFNESS
Many seniors suffer from hearing loss but few are totally deaf. As we grow older, the nerves (sound receptors) decrease in efficiency. The result is we hear less. Many times, ear wax builds up and block the ear from hearing clearly. In truly deaf people, there are physical changes in the middle ear. Infections, birth defects or injury to the middle ear can cause deafness or hearing loss.

We know that a good portion of what we hear is actually what we see. We read body language unconsciously. Have you ever heard someone tell you that a person only hears when he/she wants to? That may be due to the fact that when they want to, they are concentrating and paying attention to the body language. They may hear a little and see a lot which equals being able to understand.

Many hearing aid companies will provide free hearing tests to your clients in order to sell their hearing aids. Unfortunately, hearing aids are not covered by Medi-Care and can be extremely costly.

When the client is visiting the Attending Physician, request that he/she check the client's ear and clean them, if necessary. If you have an ASP (Appropriately Skilled Professional) on staff, you may choose to have this service performed for your clients on a regular basis.

Remember, persons with hearing disorders should be spoken to directly. Don't shout, but talk in a clear low-loud voice. Minimize the disruptive sounds when possible, like the TV and radio; shut the door, if possible.

A hearing aid is only good when it is used and adjusted properly. Usually, when a client first gets a hearing aid it is worn 1 to 2 hours a day. Most doctors recommend a gradual build up of use. We need to be patient with the client and give him assistance when needed.

TIPS ON CARING FOR HEARING AIDS:
A. Check the battery. Place the hearing aid in your hand and cover with your other hand; it should squeal if the battery is good. If the battery needs replacing, find the little latch

to pull and replace the battery with the same type that is in it. These are usually found in any Drug Store.

B. Check setting. Often the client will have it too high or too low. If you are unable to adjust it comfortably for the client, have him see the Otorhinolaryngologist.
C. Check the ear mold portion and make sure it is clean. Never use alcohol for cleaning; it can cause cracks in the mold.
D. Have the client take the hearing aid out when sitting under a hair dryer.

Types of Hearing Aids:
A. Ear mold – most commonly used
B. Behind the Ear – very compact
C. Eyeglass hearing aid – used specifically for routing signals to the good ear.

PREVENTION OF BEDSORES (DECUBITI)

For Every hour it takes to cause a bedsore, 50 hours of treatment are needed to heal it. A bedsore can appear in a few hours. The skin can become red after 30 to 60 minutes of increased pressure. The inside area of a bedsore is more widespread than the outside area. In other words, it is much worse inside than it looks outside. Bedsores are caused by continued pressure on an area, which causes that area to have decreased circulation. Death of the tissue begins after two hours of pressure.

The best way to treat a bed sore is to prevent it. Licensing prohibits decubitus in client care facilities unless an exception has been granted.

OTHER CAUSES:	PREVENTION
Urine or feces on skin	Keep client clean.
Bed wrinkles	Makes the linens smooth.
Dehydration	Encourage water and fluids
Damp skin	Pat completely dry after bathing
Soap (use only when necessary)	Rinse soap off thoroughly

AREAS TO OBSERVE:

Back of head	Backbone
Shoulder blades	Buttocks
Elbows	Front of knees
Ankles	Inside of knees
Heels of feet	Leg braces, back braces, etc.

Paralyzed or contracted areas where skin meets skin.
NOTE: Bedsores can be prevented in these areas by padding.

ALZHEIMER'S DISEASE

Alzheimer's disease is a progressive condition where the brain and substance of the brain shrinks. In the elderly, it is estimated that 75% of dementia cases result from Alzheimer's; 30% of those 85 or older are affected.

The cause of Alzheimer's is unknown but there are several proposed theories. One theory is that Alzheimer's is caused by the effects of a chronic infection. Another is that Alzheimer's is brought on by toxic poisoning by a metal such as aluminum. There is known to be a reduced level of aceytlcholine and other brain chemicals in persons with Alzheimer.

Scientific findings have proven that Alzheimer's is a disease, not an inevitable consequence of old age. Alzheimer's can affect younger adults, but far less frequently than older persons. Recent studies indicated 10% to 20% percent of Alzheimer's cases might be inherited.

The onset of Alzheimer's Disease for the majority of persons suffering from this condition is in the mid 60's with death occurring within 7 to 10 years. A person with Alzheimer's eventually has decreased abilities for self care. This increases vulnerability to pneumonia and other infections which can lead to death.

At first, the individual with Alzheimer's disease experiences only minor, and almost imperceptible, symptoms that are often attributed to emotional upsets and other physical illnesses. Gradually, however, the person becomes more forgetful-particularly about recent events – and this may be reported by anxious relatives.

The person may neglect to turn off the stove, may misplace things, may recheck to see if a task was done, may take longer to complete a chore that was previously routine, or may repeat already answered questions. As the disease progresses, memory loss and changes in personality, mood, and behavior including confusion, irritability, restlessness, and agitation are likely to appear. Judgment, concentration, orientation, writing, reading, speech, motor behavior, and naming of objects may also be affected.

The pattern of care for persons with Alzheimer's disease is not unlike the long-term care required fro many other adults with multiple chronic physical and mental impairments. In the early and middle stages of progressive dementia, relatives and friends provide most of the personal care necessary.

The same pattern often occurs when an older person has some other disease. In it's final and most debilitating stages, Alzheimer's disease often forces placement in a nursing home or long-term care institution. This can result from caregiver "burn-out", inability to provide the level of care needed or a combination of both. The same thing may happen in a family with an older member who has cancer, emphysema or some chronic disorder other than Alzheimer's.

A new brain-imaging technique, Positron Emission Tomography (PET), indicates differences in the brain metabolism of normal, depressed and demented persons. This work has shown that on the average, overall brain metabolism is normal in depressed persons; is reduced 17 percent in persons with dementia due to blood circulation problems in the brain; and is reduced 33 percent in Alzheimer's disease sufferers. Metabolic differences in particular brain regions were also found to follow distinct patterns in each type of case. Studies of these distinct patterns may provide useful data on why certain mental functions are lost inn Alzheimer's disease while other functions are spread.

The pace has accelerated dramatically in the search for an effective treatment for Alzheimer's disease. During the fast few years, several findings that may prove highly significant were reported. First, studies with cholinergic agent lecithin demonstrated that clinically modest, but reliable, brief improvements in memory can be produced in some patients with Alzheimer's disease.

Early findings from studies with lecithin combined with the "metabolic enhancer" Piracetem also suggest that this combination may be of some therapeutic utility. Research will continue and focus on the development of treatment and providing care and support to those with Alzheimer's and their families.

SIGNS AND SYMPTOMS OF DEMENTIA & MENTAL DISORDERS:

Emotional:	Physical:
Decrease in intellectual abilities	Loss of memory
Personality changes	Inability to visually
Depression – anxiety	discriminate
Lack of recall	weight increase
Communication difficulties	or loss
Delusions – hallucinations	Loss of motor ability
Irrational Suspiciousness	Body chemicals loss or

The treatment of mental disorders will depend on the diagnosis.

TIPS TO ASSIST A PERSON WITH DEMENTIA & MENTAL DISORDERS:

1. Doctor – Visit Regularly –Note Changes; treat medical problems promptly.
2. Routine – Maintain well-constructed, simple routines for daily activities; familiar persons, times of events, placement of possessions, etc.
3. Avoid stressful situations – These include unfamiliar persons, places and things.
4. Adaptation – Assist in adapting to a new environment; give reality orientation as necessary. Repeat directions specifically. Actualize a team care plan.
5. Never force or rush – Frequently, a person with dementia may not understand or cooperate with you. Do not push a subject to the point of agitation; try again later.
6. Communication – use both verbal and non-verbal communication skills. Maintain good eye contact; speak slowly with clearly understood words.
7. Agitation
    a). If the person says he/she is going to hit you. Get yourself and others out of the way and call for help.
    b) Find out why he/she is agitated and help him/her find a solution.
    c) Do not argue; do not correct harmless beliefs.
    d) Try to distract; do not over react.
    e) Do not embarrass him/her.
    f) Rummaging – give him/her a laundry basket or drawer to rummage in. Keep him/her busy with simple tasks. Make sure he/she isn't looking for something, like his/her teeth, the bathroom or towels. Let him/her have as many possessions as space will nearly and safely allow.

8. Wandering – make sure he/she has an ID bracelet, with phone number on it. Fence yards, within fire alarm, warning systems; be sure to keep a current picture of the client for identification purposes.

COMMUNICATION IN DEMENTIA
VERBAL
- Short words
- Simple sentences
- Identify yourself and call the person by name

SPEECH
- Speak slowly
- Say individual words clearly
- Lower the tone; raise the volume only for deafness, not because you do not get a response you understand
- Wait for a response
- Ask only one question at a time
- If you repeat a question repeat it exactly

NONVERBAL
- Every verbal communication is delivered with proper nonverbal gestures
- Maintain eye contact
- Move slowly
- If the person walks away while you are talking to him or her, do not try to stop him or her as your first move. Instead keep moving along in front of him and persevere.
- Listen actively. Ask for a repeat of the statement. Continue until resolution.
- Assume there is capability for insight.
- Compare notes on successes and failures.
- Treat the reaction with verbal/nonverbal techniques.
- If you have not really "gotten anywhere" in 5 minutes or less, you will probably do better to leave and either return in 5 minutes or have a colleague try.
- Finally, if you say you are going to do something, DO IT. If you forget, find the person and apologize. Assuming that the person has forgotten the episode insults both your intelligence and his/hers.
- If you need to stop a patient-patient interchange do it firmly and quickly. Get them out of each other's territory. Wait five minutes, then return and explain to each one why you acted as you did. Use factual explanations, not guilt induction.

LEVELS OF MENTAL DETERIORATION
LEVEL 1. MILD CONFUSION:
Notable decline in memory and concentration. Occasionally, gets disorientated as to place and time. Could get lost at times. Decrease in performance of activities of daily living. Difficulty in

retaining information. Forgetful and misplaces belongings. Needs some supervision to maintain living standards.

LEVEL 2: EARLY DEMENTIA:

Unable to recall some family member's names. Difficulty counting backwards. Can no longer live alone – needs general supervision. Occasionally needs assistance with activities of daily living. Inability to recall recent some past experiences.

LEVEL 3: MIDDLE DEMENTIA:

Exhibits periods of anxiety and/or agitation. May forget child or spouse's name. Needs some assistance with activities of daily living. May need to be reminded to go to the bathroom and where the bathroom is. May show signs of insecurity and/or obsessive behavior. May lose thought during course of action. An example would be forgetting the process of eating during a meal. Needs overall frequent supervision. May be living within a memory.

LEVEL 4: FINAL DEMENTIA

Diminished motor skills, may be unable to walk or feed self. Is incontinent. Speech is impaired, the majority of communication is lost. The brain is unable to tell the body what to do.

DELIRIUM

Symptoms of Delirium usually manifest themselves abruptly. They can be the sign of a serious underlying illness or disease which, if not diagnosed, can lead to death. A delirious person is described as confused and disoriented. He/she seems to have no short-term memory. Hallucinations and fears can occur. Often, the person will ramble or speak in disjointed sentences. If the symptoms are long-term, this person may need to be in a higher level of care.

SIGNS AND SYMPTOMS OF DELIRIUM:

Emotional:	Physical:
Confusion	Sleep disorders
Illusions	Sweating
Agitation	Rambling speech
Short attention span	Elevated blood pressure
Fear	

Because the person may have an underlying illness or disease or can "freak out", it is essential to seek medical help if the symptoms abruptly surface.

SCHIZOPHRENIA

Schizophrenia varies in its severity from individual to individual. Those individuals are often referred to as crazy. They show odd behavior and talk nonsense. They may show odd behavior and talk nonsense. They may suffer with delusions and hallucinations. Schizophrenia generally can be controlled with medication and medical treatment.

Schizophrenia seems to worsen or improve in cycles known as relapse and remission, respectively. Sometimes, persons suffering from schizophrenia appear relatively normal. However, during a psychotic relapse, they cannot think logically and may lose all sense of who they are, what they are doing and where they are. Their thoughts are jumbled and chaotic.

Schizophrenia is considered one of the most baffling illnesses known. A person suffering from schizophrenia usually required treatment for the rest of his/her live. Depending on the extent of the disease, relative to that person, he/she may, or may not, be appropriate for client care.

INSOMNIA

Basically, we can divide insomnia into 3 sections:

1. Transient Insomnia (1 day to 1 week);
2. Short Term (1 to 3 weeks) and,
3. Chronic (3 weeks or longer)

When a client is having sleeping problems, be sure to document and keep a record, so pattern, if any, can be established. The doctor can best assess and advise how to assist a client when accurate information is provided. The types and times medication is given can affect sleeping. Has the client started any new medications? Has the client had stressful situations occurring in his/her life.

Is he/she having leg cramps or other pains? Are there environmental problems, such as light, temperature, noise, etc?

Sometimes, a client needs reassurance. A cup of herbal tea or warm milk with someone to talk over concerns and problems may be all he needs.

The following physical conditions can contribute to insomnia:

COPD (Chronic Obstructive Pulmonary Disease)

CHF (Congestive Heart Failure)

Anxiety

Asthma

Arthritis

Diuretics given at night

Headaches or Migraines

Epilepsy

Ulcers

Liver Failure

Diabetes

Kidney Failure

Infections

And many others.

EPILEPSY AND SEIZURE DISORDERS

When a person has "spells", "fits" or "convulsions", these signs may indicate a seizure. Most seizures are unpredictable. Some people have seizures from undetermined causes, others have been diagnosed with Epilepsy. Epilepsy is noted to cause a defect in the transmission of motor impulses in the brain. Seizure disorders and Epilepsy can usually be controlled by medication and the person can live a relatively normal life. However, it is essential that regular testing of the level of medication in the blood be done and evaluated periodically. Beverages containing alcohol should be avoided.

GRAND MAL SEIZURES

Sometimes a mood change or small contractions can indicate a possible seizure. The person usually falls, if not prevented from doing so. A loss of consciousness and convulsions occur, lasting from two to five minutes. Wild movements of the arms, legs and head transpire. After the person has regained consciousness, they will usually feel tired and want to sleep. Headaches and muscle soreness can occur.

PETIT MAL or ABSENCE SEIZURES

These types of seizures are usually characterized by the fluttering of the eye lids and small tremors of the head, arms and legs. The person will usually lose consciousness for 10 to 30 seconds. The seizures may occur frequently.

STATUS EPILEPTICUS or STATUS SEIZURES

These terms are used to describe rapid recurring seizures. The person doesn't usually regain consciousness between seizures. This is a serious condition and can be life threatening: CALL FOR IMMEDIATE MEDICAL ATTENTION.

OTHER TYPES OF SEIZURES include Facial Seizures, Psychomotor Seizures and Simple-Partial Seizures. The symptoms vary from facial twitching to mental confusion.

SIGNS AND SYMPTOMS OF SEIZURES:

MENTAL:	PHYSICAL:
Withdraws	Twitching
Staring Expression	Rigidity
Blackout	Convulsions
Confusion	Tremors
Hallucinations	Shaking
Loss of Consciousness	Jerking of extremities

HOW TO ASSIST: DO NOT PUT ANYTHING INTO THE MOUTH

1. If you notice any pre-seizure symptoms, get the person to sit or lie down.
2. If a person is undergoing a seizure, they should be lying down and turned on his/her side.
3. The head should be turned sideways to prevent saliva or tongue from clogging the throat.
4. Loosen clothing and remove any obstacles from the surrounding area.
5. Keep him from hurting himself, but allow freedom of movement.

RECORDS TIME, DURATION AND SITUATION. ALWAYS MAKE SURE HE/ SHE SEES THE ATTENDING PHYSICIAN REGULARLY.

PARKINSON'S DISEASE

Parkinson's disease is a group of degenerative neurological disorders, generally characterized by uncontrolled movements of the body's extremities; i.g. shaking, tremors, rigidity of the muscles can occur. The person may show signs of sluggishness or shuffling. It occurs in a small percent of the elderly affecting both men and women.

Science has shown it is the result of the degeneration of certain types of brain cells. The production and storage of a type of neurotransmitter called Dopamine is depleted. There is also indications of Acetylcholine concentrations, another type of neurotransmitter. Anticholinergic or Dopamine medications may be used specifically or together as a treatment.

The onset of Parkinson's is usually gradual, developing over many years. Changes in posture, stiffness or shaking of the hands, weakness and slowness of movement are among some of the many symptoms. Treatment varies from each individual. Physical therapy and the use of environmental aids can often help. Support from family, friends and the care givers is fundamental. As in most types of chronic illnesses, anxiety and depression can develop. The combined treatment of medications, therapy, and supportive loving care can help the person function almost for many years.

PLEASE NOTE: Parkinson's type symptoms can result from medications used in treating mental illness and other diseases. Arteriosclerosis and other disorders may also cause Parkinson's Disease.

SIGNS AND SYMPTOMS OF PARKINSON'S

Fatigue or Weakness	Lack of Affect (facial expression)
Shaking or Tremors	Limping or Shuffling
Stoop or Poor posture	Slowed Speech
Difficult Swallowing	Muscular Rigidity
Drooling	

TIPS TO ASSIST:

1. Regular checkup by the attending physician
2. Encourage a moderate exercise program (Range of motion exercises help keep limbs limber)
3. Let the client practice reading out loud if he is having difficulty with slow or slurred speech
4. Remind person who shuffles to pick up his/her feet.
5. Remind person who is stooping or slouching to correct posture Provide easy to-get-up from chairs, beds and toilets

VISION PROBLEMS

Many older persons suffer from vision problems. The most common type of problems include cataracts, glaucoma, macular degeneration, and diabetic retinopathy.

MUCULAR DEGENERATION

The macula is the small pigmented area of the retina. Degeneration of the macula is the leading cause of severe vision loss among the elderly. The macula controls the fine vision. The deterioration leads to blurring and/or loss in central vision.

Signs and Symptoms of Macular Degeneration:

1. Vision will be fuzzy.
2. Straight lines will appear wavy or doubled.
3. Letters will appear jumbled.

If the degeneration has not caused a total loss of vision, many times a magnifying glass can still be utilized.

Policies and Procedures

MEDICATIONS

MEDICATIONS HOW, WHY, WHEN, AND WHERE.

The regulations pertaining to medications in Title 22 are should be read and frequently reviewed by Administrator and staff. It is very important to prepare a proper medication disbursement system.

OUR SYSTEM

The medications storage and preparation site is placed in the area near hand washing facilities. Anyone assisting with medications should wash his/her hands first. There will be a telephone located close to the medication storage site to relay information to Physician, pharmacist, etc... Every medication must be logged in on LIC form # 622, in the record which is to be kept for each client.

The client's records must be kept or inaccessible. The records are confidential. A separate box, basket or section, with each client's full name and room number on it, should be kept to retain his/her prescriptions and over-the-counter medications. A centralized Med Storage will be locked at all times.

ASSISTING WITH MEDICATIONS

After washing hands, staff must wear gloves and it is a good idea to use the lid of the bottle to pour the pills into and then the directed amount into the pill cup or placed in a cup separate from a drinking cup for the client to take. Paper and plastic pill cups can be purchased from some local pharmacy or a medical suppliers.

BUBBLE/BLISTER PACKS

The most efficient and controllable medication system is the bubble or blister pack, with a thirty day supply on a single card. This card can be initialed by the staff person each time the drug is punched out, certifying that the client was seen taking medication.

CLIENT'S REFUSAL OF A MEDICATION

The staff trained to provide medication is responsible for making sure that the client is properly taking his/her medications. If a client refuses a medication, which he/she can do, you must document it in their record and notify the physician. The physician may choose to discontinue the medication. But if the doctor feels that discontinuance is detrimental to the client's health, he should help AngelCare in getting the client transferred to a more appropriate .

Factual Scenario:

A once had a client, "Mr. Smith," who was found to be spitting his thyroid pills in the toilet. He was informed that the "house rules" stated that all clients must take their medicines as Doctor prescribed and that any violation of the "house rules" were grounds for eviction. Mr. Smith transferred to another . Fortunately, he did. If he had died, our home would most likely have been held responsible for his death by CCL.

STORAGE OF MEDICATIONS

All medications will be stored in a locked and centrally located storage cabinet. PRN "as needed" MEDICATIONS. PRN comes from the Latin (pro re nata) "as the need arises". In our home, it should mean "as requested by the client". Prior to admission, or prior to the start of a new medication, you must obtain a written statement from the attending physician that the client is mentally capable of determining his/her need for that PRN medicine. When a client requests a PRN medication, staff needs to document the amount taken, date, time, result and they should sign or initial it. This will eliminate the chance of overdose and provide an accurate record of usage. When a client can't determine his/her own need for a PRN medication, the Doctor must be contacted and his/her permission granted before that medication is given. If the Doctor gives specific instructions as to dose, date and time, then it is no longer considered a PRN medication. Only the Doctor, not family or friends can give you permission to give a PRN medication when the client is unable to determine this for himself/herself. Always document Doctor instructions; put the date, time and sign or initial it. Then you need to document the result on the client's record.

Clients should be cautious when using OTC's if they have any of the following conditions:

Arthritis
Diabetes
Glaucoma
Heart disease
High blood pressure
Kidney disease
Nervous condition
Sleep problems

The most common medical conditions affected by OTC's are:
Gout
Prostate problems
Ulcers

Questions which should be asked of the doctor or pharmacist regarding use of OTC's:

1. Can the client take this OTC?
2. Will it be effective?
3. How long can he/she take it?
4. Will it interact adversely with other medications the client is taking?

TIPS TO REMEMBER

1. Always keep records of OTC's and frequency of use.
2. Encourage client to drink 8 ounces of water when taking medication.
3. Antacids and laxatives are best taken 2 hours before or after taking other medications.
4. Remember to read "Warnings and Precautions"

MEDICATION POLICY

An individual medication log for each client shall be maintained. Information shall include the following:

Client's name

Physician's name prescribing the medicine

Name of medicine, date prescription is filled

Direction, strength and amount

Pharmacy name & phone number

RX number, expiration date & number of refills

This log will be kept in the client's records. All medicine, including over-the-counter medicine, shall be kept under lock and key, either in the locked cabinet or at the bedside in a locked box.

The Shift Supervisor shall give assistance with prescribed medications which are self-administered in accordance with the physician's instructions. We are not licensed for, and will not give, any injections or medication the client cannot self-administer, unless we have employed an Appropriately Skilled Professional (ASP) who is licensed or certified to perform these duties in the State of California and it is within the governing regulation for a Residential Care .

RESTRICTIONS ON "SETTING UP" AND "DRAWING UP" INJECTABLES

Insulin and other injectable medications shall be kept in their original containers until the prescribed single dose is measured into a syringe for immediate injection. Dosages of insulin and other injectable medications shall not be prepared or "set up" in advance by filling one or more syringes with the prescribed dose and storing medication in the syringe until needed. The prohibition of advance set-up does not apply to medications that are packaged by a pharmacist or a manufacturer in pre-measured doses in individual syringes.

Only the client or certified medical professionals are permitted to mix injectable medication prescribed for the client or to fill the syringe with the prescribed dose ("draw up" the medication). The medical professionals permitted to administer medications include only physicians, registered nurses and licensed vocational nurses.

HOUSE SUPPLIES
OVER-THE-COUNTER MEDS
(Before assisting the clients with these kinds of medications, get doctor's approval)
Acetaminophen (Tylenol, etc.)
Milk of Magnesia
Fleet Enema(for clients' self-use or ASP)
Metamucil
Anusol suppositories (for clients' self-use or ASP)
ExLax
Bisacodyl
Ecotrin, aspirin
Rolaids
Tums
Mineral Oil
Castor Oil
Glycerin suppositories (for clients' self-use or ASP)
Listerine
Boric Acid
Cough drops
Guituss-Dm, Robitussin (coughs and colds medicine)
NOTE: REMEMBER TO CHECK EXPIRATION DATES

FIRST AID SUPPLIES
Bandages, Plastic Strip 2" x 4 ½" (Band-Aid, etc.)
Bandages, Elastic Knee & Elbow 2" x 4" (Ace)
Bandages, Plastic, various shapes and sizes (Band-Aid, etc.)
Telfa non-stick pads 3" x 4"
Adhesive Tape, Water –proof ½" and 1" rolls
Cotton Balls
Alcohol Swabs
Cloth Tape
Butterfly Closures
Steri-strips
Tegaderm
Duo-Derm
Biolex
Disposable gloves
Providine solution
Hydrogen Peroxide
A & D ointment
Vaseline Intensive Care Lotion
Calmine lotion
Campho Phenique
Ben Gay
Muscle Rrub
Rubbing Alcohol
KY Jelly

Glossary of words

ADMINISTRATOR: "Administrator" means the individual designated by the licensee to act in behalf of the licensee in the overall management of the . The licensee, if an individual, and the administrator may be one and the same person.

ADULT: "Adult" means a person who is eighteen (18) years of age or older.

AMBULATORY PERSON: "Ambulatory Person" means a person who is capable of demonstrating the mental competence and physical ability to leave a building without assistance of any other person or without the use of any mechanical aid in case of an emergency.

APPLICANT: "Applicant" means any individual, firm, partnership, association, corporation or county who has made application for license.

APPROPRIATELY SKILLED PROFESSIONAL: means an individual that has training and is licensed to perform the necessary medical procedures prescribed by a physician. This include but is not limited to the following: Registered Nurse (RN), Licensed Vocational Nurse (LVN), Physical Therapist (PT), Occupational Therapist (OT) and Respiratory Therapist (RT). These professionals may include, but are not limited to, those persons employed by a home health , the client, or facilities and who are currently licensed in California.

Activities of Daily Living (ADLs): The physical functions necessary for independent living. These usually include bathing, dressing, using the toilet, eating and moving about (transferring).

Acute Hospital - A hospital which provides care for persons who have a crisis, intense or severe illness or condition which requires urgent restorative care.

Area Agencies on Aging (AAA): Local government agencies which grant or contract with public and private organizations to provide services for older persons within their area.

Assisted Living/Residential Care Facilities for the Elderly (RCFE) – Personal care and safe housing for people who require supervision for medication and assistance with daily living, but who do not require 24-hour nursing care.

BASIC RATE: "Basic Rate" means the SSI/SSP established rate, which does not include that amount allocated for the recipient's personal and incidental needs.

BASIC SERVICES: "Basic Services" means those services required to be provided by the in order to obtain and maintain a license and include, in such combinations as may meet need of the clients and be applicable to the type of to be operated, the following: safe and healthful living accommodations; personal assistance and care; observation and supervision; planned activities; food service; and arrangements for obtaining incidental medical and dental care.

CAPACITY: "Capacity" means that maximum number of persons authorized to be provided services at any one time in any licensed .

CARE AND SUPERVISION: "Care and Supervision" means those activities which if provided shall require the to be licensed. It involves assistance as needed with activities of daily living and the assumption of varying degrees of responsibility for the safety and well-being of clients. "Care and Supervision" shall include, but not be limited to, any one or more of the following activities provided by a person or to meet the needs of the clients:

Assistance in dressing, grooming, bathing and other personal hygiene; Assistance with taking medication, as specified in section 87575; Central storing and distribution of medications, as specified in section 87575; Arrangement of and assistance with medical and dental care. This may include transportation, as specified in section 87575; Maintenance of house rules for the protection of clients; Supervision of clients schedules and activities; Maintenance and supervision of client monies or property; Monitoring food intake or special diets.

Chronic: A lasting, lingering or prolonged illness.

Copayments: Copayments are those payments made by an individual at the time that he or she uses health care services. Copayments are generally a set amount depending upon the specific service received.

Custodial Care: Care is considered custodial when it is primarily for the purpose of meeting personal needs and could be provided by persons without professional skills or training.

COMMUNITY CARE : "Community Care " means any , place or building providing non-medical care and supervision, as defined in section 8701.c.(2).

CONSERVATOR: "Conservator" means a person appointed by the Superior Court pursuant to the provisions of section 1800 et seq. of the Probate Code to care for the person, or person and estate, of another.

CONSULTANT: "Consultant" means a person professionally qualified by training and experience to provide expert information on a particular subject.

CONTROL OF PROPERTY: "Control of Property" means the right to enter, occupy, and maintain the operation of the property within regulatory requirements. Evidence of control of property shall include, but is not limited to the following:

A Grant Deed showing ownership; or The Lease Agreement or Rental Agreement; or A court order or similar document which shows the authority to control the property pending outcome of probate proceeding or estate settlement.

DEFICIENCY: "Deficiency" means any failure to comply with any provision of the Residential Care Facilities Act for the Elderly and regulations adopted by the Department pursuant to the Act.

DEPARTMENT: "Department" is defined in Health and Safety Code, section 1569.2(b).

DIETICIAN: "Dietician" means a person who is eligible for registration by the American Dietetic Association.

DIRECTOR: "Director" is defined in Health and Safety Code, section 1569.2(c).

DOCUMENTATION: "Documentation" means written supportive information including but not limited to the Licensing Report (Form LIC # 809).

Developmental Disability (DD): Disability which originates before age 18; can be expected to continue indefinitely; constitutes a substantial handicap to the disabled ability to function normally; and is attributable to mental retardation, cerebral palsy, epilepsy, autism, or any other condition closely related to mental retardation which results in similar impairment of general intellectual functioning or adaptive behavior.

Durable Power of Attorney for Health Care: This legal document authorizes the person given the power to make decisions regarding the person's medical treatment only when the person giving the power becomes incompetent.

ELDERLY PERSON: "Elderly Person" means, for purposes of admission into a Residential Care for the Elderly. A person who is sixty-two (62) years of age or older.

EMERGENCY APPROVAL TO OPERATE: "Emergency Approval to Operate" (EAO) means a temporary approval to operate a for no more than 60 days pending the issuance or denial of a license by the licensing .

EVALUATOR: "Evaluator" means any person who is duly authorized officer, employee or agent of the Department including any officer, employee or agent of a county or other public authorized by contract to license community care facilities.

EVIDENCE OF LICENSEE'S DEATH: " Evidence of Licensee's Death" shall include, but is not limited to, a copy of death certificate, obituary notice, certification of death from the decedent's mortuary, or a letter from the attending physician or coroner's office verifying the death of the licensee.

EXCEPTION: "Exception" means a variance to a specific regulation based on the unique needs or circumstances of a specific client or staff person. Requests for exceptions are made to licensing by an applicant or licensee. They may be granted for a particular , client or staff person, but cannot by transferred or applied to other individuals.

EXISTING : "Existing " means any operating under a valid unexpired license on the date of application for a new or renewal license.

GUARDIAN: "Guardian means a person appointed by the Superior Court Pursuant to the provisions of section 1500 et seq. of the Probate Code to care for the person, or person and estate, of another.

HEALING WOUNDS: include cuts, stage one and two dermal ulcers as diagnosed by a physician, and incisions that are being treated by an appropriate skilled professional with the affected area returning to its normal state. They may involve breaking or laceration of the skin and usually damage to the underlying tissues.

HOME ECONOMIST: "Home Economist" means a person who holds a baccalaureate or higher degree in home economics and who specialized in either food and nutrition or dietetics.

IMMEDIATE NEED: "Immediate Need" means a situation where prohibiting the operation of the would be detrimental to a client's physical health, mental health, safety, or welfare. Examples of immediate need include but are not limited to:

A change in location when clients are in need of services from the operator at the new location; A change of ownership when clients are in need of services from the new operator.

INSTRUCTION: Means to furnish an individual with knowledge or to teach, give orders, or direction of a process or procedure.

Home Health (HHA): A home health is a public or private that specializes in giving skilled nursing services, home health aides, and other therapeutic services, such as physical therapy, in AngelCare.

Hospice: A hospice is a public or private organization that primarily provides pain relief, symptom management, and supportive services to terminally ill people and their families in AngelCare.

Intermediate Care (ICF): An ICF provides health related care and services to individuals who do not require the degree of care or treatment given in a hospital or skilled nursing , but who (because of their mental or physical condition) require care and services which is greater than custodial care and can only be provided in an institutional setting.

Institutes for Mental Disease (IMDs): Provide supplemental special programs for mentally disordered individuals in a locked and/or secured skilled nursing setting.

Long-Term Care Insurance: A policy designed to help alleviate some of the costs associated with long term care needs. Often, benefits are paid in the form of a fixed dollar amount (per day or per visit) for covered LTC expenses.

LICENSE: "License" is defined in Health and Safety Code section 1569.2(g).

LICENSEE: "Licensee" means the individual, firm, partnership, corporation, association or county having the authority and responsibility for the operation of a licensed .

LICENSING : "Licensing " means a state, county or other public authorized by the Department to assume specified licensing, approval or consultation responsibilities pursuant to section 1569.13 of the Health and Safety Code.

LIFE CARE CONTRACT: "Life Care Contract" is defined in Health and Safety Code, section 1771(m).

Managed Care: Medical care delivery system, such as HMO or PPO, where someone "manages" health care services a beneficiary receives; each plan has its own group of hospitals, doctors and other health care providers called a "network"; usually promote preventive health care; may have to pay a fixed monthly premium and a co-payment each time a service is used.

Medicaid (Medi-Cal in California): The state medical assistance program which provides essential medical care and services for individuals and families receiving public assistance, or whose income is not sufficient to meet their individual needs. Sixty-five percent of clients in skilled nursing facilities rely on Medicaid.

Medicare: The nation's largest health insurance program, Medicare covers 37 million Americans. Medicare provides insurance to people who are 65 years old; people who are disabled; and people with permanent kidney failure. Medicare provides only limited benefits for skilled care, and under specific guidelines, for nursing home and home health care. Only 8 percent of individuals in skilled nursing facilities rely on Medicare.

Medicare Supplementary Insurance: This insurance pays the 20% of the Medicare approved amount of which Medicare pays 80%.

Medigap Insurance: Medigap insurance are private insurance products that provide insurance protection for the costs of hospital services that are rendered to a Medicare beneficiary that exceed the amount Medicare will pay for the hospital services.

NEW : "New " means any applying for an initial license whether newly constructed or previously existing for some other purpose.

NON-AMBULATORY PERSON: "Non-Ambulatory Person" means a person who is unable to leave a building unassisted under emergency conditions. It includes, but is not limited to, those persons who depend upon mechanical aids such as crutches, walkers, and wheelchairs. It also includes persons who are unable, or likely to unable, to respond physically or mentally to an oral instruction relating to fire danger and, unassisted, take appropriate action relating to such danger.

NUTRITIONIST: "Nutritionist" means a person holding a master's degree in food and nutrition dietetics, or public health nutrition, or who is employed by a county health department in the latter capacity.

Occupational Therapy: Activities designed to improve the useful functioning of physically and/or mentally disabled persons.

Ombudsman: Individual designated by a state or a sub-state unit responsible for investigating and resolving complaints made by or for older people in long term care facilities. An ombudsman is also responsible for monitoring federal and state policies that relate to long term care facilities, for providing information to the public about the problems of older people in facilities, and for training volunteers to help in the ombudsmen program. The ombudsman program is authorized by Title III of the Older Americans Act.

Personal Care: Involves services rendered by a nurse's aide, dietician or other health professional. These services include assistance in walking, getting out of bed, bathing, toileting, dressing, eating and preparing special diets.

Physical Therapy: Services provided by specially trained and licensed physical therapists in order to relieve pain, restore maximum function, and prevent disability, injury or loss of a body part.

PHYSICIAN: "Physician" means a person licensed as a physician and surgeon by the California Board of Medical Examiners or by the California Board of Osteopathic Examiners.

PROVISION OR PROVIDE: Whenever any regulation specified that provision be made for or that there be provided any service, personnel or other requirement, it means that if the client is not capable of doing so himself, the licensee shall do so directly or present evidence satisfactory to the licensing of the particular arrangement by which another provider in the community will do so.

PROVISIONAL LICENSE: "Provisional License" means a temporary, nonrenewable license, issued for a period not to exceed twelve months which is issued in accordance with the criteria specified in section 87231.

Respite: The in-home care of a chronically ill beneficiary intended to give the care-giver a rest. Can also be provided in a hospice or nursing home (as with hospice respite care)

RELATIVE: "Relative" means spouse, parent, stepparent, son, daughter, brother, sister, half-brother, half-sister, uncle, aunt, niece, nephew, first cousin or any such persons specified in this definition, even if the marriage has been terminated by death or dissolution.

RESIDENTIAL CARE FOR THE ELDERLY: "Residential Care for the Elderly" means a housing arrangement chosen voluntarily by the clients, or the client's guardian, conservator, or other responsible person; where 75 percent of the clients are at least sixty-two years of age, or, if younger, have needs compatible with other clients as specified in section 87582; and where varying levels of care and supervision are provided, as agreed to at time of admission or as determined necessary at subsequent times of reappraisal.

RESPONSIBLE PERSON: "Responsible Person" means that individual or individuals, including a guardian, conservator, or relative, who assist the client in placement assume varying degrees of responsibility for the client's well-being. This includes the County Welfare Department, Adult Protective Services Unit, when no other responsible person can be found.

ROOM AND BOARD: "Room and Board" means a living arrangement where care and supervision is neither provided nor available.

SERIOUS DEFICIENCY: "Serious Deficiency" means any deficiency that presents and immediate or substantial threat to the physical health, mental health, or safety of the clients or clients of a community care .

Skilled Nursing Care: Care which can only be provided by or under the supervision or licensed nursing personnel. Skilled rehabilitation care must be provided or supervised by licensed therapy personnel. All care is under the general direction of a physician and necessary on a daily basis.

Therapy that is needed only occasionally, such as twice a week, or where the skilled services that are needed do not require inpatient care, do not qualify as skilled level of care.

Skilled Nursing (SNF): Provide 24-hour nursing care for chronically-ill or short-term rehabilitative clients of all ages.

Social Security: A national insurance program that provides income to workers when they retire or are disabled and to dependent survivors when a worker dies. Retirement payments are based on worker's earnings during employment.

Speech Therapy: The study, examination, and treatment of defects and diseases of the voice, speech, spoken and written language.

Sub-Acute Care Facilities: Specialized units often in a distinct part of a nursing . Provide intensive rehabilitation, complex wound care, and post-surgical recovery for persons of all ages who no longer need the level of care found in a hospital.

Supplemental Security Income (SSI): A federal program that pays monthly checks to people in need who are 65 years or older and to people in need at any age who are blind and disabled. Eligibility is based on income and assets.

SOCIAL WORKER: "Social Worker" means a person who has a graduate degree from an accredited school of social work or who has equivalent qualifications as determined by the Department.

SSI/SSP: SSI/SSP" means the Supplemental Security Income State Supplemental Program.

SUBSTANTIAL COMPLIANCE: "Substantial Compliance" means the absence of any deficiencies which would threaten the physical health, mental health, safety or welfare of the clients. Such deficiencies include, but are not limited to, those deficiencies referred to inn section 87451 and the presence of any uncorrected serious deficiencies for which civil penalties could be assessed.

SUPERVISION: means to oversee or direct the work of an individual or subordinate but does not necessarily require the immediate presence or the supervisor.

TRANSFER TRAUMA: "Transfer Trauma" means the consequences of the stress and emotional shock caused an abrupt, involuntary relocation of a client from one to another.

VOLUNTARY: "Voluntary" means resulting from free will.

WAIVER: "Waiver" means a variance to specific regulation based on a -wide need or circumstance which is not typically tied to a specific client or staff person. Requests for waivers are made to the licensing , in advance, by an applicant or licensee.

RESIDENTIAL CARE'S COMMON TERMINOLOGY: ABBREVIATIONS
DSS - Department of Social Services
CCL - Community Care Licensing
CCF - Community Care
ARF - Adult Residential
CCLD – Community Care Licensing Division
CCF - California Code of Regulations
LPA - Licensing Program Analyst
COB - Central Operations Branch
OAL - Office of Administrative Law
ASP - appropriately skilled professional

SMP - skilled medical professional

EM - evaluator manual

DD - developmental disability

IPP - individual program plan

CDER- client development evaluation report

ARM - alternative Residential model

SMA - schedule of maximum allowances

RVS - relative value scales

P & I – personal and incidental (records or money)

IHSS – in-home supportive services

CYA - cover your _ _ _!

COLA - cost of living adjustment

QUALITY ASSURANCE – Assuring services are of the highest quality

PROGRAM FLEXIBILITY – the allowance for and exception

APPRAISAL – an assessment or evaluation of a client

RETENTION – maintaining, retaining, or keeping a client

EXCEMPTION – requested for when employee has a criminal record

EXEPTION – requested for a specific client or staff person in regards to a particular circumstance, or program

WAIVER – variance for a specific regulation not tied to an individual

COMPLIANCE – obeying and properly following the law